Law for Purchasing and Supply

Law for Purchasing and Supply

Margaret Griffiths

THE
CHARTERED INSTITUTE OF
PURCHASING & SUPPLY

PITMAN PUBLISHING
128 Long Acre, London WC2E 9AN

A Division of Longman Group Limited

First published in 1994

© Margaret Griffiths 1994

A CIP catalogue record for this book can be obtained from the British Library.

ISBN 0 273 60429 5

10 9 8 7 6 5 4 3 2

Typeset by Land & Unwin (Data Sciences) Ltd
Printed and bound by Bell and Bain Ltd., Glasgow

The Publishers' policy is to use paper manufactured from sustainable forests.

For my family

CONTENTS

PART II   THE SUPPLY OF GOODS AND SERVICES

PART III   THE LAW OF TORT

PART IV   CONSUMER PROTECTION

PREFACE

This book was designed as a course text for the Legal Applications course of the Chartered Institute of Purchasing and Supply (CIPS). As such it addresses the legal areas contained within that syllabus and seeks to examine the relationship between the civil and criminal law as they apply within the field of purchasing and supply. I have included a question at the end of each chapter to encourage students to practise putting their knowledge to the test. Suggested solutions appear at the end of the book. References to the EEC should be construed as references to the EU where appropriate. To avoid tedious repetition, the masculine pronoun has been adopted throughout the book – no offence is intended.

In any work of this nature that seeks to examine such a broad range of law, the author must necessarily have access to a large number of texts for reference purposes. All the books that I have used for research are attributed at the end of the relevant chapters. However, I would like to acknowledge my particular indebtedness to Richards's *Law of Contract* and Bradgate and Savage's *Business Law* both of which proved invaluable.

As is normal in a preface, I would like to record my thanks to those who have helped me in this endeavour. My thanks go to my colleagues at the University of Glamorgan for their support and encouragement and for allowing me to pick their brains on occasions. Particular thanks are due to Corbett Spurin for his help with the chapter on International Trade and to Ann Cross, the Law Librarian, for her help with the research. Special thanks must go to my husband, Ivor, for his professional advice and guidance with the chapters on Consumer Safety, Weights and Measures and Employment Law. Thanks are also due to Penelope Woolf and Wendy Brown at Pitman Publishing for their support and patience.

On a personal note, I would like to record my special thanks to my husband, Ivor, and my parents, John and Sylvia Caddy, for their usual unfailing support. Finally, I must record my thanks to my children, Andrew and Charlotte, whose considerable patience with this venture over a period of six months is worthy of tribute.

The law stated is as I believe it to be on the 1 January 1994.

Margaret Griffiths
Caerphilly
January 1994

TABLE OF CASES

TABLE OF STATUTES

EEC legislation

PART I

The law of contract

CHAPTER 1

Contract formation

INTRODUCTION

Given the pivotal role of contract law in purchasing, it is vital to have a clear understanding of the elements that create a legally binding contract enforceable under English law. These elements are threefold; agreement (offer and acceptance), consideration (the price of the contract) and contractual intention (the intention of the parties to be contractually bound). These elements have developed through many decades of judicial interpretation with the resultant evolution of a relatively certain body of rules governing the creation of legally binding, enforceable contracts.

OFFER AND ACCEPTANCE

Agreement between the contracting parties, the *consensus ad idem*, is crucial to a contract. Thus, for example, if A is going to sell a quantity of gravel to B, they will need to agree on the quantity, quality, price, delivery date and place of delivery. Only when all these details have been agreed, will it be possible for a contract to come into being.

In practice, agreements come about when one of the contracting parties (the offeror) makes an offer which the other contracting party (the offeree) accepts. It is possible that the offer will be accepted immediately without any further discussion, as, for example, when a consumer pays the fixed price for a bar of chocolate, but, in a business context, it is more likely that some negotiation about terms will take place before agreement is finally reached.

INVITATIONS TO TREAT

It is important to distinquish at this preliminary stage between an offer and an invitation to treat, for the acceptance of one will result in a contract whereas the other is incapable of acceptance at all. Invitations to treat have no binding effect and are really a means of seeking information and inviting a prospective offeror to make a contractual offer. As such, they are in the nature of precontractual negotiations or statements.

Invitations to treat may arise in a variety of circumstances. It is well recognised that newspaper advertisements for the sale of goods and services are usually, though not always (*Carlill* v *Carbolic Smoke Ball Co* [1893] 1 QB 256), invitations to treat, this being held to be so in the case of *Partridge* v *Crittenden* [1968] 2 All ER 421. Similarly, the display of goods in a self service shop (*Pharmaceutical Society of Great Britain* v *Boots Cash Chemists (Southern) Ltd* [1953] 1 QB 401) and the display of goods in a shop window (*Fisher* v *Bell* [1961] 1 QB 394) have both been held to constitute invitations to treat only and not contractual offers. In both of these situations the display is merely the seller displaying the goods that he has available for purchase. The contractual offer is made by the prospective purchaser when he offers to buy the goods, the seller then being at liberty to accept the offer and sell the goods, or alternatively to refuse the offer and retain the goods.

In *Pharmaceutical Society of Great Britain* v *Boots Cash Chemists (Southern) Ltd*, the defendants ran a retail self service chemists shop in which customers selected the items they wished to purchase from display shelves and took them to a cash desk to pay. Among the products on display in the shop were 'over the counter' drugs which could only be sold legally under the supervision of a registered pharmacist, who was stationed near the cash desk. At issue was whether the display of the drugs on the shelves was a contractual offer or merely an invitation to treat. If it was an offer, the defendants would be guilty of an offence against the Pharmacy and Poisons Act 1933 which required any sale to be 'effected by, or under the supervision of, a registered pharmacist'. The Court of Appeal held that the display was merely an invitation to treat, the contractual offer being made by the customer at the cash desk under the supervision of the pharmacist.

TENDERS

The status of tenders illustrates well the distinction between invitations to treat and contractual offers. Any invitation inviting prospective contracting parties to submit a tender is an invitation to treat. The tender itself forms the contractual offer which is capable of acceptance or rejection. Tenders are discussed more fully at page 7.

OFFERS

A contractual offer exists when an offeror makes known the terms upon which he is prepared to contract and promises to be bound by those terms if they are accepted by the offeree. An offer can be made to an individual person or company (a bilateral offer) or alternatively can be made to the world at large (a unilateral offer) in which case it can be accepted by anyone who knows of the offer and who complies with its terms. The validity of unilateral offers was established in *Carlill* v *Carbolic Smoke Ball Co.*

The defendants were the manufacturers of a medicinal product called 'The Carbolic Smoke Ball'. They placed an advertisement in a newspaper stating that they would pay £100 to any person who contracted flu after buying and using the smoke ball correctly. They further stated that, as a token of their sincerity, they had put £1000 on deposit in the bank. The plaintiff purchased a smoke ball and used it according to the instructions but nonetheless contracted flu. She claimed £100 from the defendants who refused to pay arguing that the advertisement was merely an advertising puff and that it was impossible to contract with the world. In an action to recover the £100, the Court of Appeal held that Mrs Carlill was entitled to the money. The company had made an offer to the world at large which Mrs Carlill had accepted by her conduct.

The same principle would hold true for 'free offers' linked to the purchase of an item. Thus, for example, if a retailer places an advertisement stating that he will provide a free item to anyone purchasing his product, he is legally obliged so to do. Any person may accept his offer by conduct through the purchase of the product in question and thereafter is legally entitled to receive the free item as held in *Esso Petroleum Ltd* v *Commissioners of Customs and Excise* [1976] 1 All ER 117.

Termination of offers

An offer may come to an end in one of seven ways.

(a) **Acceptance.** The offer ripens into a contract when it is accepted unconditionally by the offeree.

(b) **Rejection.** The offeree may reject the offer after which he cannot seek to revive it.

(c) **Counter-offer.** An offer exists only as long as the terms of it remain unchanged. Thus a counter-offer proposed by the offeree in which he seeks to alter a term of the original offer will destroy the original offer. Once destroyed, the offer cannot be revived as held in *Hyde* v *Wrench* (1840) 49 ER 132.

The defendant offered to sell some real estate to the plaintiff for £1000. Two days later, the plaintiff made a counter-offer of £950 which the defendant refused. Subsequently, the plaintiff contacted the defendant agreeing to purchase the land for £1000 and sought an order of specific performance. The court refused to grant one finding that the offer to pay £950 was a counter-offer that had permanently destroyed the original offer and rendered it incapable of acceptance.

When considering counter-offers, it is important to remember two things;

first, that a counter-offer may be clothed in the garb of an acceptance and, second, that an inquiry for further information is not a counter-offer and does not effect the continued existence of the offer. In respect of the first, where an offeree seeks to accept the offer while stipulating some amendment to a term of the offer, it is really a counter-offer and not an acceptance. In respect of the second, the case of *Stevenson* v *McLean* (1880) 5 QBD 346 is instructive.

The defendants offered to sell a quantity of iron to the plaintiffs for 40s net cash, the offer being held open for two days. On the second day, the plaintiffs sent a telegram to the defendants asking if it was possible to have credit terms over two months. Not receiving a reply to their first telegram, the plaintiffs sent a second telegram to the defendants three hours later accepting the original offer. In the intervening period, the defendants had sold the iron to a third party. It was held that the defendants were in breach of contract as the first telegram was only seeking additional information and was not a counter-offer. As such, the original offer was still open at the time that the plaintiff purported to accept it.

(d) Revocation. The offeror can withdraw the offer at any time prior to acceptance (*Byrne* v *Van Tienhoven* (1880) 5 CPD 344). This is so even if the offer was stated to be available for a specified period unless the offeree has provided consideration for the offer to remain open until the specified deadline. A revocation of the offer is not effective until the offeree receives actual notice of it. However, the offeror is not required personally to inform the offeree of the revocation, it is sufficient if the offeree receives the information from a reliable third party, *Dickinson* v *Dodds* (1876) 2 Ch D 463, CA.

The defendant offered to sell a house to the plaintiff, the offer to remain open for a specified period. The day before the period was due to expire, the defendant sold the house to a third party, the plaintiff hearing of this fact that evening from another reliable person. The following day, the plaintiff delivered a letter of acceptance to the defendant. The Court of Appeal held that there was no contract as the offer had been validly revoked. The plaintiff had been aware of the sale before the attempted acceptance.

(e) Failure of a precondition. The existence of the offer may be subject to the offeree satisfying some precondition. If the offeree fails to satisfy the condition, the offer will fail to take effect as in *Financings Ltd* v *Stimson* [1962] 3 All ER 386.

In the *Stimson* decision a customer intended to buy a car and duly completed an hire purchase proposal form. The car was subsequently stolen from the dealer's premises and was badly damaged. The following day the hire-purchase company purported to accept the offer. The Court of Appeal held that there was no contract as there was a condition precedent in the offer that the goods on acceptance would be in the same condition as at the time of the offer. As they were not, the offer was incapable of acceptance.

(f) **Lapse of time.** If an offer is stated to be for a specific period, it will lapse automatically when that period expires. Otherwise, it will lapse after a reasonable time.

(g) **Death.** The death of the offeror will terminate the offer automatically as long as the offeree was aware of the death prior to acceptance. If he was not, it seems that the offeror's estate will be bound by the contract unless the offer necessarily involved some element personal to the offeror, e.g. painting a portrait. The death of the offeree terminates the offer.

TENDERS

The distinction between invitations to treat and contractual offers is most pertinent in respect of tenders, a matter of particular interest both to businessmen and in the public sector. The legal status of tenders is important. Suppose, for example, that a company issues a circular inviting tenders for a contract to supply and fit carpeting to be laid in its sixty retail premises. Is the company bound to consider any tender that it receives and thereafter bound to accept the highest bid? The decision of *Blackpool & Fylde Aero Club Ltd* v *Blackpool BC* [1990] 3 All ER 25 suggests that there is a contractual obligation to consider all tenders that are received by any deadline set and which comply with all the requirements of the invitation to submit such tender.

In *Blackpool & Fylde Aero Club Ltd* v *Blackpool BC*, Blackpool Borough Council invited tenders for a concession to run pleasure flights from Blackpool airport. The terms of the invitation were that tenders were to be submitted sealed in the envelope provided before 12 noon on a date specified. The plaintiff's tender which complied with the prescribed form was placed in the Council's letterbox at 11 a.m. on the relevant day. However, council staff failed to clear the letterbox at noon resulting in the plaintiff's tender being deemed late and not considered. The court held the council liable for breach of contract holding that the plaintiff had a contractual right to have its tender considered as it had complied in every respect with the terms of the invitation.

While there may be an obligation to consider all tenders validly submitted, the decision in *Spencer* v *Harding* (1870) 23 LT 237 suggests that there is no obligation to accept the highest bid or indeed any bid at all. There may be good reasons for deciding not to proceed with the contract or alternatively to accept a bid which, though not the highest, may offer other attractions. It is clear that the wording of the circular may be crucial.

In *Spencer* v *Harding*, the defendants issued a circular stating that they had been instructed to offer for sale by tender to the wholesale trade, the stock-in-trade of Messrs G Eilbeck & Co. The plaintiffs submitted the highest tender which the defendants refused to accept. The plaintiffs alleged that the circular constituted a contractual offer with the implication that the highest tender would be accepted. The plaintiffs had lodged the highest tender. The Court of Common Pleas held that the defendants were not liable to the plaintiffs and that the circular merely constituted an invitation to treat with no implication that they would necessarily accept any tender.

However, the Court considered that the position would have been different if the circular had continued by making a statement that the highest tender would be accepted. In that situation, the circular would have constituted a unilateral contractual offer capable of acceptance by the highest bidder. The key issue appears to be whether the circular is merely seeking information or whether it evinces a definite intention to contract on specified terms with an appropriate bidder. The distinction is illustrated in the decision of *Harvela Investments Ltd* v *Royal Trust Co of Canada Ltd* [1986] AC 207 which dealt with the issue of competitive tendering.

In the *Harvela* decision, the defendants wanted to sell some shares, the two obvious prospective purchasers being the plaintiffs and the second defendants. Both were invited to tender for the shares by a sealed competitive tender, the defendants confirming that 'if the offer made by you is the highest offer received by us, we bind ourselves to accept such offer providing that such offer complies with the terms of this telex'. In the event, the plaintiffs bid $2 175 000 while the second defendants bid $2 100 000 or $100 000 more than any other higher bid, a 'referential bid'. The defendants sold the shares to the second defendants. The House of Lords held that the defendants were obliged to sell the shares to the plaintiffs as their statement amounted to a contractual offer to accept the highest bid, i.e. that of the plaintiffs. To accept the 'referential bid' of the second defendant was contrary to the offer to accept the highest of the sealed competitive bids.

As explained earlier, if a circular or advertisement inviting tenders is merely an invitation to treat, any resultant tender is a contractual offer which the offeree can accept or reject. If accepted, the offer matures into a contract capable of enforcement.

The resultant contract may be of two types, either for the immediate supply of goods or for the supply of goods usually at a fixed price as and when ordered during a contractually agreed period, a 'standing offer'. Thus, for example, in a contract to supply a local authority with 1000 tons of rock salt to be spread on the roads in winter, the successful supplier would be obliged to provide 1000 tons of rock salt on the due delivery date. By contrast, if the contract was to supply up to 1000 tons as and when ordered by the local authority during a period of twelve months, there would be no guarantee that any order would actually be placed. Nonetheless, there would be a contractual obligation to satisfy any order placed up to a total 1000 tons during the agreed period as indicated in the case of *Great Northern Rly Co v Witham* (1873) LR 9 CP 16.

Other established invitations to treat include the issue of company prospectuses for the sale of shares in which the contractual offer is made by the prospective purchaser, and auctions where the auctioneer merely invites prospective bidders to make bids which constitute the contractual offers.

Compulsory competitive tendering

The volume and significance of tendering has increased with the advent of compulsory competitive tendering (CCT) in the public sector.

Under the Local Government, Planning and Land Act 1980, CCT applies to the allocation of construction or maintenance work (whether as a 'works contract' or 'functional work'). Its use was extended significantly by the Local Government Act 1988 which controls the ability of 'defined authorities' (defined under s.1 of the Act to include, among others, local authorities, development corporations, police authorities, fire authorities and joint education committees) to undertake contracts for the provision of 'defined activities', defined under s.2, to include, the collection of refuse, the cleaning of buildings, other cleaning, catering for purposes of school and welfare, other catering, managing sports and leisure facilities, the maintenance of ground and the repair and maintenance of vehicles. The precise extent of these activities is explained more closely in Schedule 1 of the Act.

The ability of defined authorities to undertake contracts for 'defined activities' turns on whether the contract is classed as a 'works contract' or 'functional work'. The former is defined in s.3(2) as 'a contract constituting or including an agreement which provides for the carrying out of work by a defined authority' except where it involves the discharge of the functions of a Minister of the Crown, another defined authority or (in England and Wales) a sewerage undertaker. Any work carried out by a defined authority, other than under a works contract, is classed as being functional work as is work carried out by a non-defined authority that is dependent upon, incidental or preparatory to some functional work.

Two conditions must be satisfied before a defined authority (a bidding authority) can enter a works contract. First, the other contracting party (which may well be another department from the same authority) must have invited contractual offers from at least three other persons who have expressed a preparedness to do the work and are not defined authorities. Alternatively, the other contracting party must have published a notice inviting offers in at least one newspaper circulating in the relevant locality and at least one newspaper circulating among people who carry out the appropriate type of work. The second condition is that the other contracting party has not acted in a way that would restrict, distort or prevent competition. However, a bidding authority will not be bound by a failure to satisfy the conditions unless the authority was aware of the failure before entering the contract.

Section 7 of the Act stipulates six conditions that must be satisfied before a defined authority can carry out functional work falling within a defined activity. These are that, prior to commencing the work, the authority must publish details of the work in a local newspaper and a newspaper circulating among appropriate people and include a statement inviting anyone interested in doing the work to contact the authority, that a detailed specification of the work must be available for inspection, that anyone expressing an interest should receive an invitation from the authority, that the authority through their direct labour organisation or similar organisation must have prepared a written bid, that the authority in deciding that they should carry out the work did not act in a way restricting, distorting or preventing competition and, finally, that the work carried out complied with the specifications.

Under ss.13 and 14, the Secretary of State can make provisions in respect of any failure to comply with the tendering requirements. These include the power to direct the defined authority to cease the work or to continue only if certain conditions are satisfied.

Section 8 of the Local Government Act 1992 governs the application of competitive tendering to work which falls within the definition of defined activity under the 1988 Act and consists of or involves the provision of professional advice or services or the application of any financial or technical expertise. In respect of such work, section 8 permits the Secretary of State to make by order such provisions as he considers necessary to establish both the quality of the service to be provided by anyone willing to carry out the work and their fitness to provide it. Further, provision may be made to evaluate the financial terms on which the service would be provided. To date no such provisions have been made.

Under s.9 of the 1992 Act, the Secretary of State may make regulations to identify conduct that would be deemed to restrict or prevent competition or alternatively would be presumed not to have that effect. Again, at the time of writing, no such regulations have been made.

ACCEPTANCE

A contract comes into being when the offer has been validly and unconditionally accepted by the offeree.

Certainty of terms

The underlying rationale of contract is *consensus* between the contracting parties. Thus, the acceptance must match the offer with both parties certain of the contractual terms. The contract is of no use if there is uncertainty over essential terms contained therein. Nonetheless, it is clear that an apparent uncertainty may be acceptable within a valid, legally binding contract in situations where the parties might be assumed to know the contractual terms either because of previous dealings or because of accepted business practice as in *Hillas & Co Ltd v Arcos Ltd* (1934) 38 Com Cas 23. However, if neither of these aids to construction exist, the court will have no option but to consider the terms of the agreement as they appear, and if they are too speculative or ambiguous then it would seem that no contract will exist as in *Scammel v Ouston* [1941] AC 251.

The respondent wanted to buy a motor-van on hire-purchase terms from the appellants. After some negotiations, the buyers placed an order containing the statement 'This order is given on the understanding that the balance of purchase price can be had on hire-purchase terms over a period of two years'. The hire-purchase terms were never agreed. The buyers sued the seller who appealed, the case ultimately reaching the House of Lords. The court held that there was no contract as the financial terms were not sufficiently certain. The court further held that there was insufficient evidence of contractual intention.

Letters of intent

A related issue is letters of intent whereby one party issues a document to another party making clear their intention to enter a contract with them at some point in the future. This would arise, for example, where a building company tendering to a local authority for a contract to build a new school might issue letters of intent to sub-contractors that they would wish to employ if they gained the contract. There is no intention to be bound contractually at that stage and no contractual agreement reached and yet it is possible for work to begin on the strength of a letter of intent. The leading case is *British Steel Corpn v Cleveland Bridge and Engineering Co Ltd* [1984] 1 All ER 504.

The defendants negotiated with the plaintiffs for the latter to manufacture some specialist steel nodes to be used in the construction of a bridge. During negotiations, the defendants sent a letter of intent to the plaintiffs proposing that any contract would be on the defendant's standard terms. The plaintiffs were not prepared to contract on those terms. Work was completed and the plaintiffs sued for the price, the defendants counterclaiming for damages for late delivery. The court held that there was no contract, merely a letter of intent, final terms not having been agreed. Nonetheless, the plaintiffs were entitled to claim a *quantum meruit* for the goods supplied.

Battle of the forms

Certainty of terms is of particular significance in the business world because of the widespread use of standard form contracts. The offeror may wish to contract on his standard terms while the offeree may want to accept on his own standard terms. This is the so-called 'Battle of the Forms'. The leading authority on this issue is the decision of *Butler Machine Tool Co v Ex-Cell-O Corpn* [1979] 1 All ER 965.

The plaintiff sellers offered to sell a machine tool to the defendants for £75,535 with delivery ten months later. The offer was on the plaintiff's standard terms which included a price variation clause under which the plaintiff could charge the price prevailing at the time of supply. Resultant upon this offer, the defendant buyers placed an order using their own standard form of contract the terms of which did not contain a price variation clause. The order form contained a tear off slip at the bottom confirming agreement with the buyers' terms which the sellers duly completed and returned. The sellers attempted to charge the buyers an extra £2892 relying on the price variation clause. The Court of Appeal held that the plaintiff sellers could not charge the additional sum as their return of the tear-off slip signified an agreement to contract on the buyers' terms.

Discussions about the case suggest that the party who 'fires the last shot' will win the day. This would accord with the traditional approach by holding that the submission of each standard form is, in effect, a counter-offer and thus that the last form submitted contains the final contractual terms. In practice, it is often not as clear cut as this.

Communication of acceptance

Acceptance must be communicated to be effective with the contract coming into being at the time and place where the offeror receives the communication. Certain rules apply relating to the validity and communication of acceptance.

(a) **Knowledge of the offeror.** Acceptance cannot take place where the offeree did not know of the offer. There is no *consensus.*

(b) **Silence is not acceptance.** The offeror cannot stipulate that silence by the offeree will constitute acceptance as demonstrated in *Felthouse* v *Bindley* (1862) 11 CBNS 869.

The plaintiff was negotiating the purchase of a horse from his nephew. Finally, he wrote to his nephew stating that if he did not hear further he would assume that he could buy the horse. The nephew decided to sell the horse to the plaintiff but failed to withdraw it from an auction. The defendant auctioneer, unaware of this, sold the horse and was sued in conversion by the plaintiff. The court held that mental acceptance by the nephew was not sufficient to constitute contractual acceptance.

As such, the plaintiff had not bought the horse and thus could not sue the defendant in conversion.

(c) Acceptance can be by conduct. The offeror may waive his right to receive communication of acceptance and allow acceptance to occur by the offeree's conduct, as in a unilateral offer such as occurred in *Carlill*.

(d) Method of communication. If the offeror has stipulated that a particular manner of communication must be used, it may be that any acceptance communicated by an alternative method may not be valid. However, it will depend on all the circumstances with the court considering the true intention of the offeror.

(e) Communication must be received. Thus, where the parties are dealing face to face or by telephone, the offeror must hear the acceptance for it to be valid. Likewise, if instantaneous communications such as telex are used, the acceptance occurs when and where the message is received, this being decided in *Entores Ltd* v *Miles Far East Corpn* [1955] 2 QB 327 and confirmed by the House of Lords in *Brinkibon* v *Stahag Stahl* [1983] 2 AC 34.

In the *Entores* decision, the plaintiffs made an offer by telex to the defendants' agents in Amsterdam seeking to buy goods from them. The defendants accepted by a telex received by the plaintiffs in London. The latter subsequently wished to sue the defendants for breach of contract but their ability to issue a writ was dependent on whether the contract had been made in London or Amsterdam. The Court of Appeal held that the contract was agreed in London when the telex was received by the plaintiffs.

(f) Postal acceptance. When acceptance is communicated by post, the acceptance occurs when the letter is posted. There is no requirement that it be received by the offeror who will be contractually bound from that moment even though he does not know of the acceptance and may never receive it. This was clearly established by the decision of *Byrne* v *Van Tienhoven* (*supra*). Nonetheless, it is possible for the offeror to countermand the normal 'postal rules' by stipulating in the offer that any letter of acceptance must be received to be valid, as occurred in *Holwell Securities Ltd* v *Hughes* [1974] 1 All ER 161.

CONSIDERATION

The concept of a bargain is central to English contract law, a mere agreement between the parties being insufficient. There must be evidence that a bargain has been struck. As such, consideration is necessary in all contracts other than specialty contracts and is essentially the 'price' of the contractual promise. It may consist of payment, either monetary or in kind, the doing of some action or, alternatively, the forbearance from enforcing some right.

Consideration may be classed as either executed or executory. Executed consideration occurs where the promise is made in return for the doing of an act. The most common example of this is the 'reward' situation where the offeror promises to pay money for the return of a lost item. When the offeree finds and returns the item, the monetary consideration must change hands. By contrast, executory consideration is a promise in exchange for a promise, any action being in the future. An example might be where A, a building contractor, promises to pay £1000 to B, a plant hire company, if B will promise to supply A with the use of a fork-lift truck for five days. The actual provision of the truck is in the future with only promises taking place at the time that the contract is made.

As with offer and acceptance, there are certain rules relating to the provision of consideration.

(a) **Consideration must move from the promisee.** Only a person who has provided consideration for the contractual promise has the *locus standi* to enforce it. Thus, a third party cannot enforce the contract even if it was made for his benefit.

In the case of *Tweddle* v *Atkinson* (1861) 1 B & S 393, the plaintiff's father and future father-in-law agreed to pay the plaintiff a sum of money prior to his marriage. His father-in-law died without making the payment and the plaintiff sued his estate for the outstanding money. The court held that although the contract was made for his benefit, the plaintiff did not provide any consideration for the promise and thus could not sue to enforce it.

(b) **Past consideration is no consideration.** The law will not enforce a promise when the consideration relates to a past action. In that situation, the consideration is not contractual payment but rather a subsequent *ex gratia* payment and, as such, is not enforceable.

In the decision of *Re McArdle* [1951] Ch 669, CA, Mr McArdle left his house to his widow for her lifetime and thereafter to his children. During the widow's lifetime, one of the children and his wife moved into the house and did some renovations costing £448. Subsequently, all the children signed a document agreeing to reimburse the wife when the deceased's estate was distributed finally. They failed to do so and the wife sued to enforce the promise. The Court of Appeal held that she could not enforce it as it was made after the work had been done. Hence, the consideration was in the past and did not support the promise.

However, if it can be shown that the plaintiff undertook the work at the request of the defendant and there was a reasonable assumption that payment would be made, the plaintiff can sue to enforce any promise of payment even if it was made after the work had been completed. This was the *dicta* of the decision of *Lampleigh* v *Braithwait* (1615) Hob 105, a similar finding occurring in *Re Casey's Patents, Stewart* v *Casey* [1892] 1 Ch 10.

(c) **Consideration must be sufficient but need not be adequate.** While the law is concerned with the existence of a bargain, it is not interested in the value of it and will not aid a plaintiff merely because he has made a bad bargain. *Caveat emptor*, let the buyer beware, rules as regards the value of the deal.

(i) **Sufficiency versus adequacy.** The distinction between sufficiency and adequacy is vital. Consideration will be sufficient if it is capable of legally constituting consideration, while adequacy is only concerned with the value of the consideration and thus is of no interest to the law. Thus, for example, if A agrees to sell his factory to B for £10, the agreement will be enforceable as the consideration is sufficient even if the average person would not consider it adequate. A practical example of this occurred in *Chappell & Co Ltd* v *Nestlé & Co Ltd* [1960] AC 87 in which it was held that chocolate wrappers could constitute consideration if collected by purchasers as part of the 'payment' for a contractual offer contained on the wrapper. This was so despite the fact that the wrappers had no intrinsic value and would be thrown away upon receipt.

(ii) **The performance of existing duties.** Generally, the performance of an action which the plaintiff is already obliged to perform either as a matter of public duty or because of some pre-existing contractual duty, cannot constitute consideration for a contractual promise. Examples of the first, performance of a public duty, occurred in *Collins* v *Godefroy* (1831) 1 B & Ad 950 and *Glasbrook Brothers Ltd* v *Glamorgan County Council* [1925] AC 270.

In the *Collins* decision the defendant, Godefroy, offered to pay Collins the sum of six guineas to give evidence in a court case. In fact, Collins had been subpoenaed to attend court and thus was under a public duty to do so. His action to recover the six guineas failed for lack of consideration.

The *Glasbrook* decision concerned the duty owed by a police authority to provide sufficient police officers to protect premises. The respondent requested the police to provide security for his mine during a strike. The police were satisfied that a unit of men patrolling outside the premises would be sufficient for the purpose. However, the colliery manager wanted to have a force of officers billeted at the premises. The police authority agreed to this request with the colliery manager agreeing to pay for the additional service. He subsequently refused to pay the bill and was sued for the cost of the additional cover, £2300. The House of Lords held that the police authority was able to recover the cost. While they were under a public duty to provide protection for premises, the level of such protection fell within their discretion. A charge could be made for any additional service provided.

A pre-existing contractual duty will also be insufficient to constitute consideration for a contractual promise unless it can be shown that the promisee has received some benefit or avoided some loss. The traditional approach to pre-existing contractual duty is to be found in the decisions of *Stilk* v *Myrick* (1809) 2 Camp 317 and *Hartley* v *Ponsonby* (1857) 7 E & B 872.

In *Stilk* v *Myrick* the plaintiff was employed as a sailor and was under contract to man a ship of which the defendant was the captain. During the voyage, two seamen deserted and the captain promised the remaining crew that, if they manned the ship home shorthanded, he would divide the wages of the two seamen between them. Subsequently, he refused to do so and was sued. The court found for the defendant holding that the plaintiff and the remainder of the crew were already contractually bound to man the ship back home and had not provided any consideration for the promise of the extra money.

The facts in *Hartley* v *Ponsonby* were very similar to those in *Stilk* v *Myrick* except that nearly half of the crew had deserted. This had the effect of making the voyage considerably more hazardous for the remaining crew members. They sued to recover the £40 per man that they had been promised for bringing the ship home. The court held that they were entitled to recover the additional money as the nature of the voyage had altered so drastically that their original contract had effectively been terminated leaving them free to make a new contract on different terms.

The position was reconsidered and *Stilk* v *Myrick* refined in the 1990 Court of Appeal decision of *Williams* v *Roffey Bros & Nicholls (Contractors) Ltd* [1990] 1 All ER 512. However, the *Roffey* decision did recognise a situation in which an existing contractual duty can constitute consideration for a new contractual promise.

In *Williams* v *Roffey Bros* the defendants were building contractors who gained a contract to refurbish a block of flats. They subcontracted some joinery work to the plaintiff for £20 000, the arrangement being that payment would be made in instalments as the work was completed. In practice, £16 200, over eighty per cent of the price, was paid to the plaintiff although he had not completed eighty per cent of the work. At this point, he got into financial difficulties due partly to his price being too low and partly to a failure to provide proper supervision for his workmen. The defendants, aware of his financial problems and anxious to avoid a penalty clause if the major contract was not completed on time, agreed to pay the plaintiff an additional £575 per flat on completion, a total of £10 300. The plaintiff completed a further eight flats and received a further £1500 before stopping work. The Court of Appeal, upholding the decision of the lower court, held that the plaintiff was entitled to recover the additional money due for the completed flats less a small deduction for defective or incomplete items. They held that the defendants had acquired a benefit by having the plaintiff complete the contract on time in exchange for the additional payment, namely that the defendant had avoided the penalty clause under the main contract.

(iii) Part payment of a debt. Generally, part payment of a debt is not sufficient consideration for a promise to accept the payment as full settlement of the debt, this rule being known as the rule in *Pinnel's case* (1602) 5 Co Rep 117a. Suppose, for example, that a main contractor and a sub-contractor have agreed that the latter will undertake some work for £1000. Upon completion of it, however, the main contractor, pleading cash flow problems, offers the sub-contractor £800 in full settlement of the contract debt. The sub-contractor, needing the money quickly to settle immediate commitments, accepts but later thinks better of it. Will the sub-contractor be bound by his acceptance of the lower sum? *Pinnel's case* would say not.

This rule is not as strict as it first appears and there is a variety of situations in which lesser payment will suffice. Thus, if the payment were made at an earlier date, or in a different place, or in a different form at the payee's request the payment of the lesser sum will be binding. The payee has received a benefit by receiving payment in a way other than that to which he was contractually entitled and thus consideration has been provided for his promise to accept a lesser sum. Acceptance of a lesser sum will also be binding if the part payment is made by a third party on condition that the original debt will be extinguished, as was shown in the decision of *Hiranchand Punamchand* v *Temple* [1911] 2 KB 330 in which the defendant's father offered part payment of the defendant's debt in full settlement.

Of more concern in a business context is the position regarding composition agreements whereby a debtor seeks to settle all his debts by agreeing to pay each creditor a percentage of the due debt in full settlement. Parties to such an agreement cannot sue later for the balance of the debt owed to them as this would amount to a fraud on the creditors who had accepted part payment.

The final situation in which part payment may be binding is that of promissory estoppel as enunciated in the decision of *Central London Property Trust Ltd* v *High Trees House Ltd* [1947] KB 130. It must be stressed that this doctrine can only be used as a defence to an action and never as a cause of action. Hence, it is 'a shield and not a sword'.

In *Central London Property Trust Ltd* v *High Trees House Ltd*, the plaintiffs entered into a lease with the defendants whereby the latter leased a block of flats in London from the plaintiffs for a term of ninety nine years at an annual ground rent of £2500. The lease was effective from September 1937. In January 1940, as a result of the outbreak of the war and the consequent difficulties of letting property in London, the plaintiffs wrote to the defendants agreeing to reduce the ground rent to £1250 per annum. The defendants paid rent at the reduced rate from the beginning of 1941 until 1945 when the flats were fully occupied. The plaintiffs sought to recover the difference between the rent agreed in the lease and that actually paid for the last two quarters of 1945 with the clear intention that, if the claim was successful, a further claim would be made relating to the whole of the period during which the reduced rent had been paid. Lord Denning held that the agreement about the reduced rent was only intended to apply for the duration of the war and, thus, that the plaintiffs were entitled to recover for the last two quarters of 1945, the war being over. However, no claim would be permitted in respect of the period 1941 to 1945 while hostilities existed.

The use of the doctrine as a defence requires that the plaintiff made a promise intending it to be relied upon and that the defendant acted in reliance upon it. There is no requirement that the defendant has suffered any detriment by his reliance, merely that he has altered his position. As is evident from the *High Trees* decision, the rule will suspend the plaintiff's rights for the period during which the reliance occurred but will allow them to be revived thereafter.

INTENTION TO CREATE LEGAL RELATIONS

Not all agreements are legally enforceable. Many situations occur in which people make agreements never intending that any legal liability will arise. Thus, for example, an agreement to go to the cinema with a friend would not be actionable if you fail to turn up.

The major factor in deciding whether a promise is actionable is whether the agreement is of a domestic nature or a commercial one.

Domestic agreements

There is a presumption at law that agreements of an essentially domestic or social nature will not be binding. Naturally, the presumption will be overruled if evidence is adduced demonstrating an intention to be bound as occurred in the decision of *Simpkins v Pays* [1955] 3 All ER 10 in which the three tenants of a house jointly entered a competition agreeing to share any winnings.

Commercial agreements

There is a rebuttable presumption in commercial dealings that the parties do intend to be contractually bound. It is possible, however, to rebut this presumption by the inclusion of a statement in the agreement to the effect that there is no intention to create a binding contract.

In *Rose & Frank Co* v *J.R. Crompton & Bros* [1925] AC 445, an agreement between the parties, an English company and an American company, contained an 'Honourable Pledge Clause' which provided that the agreement 'was not entered into . . . as a formal or legal agreement and shall not be subject to legal jurisdiction in the law courts either of the United States or England, but is only a definite expression and record of the purpose and intention of the parties concerned, to which they each honourably pledge themselves'. Under the agreement, the plaintiffs were to act as the sole American agents for the sale of the defendants' products. The defendants terminated the agreement without giving the agreed period of notice and refused to fulfil orders placed by the plaintiffs prior to the date of termination. The Court of Appeal held that the defendants were obliged to fulfil outstanding orders in respect of which a contract had arisen but that, because of the 'Honourable Pledge Clause', there was no contractual obligation on the defendants to continue with the agreement or accept any further orders.

A recent development with regard to intention in the commercial context has been the recognition of 'letters of comfort', most notably in the decision of *Kleinwort Benson Ltd* v *Malaysian Mining Corporation Bhd* [1989] 1 All ER 785.

The plaintiff bank agreed to provide a loan to the defendants' wholly owned subsidiary, MMC Metals Ltd, who traded in tin on the London Metal Exchange. The defendants refused to provide a guarantee for the loan but did provide two 'letters of comfort' each of which read 'It is our policy to ensure that the business of MMC Metals Ltd is at all times in a position to meet its liabilities to you under the (loan facility) arrangements'. Due to the collapse of the tin market, MMC Metals Ltd went into liquidation while still owing the plaintiff the whole of the sum borrowed. The plaintiff sued the defendants for the amount owing relying on the 'letters of comfort'. The Court of Appeal held that the defendants were not liable, the 'letters of comfort' merely being statements of fact about the defendants' present intentions and not contractual promises as to their future conduct. There was no intention to create a legal relationship as evidenced by the defendants' refusal to provide a guarantee.

Clearly, a business issuing a letter of comfort must ensure that their intention is beyond doubt because of the presumption that businesses intend to contract.

CONTRACTUAL CAPACITY

A person of full legal age, eighteen by virtue of the Family Law Reform Act 1969, has the legal capacity to enter any contract other than those which are void or illegal either at common law or by statute. The position with regard to companies and minors is not so clear cut.

Corporate capacity

Suppose, for example, that firm A supplied £20 000 worth of timber to firm B but does not receive payment. It transpires that firm B was established for the purpose of breeding pigs. Can firm A sue for the money or is firm B able to avoid the debt?

The majority of commercial companies, both public and private, are incorporated under the provisions of successive Companies Acts, the current statute being the Companies Act 1985 as amended. Traditionally, the legal capacity of companies has been governed by the doctrine of *ultra vires* which stipulates that any action by a company which falls outside the provisions of the company's 'objects clause' will be invalid. The 'objects clause' is to be found in the Memorandum of Association, the major corporate document registered at the time of incorporation, and specifies those areas of business in which the company will be involved. The *ultra vires* doctrine at its most draconian provided that contracting parties had constructive notice of the contents of any company's 'objects clause' and thus were bound by its contents. Hence, in the example above, firm A would be unable to sue firm B for the £20 000 as the latter was acting outside its declared object of pig breeding and thus was acting *ultra vires*.

The *ultra vires* doctrine, intended to protect third parties, shareholders and investors in their dealings with companies, was heavily criticised with consequent calls for its abolition. Section 35 of the Companies Act 1985, as enacted by s.108(1) of the Companies Act 1989, while not abolishing the doctrine has severely limited its impact. Section 35(1) provides:

'The validity of an act done by a company shall not be called into question on the ground of lack of capacity by reason of anything in the company's memorandum.'

In the example quoted above, therefore, firm A would now be able to recover the £20 000 for the timber from firm B, the latter being unable to plead *ultra vires*. This is clearly an advantage for anyone dealing with the company. Nonetheless, while section 35 now prevents a company hiding behind the *ultra vires* doctrine in its relationships with third parties, the doctrine has been retained as a means of internal corporate control. Thus, any shareholder may seek an injunction to prevent a company from acting *ultra vires* and restrain the directors from acting in excess of their powers.

Minors

Minors, anyone under the age of eighteen, possess restricted legal capacity, the underlying rationale being to protect them from full legal liability. Contracts with minors are void with the exception of two groups of contracts, the first of which are binding while the second group are voidable.

Binding contracts with minors comprise those for the purchase of necessaries, as defined in s.3(3) of the Sale of Goods Act 1979, and contracts of service beneficial to the minor. This includes contracts of employment, apprenticeship and education, but does not include trading contracts. Thus, a minor running his own business will not be bound by the contracts that he makes, though they will be voidable. While such trading contracts are likely to be relatively few in number, they do pose a risk in the commercial context.

Voidable contracts, i.e. those that can be ratified or avoided by the minor on attaining his majority, include trading contracts and those where he has gained an interest in something such as shares or land. A voidable contract that has been ratified becomes binding. A minor wishing to repudiate a voidable contract must do so within a reasonable period of gaining his majority, the exact length of the period depending on the facts of each individual case.

PRIVITY OF CONTRACT

If A and B enter into a contract, can C enforce it in the event of either of the contracting parties going into breach? The simple answer is 'no'. The doctrine of privity of contract provides that only a party to a contract may sue upon it, for only a contracting party will have provided consideration as in *Dunlop Pneumatic Tyre Co Ltd* v *Selfridge & Co Ltd* [1915] AC 847. Thus, a third party cannot sue on a contract even if he is the intended beneficiary of it as in the *Tweddle* v *Atkinson* (1861) 1 B & S 393 decision.

There are a few situations in which the harshness of the rule may be mitigated by some other factor.

(a) **Contracting on behalf of a group.** In *Jackson* v *Horizon Holidays Ltd* [1975] 3 All ER 92 the plaintiff who had booked a holiday on behalf of his family was entitled to claim compensation for all of them when the holiday proved unsatisfactory. However, the application of this exception is restricted to situations where there is a clear presumption that the plaintiff was acting on behalf of the group as a whole.

(b) **Collateral contracts.** This occurs where a separate contract related to the main contract exists between a third party and one of the main contracting parties.

In *Shanklin Pier Ltd* v *Detel Products Ltd* [1951] 2 KB 854 a contract existed between the plaintiff and a contractor for the painting of a pier. The plaintiff, relying on representations made by the defendant paint manufacturer, insisted that the defendant's paint should be used for the job. The contractor purchased the paint which proved unsatisfactory and did not match up to specification. It was held that the plaintiff was entitled to recover damages from the defendant manufacturer of the paint on the basis of a collateral contract.

(c) **Assignment.** This occurs where one of the contracting parties enters an agreement to transfer his rights and liabilities under a contract to a third party who may enforce it in his own behalf. Thus, if in a contract between A and B, B were to assign his contractual rights to C, the contract would then be between A and C and enforceable by both. Strictly speaking, this is not an exception to the privity rule since the contract is still a bilateral one enforceable by the parties, it is merely that the identity of the parties has changed.

QUESTION

Ace Ltd, a manufacturing company, wanted to replace all the computers in their offices with a new comprehensive system. They invited tenders for the provision and installation of the equipment from various computer companies with whom they had dealt before. The letter inviting the tenders included the statement 'if the offer made by you is the lowest offer received by us, we bind ourselves to accept such offer'. In response to the letter Niger Computers Ltd bid £360 000 while Congo Computers Ltd bid £375 000 or £5 000 less than any lower bid. The contract was awarded to Niger Computers Ltd.

Ace Ltd then placed the order stating that the contract was to be on the basis of their standard terms and conditions. However, Niger Computers Ltd purported to accept the offer but on a contract form comprising their own standard terms which included a price variation clause. On the bottom of Niger Computer Ltd's contract was a tear-off slip acknowledging the agreement to the terms. An employee of Ace Ltd duly signed and returned the slip. Advise:

(a) Congo Computers Ltd who feel that they should have been awarded the contract as they made the lowest bid.

(b) Niger Computers Ltd who want to raise the contract price to £370 000 which Ace Ltd are refusing to pay.

FURTHER READING

Furmston, M.P., *Cheshire, Fifoot and Furmston's Law of Contract* (12th ed) 1991 (Butterworth)

Downes, T.A., *Textbook on Contract* (2nd ed) 1991 (Blackstone Press)

Keenan, D. and Riches, S., *Business Law* (3rd ed) 1993 (Pitman)

Richards, P., *Law of Contract* 1992 (Pitman)

Savage, N. and Bradgate, R., *Business Law* (2nd ed) 1993 (Butterworth)

Smith, J.C., *Smith and Thomas A Casework on Contract* (9th ed) 1992 (Sweet and Maxwell)

CHAPTER 2

Contractual terms and formalities

FORMALITIES

The law stipulates few formalities in the creation of legally binding contracts. They do not even need to be in writing although there are some exceptions to this general rule. Oral contracts are equally valid to written ones although, naturally, their terms may be more difficult to prove. Consequently, it is common sense for business contracts and any contract involving a large sum of money to be written.

In contrast to the general rule, certain contracts of interest to businesses must be written. First, regulated agreements under the Consumer Credit Act 1974 must be written and in a prescribed format or they will be unenforceable against the debtor or hirer without a court order (s.65). The legal requirements for credit agreements are discussed more fully in chapter 17. Second, s.2 of the Law of Property (Miscellaneous Provisions) Act 1989 requires that any contract for the sale or other dispostion of land must be in writing, contain all the terms agreed by the parties and be signed by both parties. A contract not in this form will be void.

Contracts of guarantee are slightly different. While the contract itself does not need to be written, s.4 of the Statute of Frauds 1677 requires that there must be some written evidence of the terms of the agreement. A contract of guarantee occurs where the guarantor promises to pay the debts of a second person if that other should default. The promise must be made to the third party to whom the debt is owed. It is important to note that the guarantor is only accepting liability upon the debtor's default and not in any other situation. The written evidence of the agreement can be contained in a note but must stipulate all the terms of the guarantee and have been signed by the guarantor. There are two situations involving contracts of guarantee which fall outside the requirements of s.4. The first is where the guarantee forms part of a larger transaction, for example where the guarantor is a *del credere* agent. This occurs when an agent, usually in exchange for a larger commission, agrees to guarantee a debt owed to his principal by a third party. Here, the guarantee forms part of a larger contract of agency and falls outside the statute as held in *Couturier* v *Hastie* (1852) 8 Exch 40 in which the defendant, acting as a *del credere* agent, was held liable to his plaintiff principal on an oral contract of guarantee. The second exception occurs when the guarantee is provided by the guarantor as a way of securing property which he owns, as in *Fitzgerald* v *Dressler* (1859) 7 CBNS 374.

It is vital to distinguish between contracts of guarantee where written evidence is essential, and contracts of indemnity where there is no such requirement. Unlike contracts of guarantee which involve secondary liability, indemnity occurs where the defendant has assumed the debt in his own right.

The case of *Mountstephen* v *Lakeman* (1874) LR 7 HL 17 illustrates the point well. Mountstephen, the plaintiff builder, was to undertake some work for a Local Board of Health. In a discussion about the method of payment, Lakeman, the Chairman of the Board stated 'Go on, Mountstephen, and do the work, and I will see you paid'. The Board refused to pay for the work on the basis that they had not made any agreement with the plaintiff. The court held that, in the absence of an agreement, the Board could not be regarded as a debtor and hence Lakeman was personally liable having provided an indemnity.

In a business context, the distinction is important to contractors seeking a guarantee from a parent company that they will receive payment for goods or services provided to a subsidiary business or, alternatively, a financial institution seeking guarantees for a business loan. The agreement will need to be considered carefully as the terminology used will not necessarily determine whether the parent is merely acting as a guarantor or is providing an indemnity. Further, note the distinction between a guarantee that gives rise to legal liability and a letter of comfort (as discussed in the previous chapter) which does not.

Finally, there are some contracts which must be made by deed and 'signed, sealed and delivered'. Of prime concern are conveyances for the sale of land or the creation of a lease lasting more than three years. Of lesser interest are contracts lacking consideration which will be enforceable if made by deed.

TERMS OF THE CONTRACT

Precontractual discussions are a normal part of the business of contracting. But it would naive to assume that all the statements made during those negotiations will necessarily become embedded in the contract. Precontractual statements can best be divided into three groups; advertising puffs, representations and contractual terms. The first group involves those statements that are so wildly exaggerated that there is clearly no intention that they should be relied upon. Examples might include 'a good little runner' when applied to a car, or 'smells like spring' when applied to washing powder or other similarly exaggerated claims. For the purposes of legal liability such statements are discarded easily. By contrast, representations, sometimes termed 'mere representations', are those statements which invite reliance and are intended to induce one of the parties to enter the contract. This might, for example, include general statements about reliability or efficiency. Finally, contractual terms are those statements that both parties intend should form an integral part of their agreement and be actionable if untrue.

It is the distinction between misrepresentations and contractual terms that is of most import. Either can give rise to legal liability if they prove to be untrue, a false representation being actionable under the Misrepresentation Act 1967 (see next chapter) while a false term will give rise to an action for breach of contract. Likewise, both may give rise to some criminal liability under the Trade Descriptions Act 1968 (see chapter 13). It is often difficult to draw the dividing line between the two but various guidelines have been established. Thus the timing of the statement in the process of negotiation, whether it was later reduced into any written contract, the relative expertise of the contracting parties and the importance of the term to them all play a part in deciding the status of the relevant statement. Two contrasting decisions illustrate this.

In *Bannerman* v *White* (1861) 10 CBNS 844, a buyer of hops asked during the precontractual negotiations whether the hops had been treated with sulphur, making clear that he would not buy any hops that had been so treated. The seller confirmed that the crop had not been treated. It subsequently transpired that a small proportion of the hops had been treated with sulphur, the buyer consequently refusing to pay. The Court held that the statement that the hops were untreated was a condition of the contract having been made at a significant point in the negotiations with both parties aware of its importance.

In *Routledge* v *McKay* [1954] 1 All ER 855, the parties, both private individuals, were negotiating the sale of a motorcycle. The defendant, relying on the registration document, stated that the bike was registered in 1942. This information was not included in the written contract concluded a week later. In fact the bike dated from 1930. The court held that the statement was sufficiently remote from the final contract not to be classed as part of it. It was a mere representation.

Routledge v *McKay* is also good authority for the proposition that the statement may be classed as a mere representation if it is not contained in any later written contract.

The relevance of the skill and expertise of the contracting parties is demonstrated in the contrasting cases of *Oscar Chess Ltd* v *Williams* [1957] 1 All ER 325 and *Dick Bentley Productions Ltd* v *Harold Smith (Motors) Ltd* [1965] 2 All ER 65 both of which involved the sale of a car. The cases suggest that if the more experienced or knowledgeable of the two contracting parties makes the statement it may be classed as a term whereas if the least experienced of the two makes the statement, it is likely to be classed as a representation. It would seem that this may be so irrespective of whether the experienced party is the seller or the buyer.

One potential solution to the difficulty of deciding the status of a statement may be to class representations as collateral contracts.

EXPRESS AND IMPLIED TERMS

Thus far we have assumed that the parties are of equal bargaining power and have freedom of contract, i.e. the ability to decide for themselves what terms are to be included in their contract. In practice, this is not so.

Express terms

The express terms of a contract are those terms agreed upon by the parties and which form the nub of the contract, be it written, oral or a mixture of both. Thus, for example, the express terms might include details of the subject matter, the price, any price variation clause of the type discussed in the *Butler Machine Tool Co v Ex-Cell-O Corpn* case, any permitted exclusion clauses, a *force majeure* clause, a liquidated damages clause, a clause governing arbitration in the event of a dispute and the time of performance. If the time of performance is considered to be important, the parties must expressly agree upon this as the general contractual rule is that time is not of the essence. However, in commercial contracts, the courts may be prepared to imply that time is of the essence in order to give the contract business efficacy.

A *force majeure* clause, invariably included in business contracts for the supply of goods, constitutes an attempt by the contracting parties to stipulate what will happen if some event beyond their control interferes with contractual performance. Thus, for example, the clause might stipulate that if the supplier is prevented from delivery in accordance with the contract because of some specfied supervening event additional time for performance is to be allowed, or that the supplier can delay further performance without penalty or even terminate the contract forthwith. Supervening events outlined in *force majeure* clauses typically include Acts of God, delays in manufacture and problems with sub-contractors. The courts tend to construe such clauses narrowly but if the term does cover the event that actually occurs the term will take effect. If it does not, the contract will be frustrated instead.

In *Jackson v Union Marine Insurance Co Ltd* (1874) LR 10 CP 125, a ship was chartered to sail from Liverpool to Newport 'with all possible despatch' to load cargo for San Francisco 'dangers and accidents of navigation excepted'. The ship ran aground in Caernarvon Bay on her way to Newport and was not repaired for eight months. The court held that the clause did not cover the accident that actually occurred and that the contract was frustrated.

The parties to a commercial contract may try to genuinely calculate their likely losses in the event of contractual breach. Where agreement is reached, a liquidated damages clause may be included in the contract and will take effect when relevant. This can be used, for example, as a method for settling damages for late performance by specifying that a given percentage of the contract price is payable for each day, week or month by which delivery or completion is delayed. When a liquidated damages clause takes effect the parties receive the amount agreed by way of damages, no more and no less, irrespective of the actual damage suffered. It is vital to distinguish between liquidated damages clauses which are a genuine pre-estimate of losses and are enforceable and penalty clauses which seek to use punishment to force compliance by the contracting parties and are void. This distinction was considered in *Dunlop Pneumatic Tyre Co Ltd* v *New Garage & Motor Co Ltd* [1915] AC 79, HL in which the House of Lords established guidelines for identifying penalty clauses. A clause will be a penalty clause if

(a)   the amount to be paid on breach is extravagant as compared with the maximum loss that could be suffered as a result of the breach.
(b)   the contractual performance required consists of paying a sum of money and the clause requires the payment of a larger sum of money on breach.
(c)   the clause stipulates one sum to be paid as damages in the event of a variety of possible breaches of differing significance, some serious and some trivial. The sum cannot possibly be a realistic pre-estimate in respect of all the specified breaches.

The court will decide whether the clause is a penalty clause or not, the nomenclature used by the parties to the contract is irrelevant. It is the responsibility of the party who is liable to pay to establish that the clause is a penalty clause.

A prime example of express contractual terms in the business context is standard form contracts in which a business lays down the terms and conditions on which it is prepared to contract. Clearly, for a company contracting on a regular basis this is sound business practice for it prevents the need to negotiate a new contract with every client while also allowing it to stipulate terms that are protective of its own position (subject to statutory controls on exclusion clauses). Further, it permits relatively junior members of staff to contract on the company's behalf. A potential difficulty with standard form contracts arises, of course, when two businesses contracting together each want to use their own standard form contract. Hence the 'Battle of the Forms' as discussed in the previous chapter.

The valid incorporation of any express term must be established if it is to be enforceable. This must have occurred prior to the conclusion of the contract. Thereafter any additional term can be added to the contract only with the agreement of both parties. Unilateral alteration of the contract is not permitted as illustrated by the decision of *Olley* v *Marlborough Court Ltd* [1949] 1 All ER 127 which concerned the incorporation of an exclusion clause.

In *Olley* v *Marlborough Court Ltd* the plaintiffs, Mr and Mrs Olley, booked into a hotel, the contract for the stay being finalised at the reception desk. On their bedroom wall was a notice which read 'the proprietors will not hold themselves responsible for articles lost or stolen unless handed to the manageress for safe custody'. In their absence, a third party took the key from the reception and used it to enter the plaintiffs' bedroom and steal some furs. The defendant hotel attempted to deny liability relying on the exclusion clause. The Court of Appeal held that the exclusion clause had not been incorporated validly as it had not been included at the time that the contract had been concluded and had only come to the notice of the plaintiffs later. The hotel could not rely on it.

Implied terms

The ability of the parties to decide all the contractual terms is restricted both by the insertion of implied terms either statutorily or judicially and by the exclusion of terms that are void or illegal. Further, an inequality of bargaining power may lead to one party having terms imposed upon him with which he is not happy. This problem has been addressed to some extent by the inclusion of protective implied terms as detailed below and partly by statutory controls over exclusion clauses. Implied terms can be subdivided into those relating to fact and those relating to law.

Implied terms relating to fact will be those terms that a court may imply into a particular contract in order to give it business efficacy. The court's role is to imply those terms that the contracting parties have genuinely overlooked and not to include terms that might improve the contract. The implied terms should complete the contract intended by the parties. The test to be applied is whether, had the presence of the term been queried, both contracting parties would have agreed to its inclusion without hesitation. An unwillingness by one party to include the term would be fatal. This approach was confirmed recently in the House of Lords decision of *Scally* v *Southern Health and Social Services Board* [1991] 3 WLR 778 in which Lord Bridge opined that the test for an implied term of fact is whether it is 'necessary to give business efficacy to a particular contract'.

The same requirement of necessity exists in respect of implied terms of law, Lord Bridge stating that such a term should 'based on wider considerations . . . [be] . . . a necessary incident of a definable category of contractual relationships'. In short, the court should consider it necessary as a matter of public policy to include an implied term of the type proposed into all contracts of a particular defined group. Such terms are implied into all appropriate contracts irrespective of the wishes of individual contracting parties although reserving the right of those parties to expressly exclude the implied term to the extent that such an exclusion is legal.

Implied terms as to law may be implied by common law or statute or custom. Terms implied by the courts may cover a variety of situations. In the decision of *Lister* v *Romford Ice and Cold Storage Co Ltd* [1957] AC 555 in which Lister, a driver, was being sued by his employer for breach of contract the court implied a term that an employee would use reasonable care and skill when performing his duties. The case resulted from Lister driving his lorry negligently and injuring a workmate, his father. A similar approach was adopted in *Liverpool City Council* v *Irwin* [1977] AC 239 in which the House of Lords held that in relation to a block of flats owned by the Council, there was an implied term that the Council would take reasonable care to maintain the common areas of the property including the stairs and lifts in a reasonable condition. In the *Scally* decision the House of Lords implied a term into contracts of employment to the effect that the employers had a duty to inform their staff of the possibility of purchasing added years to gain the full benefit of a statutory superannuation scheme.

Arguably the most significant statutory implied terms are those contained in ss.12–15 of the Sale of Goods Act 1979. Sections 12, 13 and 15 are implied into all contracts of sale while s.14 is restricted to those contracts of sale in which the seller sells in the course of a business. The terms govern the seller's right to sell, sales by description, the concepts of merchantable quality and fitness for purpose and sales by sample. These implied conditions are considered in depth in chapter 7. Similar terms are implied into contracts for the supply of services together with additional terms governing the care and skill to be exhibited in the performance of contracts for services, the time of performance and a right to payment by the Supply of Goods and Services Act 1982. These terms are considered in chapter 8.

Terms implied by custom may be of significance in particular industries where neither contracting party would expressly include a term as both would assume that they would be bound by custom as in *Hutton* v *Warren* (1836) 1 M & W 466 in which it was held that a farm tenant was entitled to receive some allowance for the seeds and labour that he had spent on the land.

CONDITIONS, INNOMINATE TERMS AND WARRANTIES

Not all contractual terms are of equal significance. A longstanding distinction exists between conditions and warranties. Conditions are those terms that go to the heart of the contract, the breach of which effectively destroys the contract. By contrast, a warranty is a lesser term the breach of which would not have a major impact upon the continued existence of the contract. This distinction is reflected in the remedies available for breach, the breach of a condition giving the innocent party a right to terminate the contract whereas a breach of warranty only attracts an action for damages. In respect of a breach of condition, the injured party can elect to continue with the contract and sue for damages instead. The distinction between conditions and warranties is amply illustrated by two contrasting decisions involving similar contracts for services.

In *Poussard* v *Spiers and Pond* (1876) 1 QBD 410, the plaintiff, Madame Poussard, was under contract to the defendant to appear in an operetta. She was taken ill five days before the first performance and was not available until a week after the show had started. It was held that her failure to appear for the first performance was a breach of condition as it effectively rendered the contract incapable of performance. The defendant had been within his rights to terminate her contract and engage another singer.

By contrast, in *Bettini* v *Gye* (1876) 1 QBD 183, in which the plaintiff, Bettini, was required to be present for rehearsals six days before the first performance, it was held that his arrival three days late was only a breach of warranty for which damages were payable. He was present for the opening night and thus the substantial performance of the contract was possible. The term relating to rehearsal time was of lesser significance.

The parties may decide themselves as to the status of any particular term for which they are responsible. In respect of statutory implied terms, the statute may stipulate the nature of the term as, for example, in s.14 of the Sale of Goods Act 1979 which states that the term regarding the merchantable quality of goods is a condition. The obvious advantage of the nature of the term being made clear at the outset is that both parties are aware of the effect of any breach. There is certainty.

A more recent concept, first discussed in *Hong Kong Fir Shipping Co Ltd* v *Kawasaki Kisen Kaisha Ltd* [1962] 1 All ER 474 is that of the innominate term. These terms fall midway between conditions and warranties with the outcome of any breach being uncertain. The court has the ability to render the contract terminated or alternatively to award damages, whichever is the more appropriate remedy given the effect of the breach. It will depend upon whether the injured party has effectively been denied the benefit of the contract.

The *Hong Kong Fir Shipping* case involved a contract to charter a ship 'being fitted in every way for ordinary cargo service' for 24 months from the date of delivery. Due to the condition of the engines and the ineptitude of the crew, the ship was delayed for 20 weeks for repair. The charterers repudiated the contract and the shipowners sued for wrongful termination. The Court of Appeal held that although the ship had been unseaworthy at the outset of the contract, there were still twenty months of the charter to run at the time that the ship was ready. The contract was not frustrated being capable of substantial performance. In the circumstances, the charterers were only entitled to claim damages.

This approach of considering the effect of the breach has been followed in two other notable decisions, *Cehave NV v Bremer Handelsgesellschaft mbH, The Hansa Nord* [1975] 3 All ER 739 and *Reardon Smith Line Ltd v Yngvar Hansen-Tangen* [1976] 3 All ER 570.

In the *Cehave NV* decision, the sellers sold a cargo of citrus pellets to the buyers subject to a term that they would be shipped 'in good condition'. On arrival, part of the cargo was damaged and the buyers rejected the whole consignment. Subsequently, the original buyer bought the cargo at a substantially reduced price and used it for the original purpose of making animal feed. The Court of Appeal, rejecting the argument that all express terms about quality must be classed as conditions because of the impact of s.14 of the Sale of Goods Act 1979, held that this particular clause was an innominate term and that as the damage to the goods had not been significant, the buyer did not have a right to reject them.

In the *Reardon Smith Line* decision, the House of Lords held that a term of the contract identifying the Yard No where a ship under construction would be built was an innominate term the breach of which would only give rise to damages. It was a technical breach. The contract identified the ship as Osaka No 354, whereas because of a reallocation of work to another yard, the ship was actually built as Oshima 004. Nonetheless, the ship was built according to the agreed specifications.

It is important not to extend the principle of innominate terms too far for in cases such as *The Mihalis Angelos* [1970] 3 All ER 125 and *Bunge Corporation v Tradax Export SA* [1981] 2 All ER 513 the court, in the pursuit of certainty, has expressed a preference for stipulating that a particular term is either a condition or a warranty.

On a statutory level, innominate terms are to be found in ss.13–15 of the Supply of Goods and Services Act 1982 where the implied terms about skill and care, the time of performance and the right to payment are expressed to be implied terms as opposed to implied conditions or warranties.

QUESTION

Red-Telephones Ltd contracted to supply and install a new telephone system in the premises of Blue Manufacturing Co. The contract included two terms:

(a) that the supplier would be liable for any delay in installing the system unless such delay was due to Act of God, war, industrial action or some other reason beyond the control of the supplier;

(b) in the event of non-completion by the due date, contractual damages would be assessed at a rate of 1% of the contract price for each week or part of a week by which installation was delayed.

Some of the essential component parts for the system could only be purchased from Purple Tele-electronics Ltd, the sole supplier in the UK with whom Red-Telephones Ltd duly contracted for the purchase of sufficient parts for the system. However, due to industrial action at Purple Tele-electronics Ltd, the relevant component parts were not delivered on time with the result that Red-Telephones Ltd could not complete the system by the due date of 1 March. Contractual completion finally occurred on 15 May.

Blue Manufacturing Co are seeking to enforce the clause relating to contractual damages.

Discuss.

FURTHER READING

Downes, T.A., *Textbook on Contract* (2nd ed) 1991 (Blackstone Press)

Furmston, M.P., *Cheshire, Fifoot and Furmston's Law of Contract* (12th ed) 1991 (Butterworth)

Keenan, D. and Riches, S., *Business Law* (3rd ed) 1993 (Pitman)

Phang, 'Implied Terms in English Law – Some Recent Developments' (1993) *Journal of Business Law* 242

Richards, P., *Law of Contract* 1992 (Pitman)

Smith, J.C., *Smith and Thomas A Casebook on Contract* (12th ed) 1992 (Sweet and Maxwell)

CHAPTER 3

Vitiating factors

Apparently valid contracts agreed upon by the contracting parties may subsequently be rendered either void or voidable by some extenuating factor that existed at the time that the contract was finalised.

The effect of a contract being rendered void *ab initio* is that the contract is deemed never to have existed. It follows that neither party can acquire any rights or incur any liability under the contract and that the contracting parties must be returned to the position they occupied before the contract was concluded, the *status quo ante*. Thus, any goods that have changed hands under the contract must be returned to the original owner and any monies paid must be refunded.

By contrast, the consequences of a contract being rendered voidable are less clear cut. The contract in question remains legal and enforceable until such time as it is avoided by the innocent party. The effect of the avoidance is, *prima facie*, to terminate the contract *ab initio* with all goods and monies being returned to their original owner. However, the right to rescind the contract may be lost if either full restoration of the *status quo ante* is not possible, or an innocent third party has acquired any goods under the contract prior to the rescission or the innocent contracting party chooses to affirm the contract and carry on.

The events that may render a contract either void or voidable are:

(a) mistake
(b) misrepresentation
(c) duress
(d) illegality

MISTAKE

Only an operative mistake will have any effect upon the existence or continuance of a contract, the meaning of an operative mistake being far narrower than the meaning of mistake in common parlance. Thus, for example, in the absence of some misrepresentation by the seller, the mere fact that a purchaser has not bought what he intended to buy or has paid too much for it will not affect the validity of the contract. The basic rule of *caveat emptor*, let the buyer beware, will apply unchallenged.

Operative mistakes fall into one of two categories, the first being common mistake where both parties have made the same mistake about some fundamental aspect of the contract. They have made an agreement but based on a false premise. The second type, comprising both mutual mistake and unilateral mistake, occurs where the mistake means that there is no true agreement between the parties.

Common mistake

The essential feature of common mistake is that both parties have made the same mistake about a fundamental feature of the contract. A typical example might be where the parties have contracted for the supply and purchase of some identified goods, both unaware that the goods had perished prior to the contract being made.

The decision of *Couturier* v *Hastie* (1856) HL Cas 673 is the most commonly quoted authority for this proposition. The parties contracted for the sale of some corn which was in transit aboard ship. Unknown to both parties, a few days before the contract was made the captain of the ship had sold the corn as it had started to deteriorate and he wished to avoid loss.

A recent decision that reinforces the doctrine of common mistake is *Associated Japanese Bank (International) Ltd* v *Credit du Nord SA* [1988] 3 All ER 902, a decision of the Commercial Court.

In the *Associated Japanese Bank* decision, the plaintiff bank, Associated Japanese Bank (International) Ltd, agreed a sale and leaseback transaction with B under which the bank bought four specified precision engineering machines from B and then leased them back to him. Under this arrangement, the plaintiff bank paid £1 020 000 to B. The agreement was subject to a condition that B's obligations were to be guaranteed by the defendant bank, Credit du Nord. Both banks believed that the four machines existed and were in B's possession. When B defaulted on the agreement, the plaintiff bank sought to enforce the guarantee. It transpired that the machines did not exist and the defendants denied liability arguing that the contract was void *ab initio* for common mistake. The court held that there was both an express and implied condition in the guarantee that the machines did exist. As they did not the guarantee was void for common mistake.

It is vital to recognise the distinction between the non-existence of goods and the fact that they are of a different quality from that envisaged. The leading case is that of *Bell* v *Lever Bros* [1932] AC 161 relating to the termination of a contract of employment, in which Lord Atkin propounded the view that a mistake about the quality of the subject matter of a contract will only be an operative mistake if it involves 'the existence of some quality which makes the thing without the quality essentially different from the thing as it was believed to be'.

In respect of the sale or supply of goods, if the goods have been described as possessing some quality which they do not and the seller has warranted the truth of the statement, then a contract action will lie for a breach of s.13 of the Sale of Goods Act 1979 (or other similar provision under another statute depending on the nature of the supply of the goods). A misdescription of this nature would also give rise to criminal liability under s.1 of the Trade Descriptions Act 1968 if applied in the course of a trade or business.

The third way in which common mistake may arise is where both parties have made the same mistake about the ownership of the subject matter of the contract, typically where the seller purports to sell or supply something which, unknown to both parties, already belongs to the buyer.

Mutual mistake

Mutual mistake occurs when the parties are dealing at cross purposes with no real *consensus* as, for example, if there is confusion about the subject matter of the contract.

In *Raffles* v *Wichelhaus* (1864) 2 H & C 906, the buyer agreed to buy some cotton to be transported on the ship 'Peerless'. In fact, there were two ships of that name one sailing in October and the other in December. The buyer believed that he was buying the cotton to be transported in October while the seller believed that he was selling the December shipment. The court held the contract void for mistake. There was no agreement.

Unilateral mistake

Unilateral mistake occurs where one party has made a mistake about a fundamental facet of the contract with knowledge of the other party. This may arise in two situations, a mistake as to the terms of the contract or a mistake as to the identity of one of the contracting parties.

(a) **Mistake as to terms.** This rare situation occurs when one of the parties has misunderstood a fundamental term of the proposed contract, this mistake being known to the other contracting party.

In the decision of *Hartog* v *Colin & Shields* [1939] 3 All ER 566 the defendants offered to sell some hare skins and negotiated on the basis of a unit price per piece as was the trade custom. Subsequently, the contract was for a sale at a unit price per pound which the plaintiffs purported to accept. They were prevented from enforcing the contract on the basis that they must have been aware of the defendants' mistake.

(b) Mistake as to identity. Identity cases are most likely to arise when one of the contracting parties has been the victim of a fraud. The typical scenario is that the plaintiff seller has sold goods to a fraudster who has in turn sold them to the defendant purchaser who has bought them innocently and in good faith unaware of the fraud.

Whether the contract will be void for mistake or merely voidable for fraudulent misrepresentation will depend on the facts of the individual case and the extent to which the identity of the fraudster was central to the negotiations. Clearly, whether the contract is void or voidable has a significant impact on the rights of the innocent seller and purchaser and upon the ownership of the goods. If the contract is void, the original owner, the plaintiff seller, will be able to recover the goods from the defendant on the basis that the fraudster never acquired any title to the goods and thus was incapable of passing title to the defendant buyer. The buyer is liable for conversion of the goods and is left with the unenviable task of locating the fraudster and suing him under s.12(1) of the Sale of Goods Act 1979 for breach of the implied condition of the right to sell (see chapter 7). By contrast, if the contract is voidable, the plaintiff seller can recover the goods only if he has avoided the contract before the fraudster sold the goods to the innocent defendant buyer. Otherwise, the buyer will be protected under s.23 of the Sale of Goods Act 1979 and gain valid title to the goods leaving the seller with the equally unenviable task of suing the fraudster for the purchase price (see chapter 10 for a full discussion of the s.23 provision).

Identity cases are subject to a rebuttable presumption that the seller who was the victim of the fraud intended to deal with the person with whom he actually dealt, i.e. the fraudster. In practice, this presumption is extremely difficult to rebut. For the contract to be held void for mistake the seller must prove that the identity of the person with whom he was dealing was of fundamental importance to him and that he intended to deal only with the person of the specified identity. Further, he must show that he took reasonable steps to confirm the identity of the buyer.

The case of *Cundy v Lindsay* (1878) 3 App Cas 459, HL, is a rare example of the successful rebuttal of the presumption. The fraudster, Blenkarn, ordered some handkerchiefs from Lindsay. He signed the order in such a way that it looked like 'Blenkiron & Co' a reputable company known to Lindsay who traded from the same street as Blenkarn. Lindsay despatched the goods to Blenkarn who duly sold them to Cundy. The court held that the contract was void for mistake as Lindsay had intended to sell only to Blenkiron & Co. Lindsay was able to recover the cost of the goods from Cundy.

This case is of particular interest in the business context given that a large percentage of contracts are negotiated by letter or fax without the parties ever meeting face to face. Nonetheless, the importance of the case should not be overstated and must be contrasted with decision of *Kings Norton*

Metal Co Ltd v Edridge, Merrett & Co Ltd (1897) 14 TLR 98, CAB.

In the *Kings Norton* decision, the plaintiffs sold goods to a fraudster named Wallis who for the purposes of perpetrating the fraud had letterheads printed with the name 'Hallam & Co'. He then ordered the goods on headed paper. He subsequently sold them to the defendant who acted in good faith. The court held that the contract was not void. The plaintiffs had always intended to contract with the fraudster and had done so.

The distinction between the two cases is vital. While the identity was crucial in *Cundy v Lindsay*, in the *Kings Norton* decision it was held that it was merely his ability to pay that mattered. His true identity was irrelevant.

The difficulty of rebutting the presumption is demonstrated further by the decision of *Lewis v Averay* [1971] 3 All ER 907 in which the parties dealt face to face, as well as in the recent Commercial Court decision of *Citibank NA v Brown Shipley & Co Ltd* [1991] 2 All ER 690.

In *Lewis v Averay*, Lewis sold his car to a fraudster who claimed to be Richard Greene an actor and star of the television series 'Robin Hood'. When paying by cheque, the fraudster produced what appeared to be a pass to Pinewood Studios as proof of identity. He then sold the car to Averay. The court held that the contract was not void for mistake but voidable for fraudulent misrepresentation, the identity of the fraudster not being important to the seller at the time of the contract. As the fraudster had sold the car to Averay before Lewis avoided the contract, Averay had acquired good title to it.

In *Citibank NA v Brown Shipley & Co Ltd* a fraudster purporting to be a signatory of a company account at Citibank NA phoned the defendant, Brown Shipley, and ordered large amounts of foreign currency, payment to be made by a banker's draft drawn on Citibank NA. He then contacted Citibank and asked them to draw up a banker's draft in favour of the defendant bank and drawn on the company's account. Citibank handed the banker's draft to the fraudster who cashed it with Brown Shipley. The Commercial Court held that the contract was not void for mistake, only voidable and that Citibank could not recover the money from the defendant. The identity of the fraudster had not been fundamental in the contract and title to the draft had passed to the defendant.

As indicated earlier, the identity situation is most likely to arise where a fraud has been perpetrated. However, this is not necessarily so and may occur quite innocently as, for example, where a business has changed hands and a buyer continues to order goods from the business unaware of the change of ownership. If the buyer can establish that the identity of the proprietor of the business was of particular importance to the contractual relationship, the contract with the new proprietor would be void for mistake.

Mistake in documents

There are two further situations in which it may be possible to plead mistake. The first is where a contract has been reduced into writing but does not accurately reflect the terms of the agreement. The parties can seek the equitable remedy of rectification to have the document amended to record the agreement accurately.

The second involves the plea of *non est factum*, it is not my deed. This exception is limited to those situations where the plaintiff can show that the document he signed is essentially different in nature and effect from that which he thought he was signing as in the recent decision of *Gibbon* v *Mitchell* [1990] 3 All ER 338. Generally, the rule is that any contracting party is bound by what he has signed and will not be relieved of his liabilities. Thus, in *Saunders* v *Anglia Building Society* [1970] 3 All ER 961, HL, an elderly widow was bound by the terms of a document which she had not bothered to read. Similarly, a plaintiff cannot plead mistake if he has signed a blank contract and allowed the blanks to be filled in later although, if such a contract falls within the provisions of section 61 of the Consumer Credit Act 1974, the contract will be unenforceable against the debtor without a court order.

MISREPRESENTATION

As discussed previously, a representation is a statement that occurs prior to a contract and which induces one of the parties to enter the contract. Should the representation prove false, a remedy will lie for misrepresentation, the precise outcome depending on whether the the misrepresentation was fraudulent, negligent or innocent.

Three factors must be established for an action in misrepresentation:

(a) a misrepresentation of fact not law
(b) the misrepresentation was material
(c) it induced the contract

A misrepresentation of fact

The misrepresentation must involve some pertinent fact, must be distinguished from a mere 'advertising puff' and must be a verifiable statement about an existing fact. A misrepresentation of law will not suffice as everyone is assumed to have equal access to the law.

Further, a distinction must be drawn between statements of fact and mere expressions of opinion. There is no liability for opinion unless the person either did not genuinely hold that opinion or had no reasonable grounds on which to base it. Opinion includes statements that cannot be verified such as the projected turnover in a business or the likely sales figures for a new untried product. A seemingly good product may fail spectacularly.

The decision of *Esso Petroleum Ltd* v *Mardon* [1976] 2 All ER 5 confirms the view that opinion must be held reasonably. Esso wanted to sell a petrol site to Mardon and stated that the petrol sales for the site should reach 200 000 gallons per year. However, due to restricted access to the site, actual sales never exceeded 78 000 gallons a year. Esso were held liable for misrepresentation, the Court of Appeal holding that given their experience and skill in market research, their expressed opinion of likely sales was not reasonable.

Similarly, a statement about future conduct is not actionable unless it can be shown that the person had no intention of acting that way as in *Edgington* v *Fitzmaurice* (1885) 29 Ch D 459, in which the directors of a company stated in their prospectus that the money to be raised from the sale of debentures would be used to buy premises and develop the company. In fact, they intended to use it to pay off debts. The plaintiff subscriber was able to rescind the contract for misrepresentation as the directors had deliberately misled prospective subscribers as to their intentions. Naturally, this does not affect the situation where the statement about future conduct is a term of the contract and is actionable as such as, for example, terms about future manufacture or delivery of goods.

Generally, silence will not be classed as a misrepresentation. However, there are some exceptions to this, namely where any statement actually made reveals only half the truth, where a true statement subsequently becomes untrue and where the relationship is *uberrimae fidei* (of the utmost good faith). A prime example of the last situation would be an insurance contract where the policyholder is obliged to disclose all relevant matters to the insurance company with silence constituting a misrepresentation which could render the policy invalid (see chapter 21). It was confirmed recently in the Court of Appeal decision of *Banque Financière de la Cité SA* v *Westgate Insurance Co Ltd* [1989] 2 All ER 952 that the duty is reciprocal being placed on both insurer and insured.

The misrepresentation must be material

To be actionable, the misrepresentation must have related to a material fact rather than mere trivia. A statement will be classed as material if a reasonable man would have been affected by it when deciding whether to enter the contract. Note that the test is objective and is not concerned with whether the particular plaintiff was influenced. That factor is considered separately.

J.E.B. Fasteners Ltd v *Marks Bloom & Co* [1983] 1 All ER 583 demonstrates this distinction. The plaintiffs wanted to launch a takeover bid for J.E.B. Fasteners Ltd, largely to acquire the services of two of the directors. As part of the takeover bid, the plaintiffs looked at the company's accounts which it transpired were inaccurate because of the negligence of the defendant accountants. It was held that the accounts were a material representation as a reasonable man would be influenced by them when deciding whether to launch a takeover bid. However, it was held on the facts that the plaintiffs could not recover as they had not relied on them, being interested only in the directors.

The misrepresentation induced the contract

It is here that subjective reliance must be shown. As demonstrated by the *J.E.B. Fasteners* decision, it is insufficient merely to show that a reasonable man would have relied on the misrepresentation, the plaintiff must show that it actually induced him to enter the contract. The plaintiff will fail if either he was unaware of the misrepresentation or, alternatively, he knew it was untrue.

Remedies for misrepresentation

The available remedies for misrepresentation are rescission and damages although the availability of the latter will depend to some extent on whether the misrepresentation was fraudulent, negligent or innocent.

(a) **Rescission.** When a misrepresentation is proved the contract is usually voidable and thus the innocent party can rescind it and seek to restore the *status quo ante*. As explained previously, the innocent party's ability to recover any goods that have been transferred under the contract will be defeated if an innocent third party has acquired the goods before the act of avoidance. An action for damages would then lie.

To constitute a valid rescission, the innocent party must take some positive action, mental rescission will not suffice. However, there is no obligation to contact the other contracting party directly, it is sufficient that the innocent third party has undertaken some action that demonstrates a intention to rescind. Thus in *Car and Universal Finance Co Ltd* v *Caldwell* [1964] 1 All ER 290, CA, a case involving a car obtained by fraudulent misrepresentation, it was held sufficient to have informed the police and the AA of the fraud.

(b) **Damages.** The ability to claim damages for misrepresentation will depend on the nature of the misrepresentation.

Fraudulent misrepresentation occurs when the person making the statement either knows it to be false, or does not believe it to be true or is reckless as to whether it is true. Damages are payable irrespective of the statement's impact on the contract. There must be clear evidence of dishonesty as held in *Derry* v *Peek* (1889) 14 App Cas 337, HL, in which the directors of a company were found not liable for fraudulent misrepresentation in respect of a statement in a prospectus which they had genuinely believed to be true.

Damages for negligent misrepresentation arise in both contract and tort. Under s.2(1) of the Misrepresentation Act 1967 'where a person has entered into a contract after a misrepresentation has been made to him by another party' the innocent party can claim contractual damages as long as the guilty party would have been liable to pay damages if the misrepresentation had been made fraudulently. The right to damages will be lost however if the defendant can show that 'he had reasonable grounds to believe up to the time the contract was made that the facts represented were true'. Thus if the defendant can establish that he was not negligent the claim will fail. Damages for a negligent misstatement can also be founded in tort under the authority of *Hedley Byrne & Co Ltd* v *Heller & Partners Ltd* [1963] 2 All ER 575, HL, which is discussed in chapter 11. Where a plaintiff makes concurrent claims in negligence at common law and under the Misrepresentation Act 1967, any claim that the plaintiff was contributorily negligent such as to reduce damages under the Law Reform (Contributory Negligence) Act 1945 will apply both to the negligence claim and to the claim under the Misrepresentation Act as held in *Gran Gelato Ltd* v *Richcliff (Group) Ltd* [1992] 1 All ER 865.

Under s.2(1) of the Misrepresentation Act 1967, damages for innocent misrepresentation are available for any loss flowing from the misrepresentation even if that loss was not foreseeable as held by the Court of Appeal in *Royscott Trust Ltd* v *Rogerson* [1991] 3 All ER 294. Further, while the normal remedy for innocent misrepresentation is rescission the court has the power under s.2(2) of the Act to declare the contract subsisting and award damages instead if it is of the opinion that it would be just in all the circumstances. Note that there is no right to damages under this section, it is merely a discretion available to the court. In exercising it, the court must balance the nature of the misrepresentation and the loss that would be caused by upholding the contract against the loss that rescission would cause to the other party. This discretion can never be used in respect of fraudulent misrepresentations.

DURESS AND UNDUE INFLUENCE

Agreement assumes the voluntary consent of both contracting parties. Naturally, if the consent of one party is involuntary because his agreement has been induced by duress, the contract should be voidable. Originally duress was restricted to actual or threatened violence such as to cause fear of physical injury or death. More recently, duress has been extended to cover illegitimate threats to goods, i.e. economic duress. In *Pau On* v *Lau Yiu Long* [1979] 3 All ER 65 Lord Scarman summarised the position thus:

there is nothing contrary to principle in recognising economic duress as a factor which may render a contract voidable, provided always that the basis of such recognition is that it must always amount to a coercion of will, which vitiates consent.

It seems that there are two criteria which must be satisfied to prove duress, first, did the victim of the duress complain at the time and, second, did the victim intend to repudiate the agreement. A recent example of economic duress occurred in *Atlas Express Ltd* v *Kafco (Importers and Distributors) Ltd* [1989] 1 All ER 641 and would suggest that the concept is now firmly established.

The plaintiff company, Atlas Express Ltd, contracted with the defendants, Kafco, to transport cartons of basketware for them to retail premises nationwide. The agreed rate was £1.10 per carton, the plaintiffs' expectation being that each load would comprise 400–600 cartons. The first load contained only 200 cartons and the plaintiffs refused to carry any more loads unless the defendents agreed to a minimum price of £440 per load. Unable to find an alternative carrier and thus dependent on the plaintiffs, the defendants agreed reluctantly to pay the new rate. When they subsequently refused to pay, the plaintiffs sued to enforce the new agreement. The Commercial Court, dismissing the claim, held that the pressure applied by the plaintiffs to force the defendants to renegotiate the contract was economic duress which vitiated the contract.

It should be stressed that economic duress does not extend to situations where the contracting parties have voluntarily agreed to enter a contract, the terms of which seem unfair or unduly onerous to one party. The law will not interfere with bargains agreed voluntarily.

Allied to the concept of duress is that of undue influence and the inequality of bargaining power. Undue influence typically occurs where one of the contracting parties holds a position of influence over the other and thus is in a position to influence the weaker to enter a contract against their own best interests. This would include relationships such as doctor/patient, solicitor/client and priest/parishioner. Any contract entered as a result of undue influence is voidable.

Despite Lord Denning's attempts in *Lloyds Bank Ltd* v *Bundy* [1975] QB 326, inequality of bargaining power is not recognised as a ground for rendering contracts voidable. Nonetheless, in the area of consumer law, there are a few examples of statutory protective measures that rely on that general idea. The most notable is in ss.137–138 of the Consumer Credit Act 1974, discussed more fully in chapter 12, in which the court has the power to reopen extortionate credit bargains if certain criteria are satisfied.

ILLEGALITY AND INVALIDITY

A total of nine different categories of contract are either illegal or void at common law. Two are relevant here, contracts that oust the jurisdiction of the courts and contracts in restraint of trade.

(a) Ousting the jurisdiction of the court. Contracts to oust the jurisdiction of the courts are void. However, contractual terms agreeing to submit disputes to arbitration are valid as are agreements to use some form of alternative dispute resolution. Such agreements are enforceable.

(b) Contracts in restraint of trade. Generally, it is in the public interest to allow individuals to follow their trade or profession, any contract that interferes with this freedom being *prima facie* void. Nonetheless, there are situations in which it may be reasonable to permit some fetter to be placed on an individual's ability to trade freely. These are

(a)   the right of a purchaser of a business to protect the goodwill from abuse by the previous owner
(b)   an employer's right to protect legitimate business interests, i.e. trade secrets and customer lists, from past employees (see also chapter 19)
(c)   agreements whereby a trader agrees to restrict his sources to one manufacturer or wholesaler, and
(d)   contracts contrary to the Restrictive Trade Practices Acts 1976–77 and the Resale Prices Act 1976 (see also chapter 18).

A restraint of trade clause is *prima facie* void, it being the responsibility of the person relying on it to demonstrate its validity by showing that it is both in the public interest and reasonable as between the parties.

   In respect of the first two their validity will depend largely on the geographic area of the restriction and its duration, although in respect of controlling past employees other factors such as their position in the firm may be relevant in determining their access to trade secrets or their ability to influence customers. The clause must not merely seek to prevent competition, it must protect some legitimate interest.

In *Nordenfelt* v *Maxim Nordenfelt Guns and Ammunition Co* [1894] AC 535 it was considered reasonable for an armament manufacturer to be bound by a clause agreed when he sold his business in which he agreed not to deal in arms worldwide for a period of twenty five years.

Similarly, in *Forster & Sons Ltd* v *Suggett* (1918) 35 TLR 87, a manager who had acquired trade secrets regarding the manufacture of glass was prevented from being involved in glass making anywhere in Britain for five years.

By contrast, in *M & S Drapers (a firm)* v *Reynolds* [1956] 3 All ER 814 a five year restraint against a salesman was not enforced.

Restraint of trade clauses preventing former employees of a company from soliciting customers of the company for a given period are capable of being enforced by a subsequent purchaser of the company.

In *Morris Angel & Son Ltd* v *Hollande* [1993] 3 All ER 569 the Court of Appeal held that where the plaintiff had purchased a company and then immediately sacked the defendant, the managing director of the company, the plaintiff was entitled to enforce the restraint of trade clause contained in the defendant's contract. The plaintiff had acquired all the rights and obligations of the company at the time of purchase including the right to enforce the restraint of trade clause. This would also be true of companies to which the Transfer of Undertakings (Protection of Employees) Regulations 1981 apply (see chapter 22).

'Vertical agreements' or 'solus agreements' whereby a trader agrees to restrict his source of supply to one manufacturer may be upheld if their duration is reasonable and the trader derives some benefit from the contract.

In *Esso Petroleum Co Ltd* v *Harper's Garage (Stourport) Ltd* [1967] 1 All ER 699 Harpers entered into two agreements with Esso whereby Harpers agreed to buy all the petrol for two garages from Esso. They further agreed to keep the garages open at all reasonable hours and to ensure that anyone buying the garages would abide by the solus agreements. In return, Harpers received a discount on all their petrol and the second garage was mortgaged to Esso to cover a loan of £7000. The agreements were to last for four and a half years for the first garage and twenty one years (the term of the mortgage) for the second garage. The House of Lords held that the first agreement was valid but that the second one was unreasonable and hence void.

Contracts which are contrary to the Restrictive Practices Act 1976–77 and the Resale Prices Act 1976, both of which seek to control anti-competitive practices, are considered fully in chapter 18.

QUESTION

Hippo Ltd wholesalers of clothing, entered two contracts:

(a)   they contracted to sell 20 coats valued at £1400 to Jones Bros. The order for the coats was received on paper headed 'Jones Bros, Wholesale Clothier, 15 Forest Hill, Blanktown'. Hippo Ltd had not dealt with Jones Bros in the past. Hippo Ltd have not received payment and an investigation has revealed that Jones Bros do not exist. The coats had actually been ordered by Jeremy, a fraudster.

(b) they contracted to buy designer lingerie from a distributor, Worm Silks Ltd, at a cost of £3000, delivery to be made in five instalments. Hippo Ltd have already contracted to sell the lingerie to various retail outlets. After three instalments had been delivered, Worm Silks Ltd announced that they were raising the contract price to £3800. Unable to get replacement goods elsewhere with which to fulfil the retail contracts, Hippo Ltd have had no alternative but to pay the extra £800.

Advise Hippo Ltd about possible remedies available to them in respect of each of the two contracts.

FURTHER READING

Downes, T.A., *Textbook on Contract* (2nd ed) 1991 (Blackstone Press)
Furmston, M.P., *Cheshire, Fifoot and Furmston's Law of Contract* (12th ed) 1991 (Butterworth)
Richards, P., *Law of Contract* (Pitman)
Savage, N. and Bradgate, R., *Business Law* (2nd ed) 1993 (Butterworth)
Smith, J.C., *Smith and Thomas A Casebook on Contract* (12th ed) 1992 (Sweet and Maxwell)

CHAPTER 4

Exclusion clauses

Inequality of bargaining power in a contract is at its most obvious in relation to limitation and exclusion clauses, whereby the stronger party may seek to limit or totally exclude his liability to the weaker party in the event of breach. Such clauses, in common use in business contracts, have been subjected to control by common law and more recently and effectively by statute.

COMMON LAW CONTROL

Attempts by the common law to control exclusion clauses have revolved around three strategies, incorporation, interpretation and the now defunct doctrine of fundamental breach.

Incorporation

The same requirements for incorporation apply to exclusion clauses as to any other express clause; namely that the clause must be validly incorporated at the time that the contract is made as in *Olley* v *Marlborough Court Ltd* [1949] 1 All ER 325. Methods of incorporation vary along with the emphasis that any clause must receive for effective incorporation.

(a) **Signed documents.** The parties to a signed agreement are bound by the terms of the agreement irrespective of whether they have read the document. It follows therefore, that if the contract includes a limitation or exclusion clause the parties will be bound by it as it will have been validly incorporated. This would not extend, of course, to situations where *non est factum* has been pleaded successfully (see chapter 3).

In *L'Estrange* v *Graucob* [1934] 2 KB 394 the plaintiff, Miss L'Estrange bought a cigarette vending machine and signed a sales agreement. In the small print of the agreement was a clause reading 'Any express or implied condition, statement or warranty, statutory or otherwise, not stated herein is expressly excluded'. Miss L'Estrange signed the agreement without reading it. The machine proved unfit for its purpose but the court held that Miss L'Estrange was still liable to pay for it as she had signed away her rights.

The draconian exclusion clause in this case is typical of those that led to a demand for the controls ultimately contained in the Unfair Contract Terms Act 1977.

(b) Notices. Where there is no signed contract, merely an unsigned notice or ticket, it is still possible to incorporate an exclusion clause as long as two criteria are satisfied. First, the person to whom the unsigned document was given either knew or should have realised that it had contractual effect and, second, sufficient notice of the exclusion clause has been given. The description given to the document by the parties, e.g invoice, receipt etc., is not conclusive, the correct test being the objective one of whether the reasonable man would have assumed the document to contain contractual terms as opposed to being a mere acknowledgement or receipt for payment.

In *Chapelton* v *Barry UDC* [1940] KB 532 the plaintiff, Chapelton, was given a ticket when he hired a deck chair. There was an exclusion clause on the reverse of the ticket which read 'The Council will not be liable for any accident or damage arising from hire of the chair'. The canvas of the chair gave way and Mr Chapelton was injured. The court held the Council liable holding that the document was a mere receipt which no reasonable man would have considered to be a contract.

The issue of notice must be resolved on a case by case basis. Reasonable notice of the existence of the clause must have been given to the party bound by it with a greater degree of notice being demanded if the clause is particularly onerous or unusual in its effect.

In *Thornton* v *Shoe Lane Parking Ltd* [1971] QB 163 the plaintiff, Thornton, when parking his car in the defendant's car park received a ticket which stated on the reverse 'issued subject to the conditions of issue displayed on the premises'. Inside the car park was a separate notice purporting to exclude the defendant's liability for 'loss, mis-delivery of or damage to the vehicle or injury to the customer'. Mr Thornton was subsequently injured in an accident caused partly by the defendant's negligence. The Court of Appeal found the defendant liable holding the exclusion clause ineffective as it was sufficiently unusual to justify it being explicitly drawn to the plaintiff's attention.

A similar approach was adopted in *Interfoto Picture Library* v *Stiletto Visual Programmes Ltd* [1988] 1 All ER 348 which related to an unusually onerous penalty clause. The Court of Appeal held that the the clause contained in a standard form contract had not been incorporated due to a lack of appropriate notice. Nonetheless, the plaintiffs were awarded some damages on a *quantum meruit* basis.

The most telling and oft-quoted comment on the requirement of notice was given by Lord Denning in *Spurling* v *Bradshaw* [1956] 2 All ER 121 when he stated that some clauses would need to be printed in red ink on the face of the document with a red hand pointing to it before the notice could be held to be sufficient.

(c) Previous course of dealings. Trade custom or a longstanding course of dealing between two parties may give rise to the incorporation of a limitation or exclusion clause. In practice, this is more likely to arise in a commercial context where regular dealings between two parties are more likely to occur. The involvement of a consumer in a regular course of dealing is less likely. This distinction is illustrated by contrasting the decisions of *Kendall (Henry) & Sons (a firm)* v *William Lillico & Sons Ltd* [1969] 2 AC 31 and *Hollier* v *Rambler Motors (AMC) Ltd* [1972] QB 71.

In the *Kendall* decision, a course of dealing involving over a hundred transactions over a three year period was held to be sufficient to incorporate an exclusion clause. The sellers sold some animal feed to the buyer in an oral contract followed up by a written 'sold note' containing an exclusion clause on the reverse. When the goods proved unfit, the House of Lords held that the exclusion clause protected the defendant from liability. Although the sold note had not been incorporated as it occurred after the oral contract, the previous course of dealing on the same terms demonstrated a preparedness by the parties to be bound by those terms including the exclusion clause.

By contrast, in *Hollier* v *Rambler Motors (AMC) Ltd* three or four transactions in the previous five years was not sufficient to found a course of dealing. The plaintiff, Hollier, had left his car at the defendant's garage to be repaired. It was damaged in a fire caused by the defendant's negligence. The plaintiff had used the garage three or four times in the previous five years and on two occasions had signed invoices containing a clause excluding the defendant's liability in the event of fire. The Court of Appeal held that the exclusion clause had not been validly incorporated.

Interpretation

Traditionally, the courts have taken a strict view to the interpretation of exclusion clauses. The basic tenet of interpretation is that the clause will be construed *contra proferentum* (against the person seeking to rely on it). One effect of this approach is that the clause will only apply to matters expressly covered by it and any ambiguity will be construed in favour of the innocent party.

Thus in *Andrews Bros (Bournemouth) Ltd* v *Singer & Co* [1934] 1 KB 17, the plaintiff entered a contract to buy 'new Singer cars' from the defendant. The contract contained an exclusion clause which excluded all liability for implied terms. One of the cars supplied was not new. The Court of Appeal held that the exclusion clause was not valid as the term 'new Singer car' was a condition of the contract and the exclusion clause only covered warranties.

A further effect of this approach is that where liability may arise under either contract or negligence, only the contractual liability will be covered by the clause unless it expressly refers to negligence. However, if the only liability that can arise is in negligence, no contract action being possible, the clause will be presumed to apply to the negligence claim.

In *White* v *John Warwick & Co Ltd* [1953] 2 All ER 1021 White hired a bicycle from the defendants. The hire agreement included an exclusion clause stating 'nothing in this agreement shall render the owners liable for personal injury'. While riding the bike, White was injured when the saddle tipped forward. The Court of Appeal held that the defendants were liable in negligence and could not claim the protection of the exclusion clause. A contractual liability existed regarding the merchantability of the bike and the effect of exclusion clause was limited to that liability.

Finally, an exclusion clause will not be upheld if the party seeking to rely upon it misrepresented its effect to the other contracting party as in *Curtis* v *Chemical Cleaning & Dyeing Co* [1951] 1 KB 805.

Doctrine of fundamental breach

The doctrine of fundamental breach stipulated that an exclusion clause could never negate liability for the breach of a fundamental term of the contract, i.e. a term going to the heart of the contract. This doctrine was finally and firmly laid to rest by the House of Lords in *Photo Production Ltd* v *Securicor Transport Ltd* [1980] AC 827, Lord Wilberforce stating

> After (the Unfair Contract Terms Act 1977), in commercial matters generally, when the parties are not of unequal bargaining power, and when risks are normally borne by insurance ... there is everything to be said ... for leaving the parties free to apportion the risks as they think fit and for respecting their decisions.

This is of particular importance in contracts between businesses who are given the power to determine their own contract terms subject to the provisions of s.3 of the Unfair Contract Terms Act 1977.

STATUTORY CONTROL

Statutory control of exclusion clauses is governed largely, though not exclusively, by the provisions of the Unfair Contract Terms Act 1977. This Act, which governs clauses used by businessmen, renders some clauses void and subjects others to a test of reasonableness. The Act's title is misleading in that it only covers limitation and exclusion clauses and not all contract terms that might be deemed unfair. Further, it extends to both contract and tort, notably negligence.

The Act applies to contracts entered into on or after 1 February 1978 and covers business liability defined as being obligations or duties arising :

(a) from things done or to be done by a person in the course of a business (whether his own business or another's); or
(b) from the occupation of premises used for the business purposes of the occupier.

Business includes a profession and any activities of any government department or local or public authority.

Dealing as a consumer

The protection the Act provides to the other contracting party depends to a significant extent on whether that person is 'dealing as a consumer'. This status depends on three factors to be found in s.12 which states:

A party to a contract 'deals as a consumer' in relation to another party if:
(a) he neither makes the contract in the course of a business nor holds himself out as so doing; and
(b) the other party does make the contract in the course of a business; and
(c) in the case of a contract governed by the law of sale of goods or hire-purchase, or by section 7 of this Act, the goods passing under or in pursuance of the contract are of a type ordinarily supplied for private use or consumption.

This definition gives rise to two issues of interpretation; first, what does 'in the course of a business' mean and, second, when are goods 'of a type ordinarily supplied for private use and consumption'? In respect of the first, the courts seem to be adopting the same approach as under the Trade Descriptions Act 1968 by holding that the mere fact that the purchaser is a business does not necessarily prevent it acting as a consumer in any particular transaction. The nature of the transaction will depend on whether the purchase was integral to the purchaser's business or merely incidental.

In *R & B Customs Brokers Co Ltd* v *United Dominions Trust Ltd* [1988] 1 All ER 847 the plaintiff company bought a second hand car for one of their directors, to be used partly for business and partly for private motoring. The purchase was financed through the defendant finance company with an agreement which contained an exclusion clause. When the car leaked, the plaintiff sought to recover the purchase price. The Court of Appeal found that car was not fit for the purpose contrary to s.14(3) of the Sale of Goods Act. Further, as the car was only the second or third bought by the plaintiff on credit terms, the practice was not integral to the business. As such, the plaintiff should be classed as a consumer against whom the exclusion clause was void.

This approach, which is similar to that adopted in ss. 1 and 14 of the Trade Descriptions Act 1968 and in the decisions of *Havering London Borough* v *Stevenson* [1970] 3 All ER 609 and *Davies* v *Sumner* [1984] 3 All ER 831, would mean if taken to its logical conclusion that a business will only act as a business in respect of stock-in-trade items. All ancillary items not essential to the business would be bought 'as a consumer'.

Which goods are of a type 'ordinarily supplied for private use or consumption' is also not as clear cut as might first appear. Heavy manufacturing plant is obviously not for private use, curtains for one's home clearly are. The difficulty lies with those items that straddle the divide such as company cars used for private purposes and personal computers/word processors used for both business and private correspondence. It can only be decided on a case by case basis.

Reasonableness

A recurring theme of the Act is that some exclusion clauses may be valid to the extent that they are reasonable. This clearly begs the question what is reasonable? There are no clear guidelines other than those contained in Schedule 2 which relate specifically to liability when goods are covered by ss.6 and 7 although s.11 does refer to some general factors that should be considered. These include that the burden lies on the person seeking to rely on the clause to show that it is reasonable, that reliance on a non-contractual notice should be fair and reasonable in all the circumstances and that where limitation clauses are concerned the court should consider the resources open to the contracting party to cover his potential liability and the availability of insurance.

Schedule 2 lays down five criteria to be considered in relation to liability under ss.6(3) and 7(3) when clauses are being used in business to business sale or supply. These are:

(a)   the relative bargaining strength of the parties including any alternative means of satisfying the customer's requirements. This would be relevant if for example a multi-national company was imposing an exclusion clause on a small manufacturer.

(b)   whether the party received any inducement to accept the term or whether he had the opportunity to gain a similar contract elsewhere without the term. It may be that the customer received a discount on the price or the opportunity to buy on credit in exchange for accepting the exclusion clause.

(c)   whether the customer knew or ought to have known of the existence of the term. Was the term drawn to the customer's attention or was there a previous course of dealing such as to assume knowledge of incorporation.

(d)   where the clause excludes liability for the non-compliance with a contractual term, whether such compliance was practical. For example, can a customer be required to give notice of any defect before it would become apparent as in *R.W. Green Ltd* v *Cade Bros Farm* [1978] 1 Lloyd's Rep 602 in which the buyer was required to inform the seller of seed potatoes of any defect in the product within three days of delivery?

(e)   whether the goods were manufactured, processed or adapted to the special order of the customer. If this is so, it may be reasonable for the supplier to exclude liability for merchantability and/or fitness for purpose.

Section 2 – Negligence liability

Section 2 of the Act prohibits the use of contract terms or notices to exclude liability for death or personal injury caused by negligence. In respect of any other loss or damage caused by negligence it is possible to exclude liability to the extent that the exclusion is reasonable.

Section 3 – Contractual liability

Section 3 covers two situations where there is potential for an inequality of bargaining power. First, where one of the contracting parties is dealing as a consumer and, second, where one of the parties deals on the other's standard terms. In either of these situations the other party cannot use a contract term to exclude or restrict his liability in the event of a breach of contract. Section 3 further provides that a trader cannot claim to be entitled to render either no contractual performance at all or a substantially different performance from that expected unless the contract term is reasonable.

Section 4 – Unreasonable indemnity clauses

Under s.4 a person dealing as a consumer cannot by reference to a contract term be made to indemnify another person (whether a party to the contract or not) in respect of liability that may be incurred in contract or negligence unless the term is reasonable.

Section 5 – Manufacturer's guarantees

Section 5 defines a guarantee as being 'anything in writing ... if it purports to contain some promise or assurance (however worded or presented) that defects will be made good by complete or partial replacement, or by repair, monetary compensation or otherwise'. A manufacturer cannot use a contract term or notice related to the guarantee to exclude liability for loss or damage to goods ordinarily supplied for private use or consumption if the loss or damage has arisen from the goods proving defective while in consumer use and results from the negligence of the manufacturer or a person involved in the distribution process. This section resolves the problems caused by manufacturers using guarantees ostensibly to provide consumers with additional rights while actually using them to deprive the consumer of some of his legal rights both contractual and tortious.

Section 6 – Sale of goods and hire-purchase

Section 6 contains some of the central provisions of the Act. It concerns the extent to which it is possible to exclude liability for the implied conditions of title, description, merchantability, fitness for purpose and sale by sample contained in ss.12–15 of the Sale of Goods Act 1979 and ss.8–11 of the Supply of Goods (Implied Terms) Act 1973. The former provisions relate to contract for the sale of goods while the latter imply the same terms into hire-purchase contracts. Section 6 deals with both categories of contract simultaneously.

The condition as to title receives separate treatment under s.6(1) of the Unfair Contract Terms Act which provides that it cannot be excluded by reference to any contract term.

The legitimacy of exclusion clauses relating to description, merchantability, fitness for purpose and sale by sample depend upon whether the purchaser was 'dealing as a consumer'. If he was, s.6(2) provides that the implied terms cannot be excluded. While this protects the consumer from business sellers, it offers no protection at all if the item was sold by a private individual who would not satisfy the s.12 UCTA requirement of being 'in the course of a business'.

If the purchaser is not 'dealing as a consumer' because he is in the course of a business as is the seller, then exclusion clauses are permissible under s.6(3) to the extent that they are reasonable. This will depend upon the application of the Schedule 2 guidelines discussed above. Note, however, that a private seller can never be held liable in respect of the condition of merchantability and fitness for purpose as those conditions only apply if the seller sells 'in the course of a business' (see chapter 7). As such, any discussion of the exclusion of that liability by private sellers is irrelevant.

Section 7 – Contracts for the supply of goods

Part I of the Supply of Goods and Services Act 1982 makes provision for the implied terms of title, description, merchantability, fitness for purpose and sale by sample to be implied both into other contracts under which goods are supplied and into hire contracts. This covers, for example, contracts for the repair of goods under which spare parts are to be provided by the repairer together with contracts of barter for which the consideration is not money but in kind. In respect of contracts under which the ownership of goods will pass, any exclusion of the condition as to title is void. However, in hire contracts, it can be excluded to the extent that the exclusion is reasonable. The remaining implied conditions are dealt with in the same way as under s.6, namely that under s.7(2) they cannot be excluded against a person 'dealing as a consumer' but otherwise can be excluded under s.7(3) subject to the test of reasonableness.

Section 8 – Liability for misrepresentation

Section 3 of the Misrepresentation Act 1967 as amended by section 8 of the Unfair Contract Terms Act 1977 prevents the exclusion of liability for misrepresentation except to the extent that the exclusion is reasonable.

EEC REFORM

Reform of the law on exclusion clauses will follow from the passage of the EEC Directive on Unfair Terms in Consumer Contracts, Directive 93/13/EEC. This Directive which must be adopted by Member States no later than 31 December 1994 lays down new requirements for the control of exclusion clauses in contracts concluded between a seller or supplier and a consumer. For this purpose a consumer is 'any natural person who is acting for purposes which are outside his trade, business or profession'. Thus, unaccompanied associations and incorporated companies, not being natural persons, cannot be consumers for this purpose. By contrast, a seller or supplier is defined as being 'any natural or legal person who is acting for purposes relating to his trade, business or profession, whether publicly owned or privately owned'.

Under Art. 3 a contractual term which has not been individually negotiated shall be regarded as unfair if, contrary to the requirement of good faith, it causes a significant imbalance in the parties' rights and obligations arising under the contract, to the detriment of the consumer. Terms are deemed not to have been individually negotiated if they have been drafted in advance with the consumer unable to influence the substance of the term. Particular mention is made of pre-formulated standard contracts which will be covered even if certain aspects of a term or one specific term have been individually negotiated. The Annex to the Directive provides a non-exhaustive list of seventeen different types of contract term that may be classed as unfair. Included amongst these are terms that exclude or limit liability in the event of the death of or personal injury to the consumer; retaining money from the consumer should he cancel the contract while not permitting the consumer to receive an equivalent amount from the supplier should he cancel; automatically extending contracts of fixed duration where the consumer has not indicated otherwise; enabling the supplier to alter the terms of the contract unilaterally without valid reason and obliging the consumer to fulfil all his contractual obligations while the supplier does not fulfil his.

When assessing the unfairness of a contractual term, the nature of the goods or services will be taken into account as will all the other terms of the contract and all the circumstances pertaining at the time the contract was concluded. Any unfair terms will not be binding on the consumer although the contract will continue to exist without the unfair terms if this is possible.

Where any contractual terms are provided to the consumer in writing they must be in plain, intelligible language with any ambiguity being interpreted in favour of the consumer.

Article 7 provides a further measure of consumer protection in that it requires provisions to be made whereby persons or organisations, having a legitimate interest in protecting consumers, will be able to take action before the courts or other appropriate administrative body for a decision as to whether contractual terms drawn up for general use are unfair. This will permit appropriate means to be adopted to prevent their further use. Clearly, in the United Kingdom, the Office of Fair Trading is the most appropriate body to undertake this function as a means of controlling unfair standard terms promulgated either by individual suppliers within the same economic sector or trade associations recommending the same general contractual terms.

CRIMINAL CONTROL

Running parallel to the civil law controls over exclusion clauses found in the Unfair Contract Terms Act 1977 are criminal law controls promulgated under the Fair Trading Act 1973. It is an offence contrary to the Consumer Transactions (Restrictions on Statements) Order 1976 as amended for a trader to display a notice which would contravene ss.6 and 7 of the Unfair Contract Terms Act 1977. Thus an exclusion clause displayed in this way would be both void and illegal.

QUESTION

Leopard Ltd, a manufacturer of electrical equipment, bought some new office furniture from Tiger Office Furniture Ltd. Among the items purchased were some chairs with upholstered seats and stainless steel frames. The contract of sale for the furniture included the term 'Tiger Ltd accept no liability for any damage howsoever caused'.

Emily, an employee of Leopard Ltd, was injured when one of the welds failed on the leg of the chair on which she was sitting. She fell to the floor and injured her back. It transpired that the weld was faulty because of negligent workmanship by an employee of Tiger Office Furniture Ltd.

Emily wishes to claim for the injury caused to her while Leopard Ltd want to claim a refund for the faulty chair. Tiger Office Furniture Ltd are denying liability relying on the exclusion clause.

Discuss.

FURTHER READING

Furmston, M.P., *Cheshire, Fifoot and Furmston's Law of Contract* (12th ed) 1991 (Butterworth)

Keenan, D. and Riches, S., *Business Law* (3rd ed) 1993 (Pitman)

Pitt, G. (ed) *Butterworths Commercial Law Handbook* (Butterworth)

Richards, P., *Law of Contract* 1992 (Pitman)

Savage, N. and Bradgate, R., *Business Law* (2nd ed) 1993 (Butterworth)

Smith, J.C., *Smith & Thomas A Casebook on Contract* (9th ed) 1992 (Sweet and Maxwell)

CHAPTER 5

Termination and remedies

INTRODUCTION

There are four methods by which a contract may be terminated: performance, agreement, frustration and breach.

PERFORMANCE

The majority of contracts will be terminated by performance when both parties have completed successfully their contractual obligations as per the terms of the contract. Thus, in a contract for the purchase and delivery of a piece of machinery, the contract will be terminated by performance when the correct machine in working order has been delivered to the correct premises and the contractual price has been paid.

Substantial performance

Strictly, the law requires full performance of all the contractual obligations by both parties. Either party failing in any aspect of contractual performance would be sufficient to prevent the successful termination by performance of the agreement. This potentially draconian rule has been mitigated, however, by the evolution of the doctrine of substantial performance. Under this doctrine, a contract may be deemed concluded if substantial performance of the contractual obligations has occurred and the contractual price must be paid less an appropriate amount for the uncompleted work. This doctrine is a major step forward from the position that existed previously whereby nothing other than full performance would suffice to establish an action for the contract price as evidenced in the decision of *Cutter* v *Powell* (1756) 6 Term R 320.

Hoenig v *Isaacs* [1952] 2 All ER 176 is the most commonly quoted decision demonstrating the impact of contractual substantial performance. The plaintiff agreed to decorate the defendant's flat and undertake some refurbishment including providing a wardrobe and bookcase at a total cost of £750. The defendant paid £400 but refused to pay the balance stating that the work was negligently done and that the wardrobe and the bookcase needed further work. The plaintiff sued for the remaining £350. The Court of Appeal found that the contract had been substantially performed and that the plaintiff was able to recover the £350 less a reduction of £55 to cover the cost of the remedial work necessary to the wardrobe and bookcase.

Part performance

It is important to distinguish between substantial performance as illustrated in the *Hoenig* decision and partial performance which occurs when one of the parties fails to complete the contract. The innocent party has the option of rejecting the work performed or alternatively accepting the partial performance and paying for it on a *quantum meruit* basis.

The assumption has been made that the promisee is prepared to allow full contractual performance to take place. Clearly, it would be inequitable to allow him to avoid the contract or use non-performance as a defence in an action for the price if he has prevented performance taking place. In this situation, the promisor is entitled to treat the contract as terminated and sue for the value of the work actually performed on a *quantum meruit* basis as in *Planche* v *Colburn* (1831) 8 Bing 14 where an author was entitled to receive payment for the research and writing undertaken for a book before the publisher decided to abandon the project.

Divisible contracts

A further example of the mitigation of the performance rule is to be found with divisible contracts. A divisible contract is one whereby each stage of performance brings with it an entitlement to receive part of the contract price. Thus, for example, if a large quantity of goods is to be delivered in instalments over an extended period of time each instalment might carry a right to payment in respect of it. Where this is the case the contractor providing the goods would be entitled to receive payment for the deliveries actually made even if the contract is not fully performed.

AGREEMENT

In the same way that the contracting parties agree to enter a contract so they can agree to terminate it. This may occur in two ways, either as a result of an express contractual term or because one or both of the parties wish to terminate the contract before performance has been completed.

The first situation would occur, for example, where the contract is for a fixed period as in the hire of machinery for three months. At the conclusion of the period the contract will terminate automatically. Similarly, if the agreement was to last until some specified event took place, the occurrence of the event would cause automatic contractual termination. Finally, it would also include contracts the terms of which provide for either party to terminate the contract by notice as, for example, in a tenancy agreement, a contract of employment or a hire agreement of indeterminate length.

Agreements to terminate once contractual performance has started but not been completed pose some difficulties, the major one being that the agreement to terminate must itself satisfy the requirements of a binding contract. In particular, this means that consideration must be present. When neither party has completed their contractual performance, i.e. a bilateral agreement, the consideration provided by each party which releases him from further contractual performance is the promise to release the other party from their remaining obligations. Both parties benefit from the new agreement.

By contrast, when only one party has outstanding contractual obligations, the other party having completed performance, i.e. a unilateral agreement, there is no consideration provided by the party who has not completed his contractual performance. While the parties may agree to terminate the contract and not require any further performance, the promise received by the party with outstanding obligations is gratuitous and, as such, not enforceable unless contained in a deed.

FRUSTRATION

Impossibility of performance

A contract is deemed to be frustrated when further performance becomes impossible due to some intervening factor beyond the control of the contracting parties. Examples would include the destruction of the subject matter of the contract, the cancellation of an event central to the contract and the contract subsequently becoming illegal. Decisions in which contracts have been frustrated include the following.

In *Taylor* v *Caldwell* (1863) 3 B & S 826, the plaintiff hired a music hall from the defendant in order to give some concerts. After the contract was agreed but before the date of the first concert, the hall was destroyed by fire. The plaintiff sued the defendant in an attempt to recover all the expenses that he had accrued in arranging the concerts. The Court of Appeal found the defendant not liable, the contract having been frustrated.

In *Krell* v *Henry* [1903] 2 KB 740, the plaintiff owned a flat which he hired to the defendant for Edward VII's coronation day to enable the defendant to watch the coronation procession. The coronation was cancelled due to the king's illness and the defendant refused to pay for the flat. The court held that the defendant was not liable for the hire fee as the primary purpose of the hire was to watch the coronation procession. As it did not take place the contract was frustrated.

Contrast, however, the decision of *Herne Bay Steamship Co* v *Hutton* [1903] 2 KB 683, another of the 'coronation cases' in which a contract for the hire of a boat to watch the coronation review of the fleet at Spithead was not frustrated even though the review was cancelled because it was still possible to view the fleet.

It is important to distinguish between those cases where further performance genuinely becomes impossible and frustration is likely to occur and those instances where performance merely becomes more expensive or time-consuming and frustration will not take place.

An example of this situation occurred in *Tsakiroglou & Co Ltd* v *Noblee Thorl GmbH* [1962] AC 93 in which a contract of shipment under which goods were to be transported from Port Sudan to Hamburg was not frustrated by the closure of the Suez Canal. Shipment would take longer and be considerably more expensive than envisaged originally by the seller but this was insufficient to frustrate the contract as delivery of the goods was still possible.

Restrictions on application

Application of the doctrine of frustration is restricted and will not occur if the parties have foreseen the frustrating event and made provision for it in the contract by, for example, the use of a *force majeure* clause as discussed in chapter 2. Likewise, the contract will not be frustrated if the frustrating event has been induced by one of the contracting parties, e.g. a contract whereby A agrees to service B's car for a year would be terminated but not frustrated by B selling the car.

The effect of frustration

The effect of contractual frustration is that the contract is avoided from the date of the frustrating event and the parties are released from any further contractual performance. This leaves the issue about the possible recovery of monies paid before the event and payment for any contractual performance that preceded the frustrating event. This is governed by s.1 of the Law Reform (Frustrated Contracts) Act 1943 which provides that any monies paid before the frustrating event can be recovered subject to the payee's right to receive reimbursement in respect of any appropriate expenses incurred prior to the frustration. Similarly, where one of the contracting parties has received a valuable benefit under the terms of the contract before the contract was discharged, he is liable to pay the other contracting party a sum that the court considers fair in all the circumstances. In deciding a figure the court must take account of expenses incurred legitimately by the benefited party when seeking to perform the contract and the effect of the frustrating event upon the benefit received.

BREACH

A failure by either contracting party to fulfil his contractual obligations either wholly or in part may cause the contract to be terminated by breach. This leaves the innocent party with the right to claim contractual damages and the potential to deem the contract at an end depending on the circumstances.

Anticipatory breach

Breach may occur during the lifetime of the contract or, alternatively, may happen after the contract has been agreed but before the date for performance. This latter possibility is termed anticipatory breach and gives the innocent party the right to seek contractual damages immediately as in *Hochester* v *De La Tour* (1853) 2 E & B 678. For an action in anticipatory breach to succeed, it must be clear that the guilty party has decided irrevocably not to perform his contractual obligations. If there is any doubt about his intentions, the innocent party should wait until the date for contractual performance has passed before commencing any action.

In *Hochester* v *De La Tour* the plaintiff was employed by the defendant to act as a courier with effect from 1 June, the contract having been concluded in April. On 11 May, the defendant wrote to the plaintiff stating that his services would not be needed. The plaintiff sued on 22 May seeking contractual damages for the breach, the court holding in his favour on the basis that the plaintiff's letter was actionable as an anticipatory breach.

Effect of the breach

The effect of the breach will be dictated by the status of the term breached. If the term is a condition, the breach of which has effectively destroyed the contract, the innocent party will have a right to repudiate the contract and seek damages. Alternatively, the innocent party may elect to continue with the contract and merely seek damages by way of compensation. If he chooses the latter option, he will himself continue to be bound by the terms of the contract and would be liable for breach if he failed to fulfil his contractual obligations properly. If the breached term is merely a warranty, damages are the only remedy available, there being no right of repudiation. The more complex position arises in respect of innominate terms where, ultimately, the court has the power to decide upon an appropriate remedy depending on the effect of the breach (see chapter 2).

REMEDIES

Remedies for contractual breach fall into two categories: damages, the normal legal remedy, and the equitable remedies of specific performance and injunctions. The essential distinction is that while damages are awarded to the innocent party as of right, the award of the equitable remedies of specific performance and injunctions is discretionary with the plaintiff having no right to insist on them.

Damages

(a) **Liquidated damages.** As discussed in chapter 2, businesses may use a liquidated damages clause in a contract to stipulate the amount of damages payable in the event of breach. Such a clause is for an agreed sum and, provided that the court is satisfied that the clause is a genuine pre-estimate of loss and not a penalty clause as outlined in the *Dunlop Pneumatic Tyre Co Ltd* decision, it will be upheld and enforced. Where a liquidated damages clause is upheld, the plaintiff will receive the agreed sum irrespective of the actual loss suffered.

(b) **Unliquidated damages.** Where there is no agreed figure for the damages, the plaintiff will sue for unliquidated damages, this being the sum that the court considers appropriate to compensate the injured party for the loss that he has suffered as a result of the breach. If no loss has been sustained, the court will award nominal damages to acknowledge the breach. The recent Court of Appeal decision of *Surrey County Council* v *Bredero Homes Ltd* [1993] 3 All ER 705 confirmed that the function of contractual damages is to compensate the victim for his loss, not to transfer to the victim the benefit which the wrongdoer gained by his breach.

To be recoverable the damages must relate to loss that was foreseeable at the time that the contract was made as stipulated in *Hadley* v *Baxendale* (1854) 9 Exch 341.

In the *Hadley* decision, the plaintiff mill-owner employed the defendant to transport a broken crankshaft to the shaft manufacturer to enable it to be used as a pattern for the construction of a new, replacement part. The defendant negligently delayed delivery of the shaft resulting in the mill being closed longer than would otherwise have been the case. The plaintiff sued for his loss of profits due to the mill being out of use. The court held that the defendant was not liable as there was nothing to suggest that he should have been aware of the special losses that the plainitff would suffer as a result of the dalay. The plaintitff might have had a spare shaft.

The rules emanating from the *Hadley* decision mean that recoverable damage is limited to that which falls within two specified criteria:

(a)   such damage as arises naturally from the breach, i.e. in the usual course of events, and
(b)   that which, while not arising naturally, 'may reasonably be supposed to have been in the contemplation of both parties at the time they made the contract' as being the probable result of the breach.

Applying these rules, it follows that the defendant in the *Hadley* decision would have been liable for the plaintiff's loss of profits if he had known that the plaintiff did not have a spare shaft and thus that any delay would cause increased damage.

This approach was subsequently approved and applied in the decision of *Victoria Laundry (Windsor) Ltd* v *Newman Industries Ltd* [1949] 2 KB 528.

If the damage is not too remote the plaintiff can recover for death and personal injury, damage to property, financial loss and, in some situations, distress and disapppointment occasioned by the breach as in *Jarvis* v *Swans Tours* [1973] 1 QB 233 in which the plaintiff was awarded damages for the disappointment he suffered when a holiday did not live up to the description applied in a holiday brochure. Similarly in *Cox* v *Phillips Industries Ltd* [1976] 3 All ER 161 an employee was allowed to recover for the distress caused by his wrongful demotion.

The purpose of damages is to compensate the innocent party for the loss that he has sustained and attempt to put him in the same position he would have achieved but for the breach. Note however, that while the innocent party has a right to receive appropriate compensatory damages, he is under a duty to mitigate (reduce) his loss as far as is reasonably possible. He cannot recover damages for losses that he could have avoided through reasonable actions.

Punitive or exemplary damages, the primary purpose of which is to punish the wrongdoer, are not normally awarded in contract actions.

Specific performance

An order of specific performance requires the defendant to perform his contractual obligations according to the terms of the contract. The order is discretionary and will be awarded only when the court considers it just and equitable so to do. Breach of such an order is actionable as a contempt of court. Certain criteria must be satisfied if specific performance is to be granted:

(a) Damages must be inadequate as a remedy. In many contracts damages would suffice as a remedy but there are some contracts where mere money would prove inadequate. This situation is most likely to pertain where the subject matter of the contract is unique. A contract for the purchase of land is a prime example as all land is unique if only because of its location and thus the court would be likely to award specific performance to enforce a contract for the sale of land. Similarly, specific performance might be awarded to enforce a contract for the sale of goods if the goods are unique as, for example, if the contract were for the sale of the Mona Lisa. By contrast, if the contract were for the sale of an item that is widely available such as a washing machine, specific performance would be refused as damages would be sufficient to allow the innocent party to obtain the goods elsewhere. (Other remedies relating to contracts for the sale of goods are discussed in chapter 7.)

(b) Specific performance must be available to both parties. The court will not award specific performance to one contracting party if the remedy would not be open to the other party. Thus, for example, as specific performance cannot be awarded against a minor, a minor cannot claim it against an adult.

(c) The court must be capable of supervising the order. The court will not award specific performance if it is incapable of supervising the enforcement of the order as this would bring the law into disrepute. Similarly, it is unlikely to award specific performance in respect of personal contracts such as employment contracts as it would be potentially inequitable to force an employee to work for an employer with whom he has disagreed in the past.

Injunctions

While specific performance enforces the positive terms of a contract, injunctions are used to enforce the negative ones as for example to enforce a legitimate restraint of trade clause as in the *Nordenfelt* decision (see chapter 3).

In respect of the use of injunctions in employment contracts, the decisions of *Lumley* v *Gye* (1852) 1 De GM & G 604 and *Warner Bros Inc* v *Nelson* [1937] 1 KB 209 both support the notion that an injunction can be used against an employee to enforce a clause under which he has agreed not to work for someone else. However, the court will not allow an injunction to be used as a way of forcing an employee to continue working for his present employer. Finally, they may be used by an employer to protect confidential information by restraining an employee from disclosing it (see also chapter 19).

Limitation of actions

Whether seeking damages or one of the equitable remedies, the plaintiff must commence his action within the appropriate time period as specified in the Limitation Act 1980. This is six years from the time of the breach for simple contracts (s.5) and twelve years in respect of contracts under seal (s.8).

Section 32 of the Act provides that where a fraud, concealment or mistake is alleged, the limitation periods will not begin to run until the plaintiff has discovered the fraud, concealment or mistake or could with reasonable diligence have discovered it.

Of particular interest in the commercial context is that under s.29 when an action has accrued in respect of a debt or a liquidated damages claim, the limitation period begins afresh every time that the debt is acknowledged in writing by the debtor or his agent or a part payment of it is made in respect of it. This only applies however if the original claim was commenced within the appropriate limitation period.

QUESTION

Danny, a house building contractor, entered three different contracts:

(a) to buy some window frames from Eric Ltd. The frames were to be delivered in six instalments, each instalment to be paid for on arrival. After four instalments had been delivered, Eric Ltd announced that they were in financial difficulties and did not intend to deliver the rest.

(b) Plumbers Ltd were employed to install all the plumbing in the houses at a total cost of £30 000. While they completed the job, some of the work was unsatisfactory and Danny had to get another plumber to do the remedial work at a cost of £350. Consequently, Danny has not paid the last £1000 due on the original agreement.

(c) a contract with Flooring Ltd to supply ceramic floor tiles for the kitchen. The contract contained a liquidated damages clause stating that a payment of £100 would be due for every day by which delivery was delayed. The tiles were three days late arriving.

Advise Danny about his rights and liabilities in respect of each of the three contracts.

FURTHER READING

Furmston, M.P., *Cheshire, Fifoot and Furmston's Law of Contract* (12th ed) 1991 (Butterworth)
Keenan, D. and Riches, S., *Business Law* (3rd ed) 1993 (Pitman)
Richards, P., *Law of Contract* 1992 (Pitman)
Smith, J.C., *Smith & Thomas A Casebook on Contract* (9th ed) 1992 (Sweet and Maxwell)

CHAPTER 6

The law of agency

INTRODUCTION

While the doctrine of privity stipulates that only the contracting parties have the right to enforce a contract, there is no requirement that they be the only people involved in the pre-contractual negotiations in which the terms of the contract are agreed. It is commonplace, particularly in business, for a contracting party to use another person, an agent, to negotiate on his behalf. Thus, an employee is the agent of his employer, an estate agent is the agent of the vendor and a stockbroker is an agent for the purposes of buying and selling stocks and shares. Their use by businesses and financial institutions to advise and act on financial matters, market research agencies to advise on marketing trends and practice and advertising agencies to advise on popular presentation all bear testimony to the continued use and importance of agents in the commercial sector. There is no need, however, for such formal arrangements as these situations suggest, it is sufficient that the agent is acting on behalf of his principal with the latter's authority.

THE ROLE OF AN AGENT

The function of an agent is to bring about a valid, binding contract between his principal and a third party. Essentially, his role is that of negotiator, there being no intention that he should be bound contractually himself by the deal. The limit of the agent's contractual involvement is that a contract of agency exists between himself and his principal. It is from this contract that the agent derives his authority.

While in the vast majority of situations the agent drops out of the picture after arranging the contract, there are some exceptions, discussed later, in which the agent may become contractually bound to the third party.

The contractual relationships between the principal, the agent and the third party are as illustrated in Fig. 1.

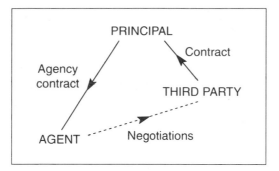

Figure 1   Agency/contractual relationship

THE CREATION OF AN AGENCY

There are no formal requirements at common law for the formation of an agency unless the principal wishes to give his agent the authority to enter deeds on his behalf in which instance a power of attorney will need to be created under the provisions of the Powers of Attorney Act 1971.

The only restriction on an ability to appoint someone as an agent is that the principal must both exist and have the contractual capacity to enter the contract. Thus, a company cannot create an agency to enter a contract prior to its incorporation, s.36(4) of the Companies Act 1985 providing that where a company purports to enter a pre-incorporation contract, the person acting on behalf of the company, i.e. the supposed agent, will be personally liable on the contract unless it provides otherwise. Similarly, a minor cannot create an agency for a contract other than a contract for necessaries and any adult purporting to act as a agent in this situation would, in fact, enter the contract as a principal in his own right.

AUTHORITY

The scope of an agent's power is delineated by the level of authority that the principal has bestowed on him. Authority may be actual or apparent, express or implied.

Actual authority

As the name suggests, this is the level of authority that actually exists between the principal and the agent and the authority for which the agent is entitled to receive his remuneration. If the agent acts in excess of this authority he may be liable to the principal for breach of agency particularly as, depending on the circumstances, the principal may be bound by a contract negotiated by his agent when he was acting outside his actual authority.

Actual authority may be either express or implied.

Express authority

If the agency has been created by a written contract of agency, the scope of the express authority can be determined from the construction and wording of the document. In an oral agency agreement, it will depend on what the parties agreed the agent should have the authority to do.

Implied actual authority

The scope of implied actual authority is more difficult to determine as it must be deduced from all the surrounding circumstances. Typically, it will arise from the extension of a pre-existing express authority although this is not necessarily the case as, for example, in the implied authority existing between a husband and wife.

The decision of *Hely Hutchinson* v *Brayhead Ltd* [1968] 1 QB 549, a Court of Appeal decision, examined the scope of implied authority. The chairman of the defendant company acted as its 'de facto' managing director with the acquiescence of the other directors although he had not been formally appointed to that position. He issued two letter of guarantee to the plaintiffs which they subsequently sought to enforce, the defendants denying liability on the grounds of lack of authority. The court held that the 'managing director' had implied actual authority exercised with the defendants' agreement.

An agent will also have implied authority for any acts that are necessarily incidental to the exercise of his express authority. Thus, for example, if an agent is instructed to buy an item for his principal, there would be an implied authority to pledge the principal's credit such as to bind him to the debt.

Usual authority

The exact location of usual authority within the law of agency has given rise to much academic debate, but this author supports the widely held view that it is a subdivision of implied actual authority.

Usual authority is the authority which an agent acquires by virtue of his profession. It results from an assumption that a principal when appointing an agent to a recognised job or profession impliedly provides him with the authority to undertake all the duties that would normally fall within such a job or profession. It follows that it does not have a general application but is limited to those situations where the agent occupies an identifiable job or profession.

In *Panorama Developments (Guildford) Ltd* v *Fidelis Furnishing Fabrics Ltd* [1971] 3 All ER 16, CA, it was held that a company secretary has the implied authority to enter contracts 'dealing with the administrative side of the company's affairs'. This included the authority to hire cars and thus the company was liable in respect of such contracts even though the company secretary had hired them for his own purposes. From the *Panorama* decision, a company secretary would clearly also have authority to buy office equipment, hire staff, rent accommodation etc.

Given the breadth of the powers that an agent might acquire under usual authority, it is appropriate that a principal should have the ability to limit the extent of those powers if he sees fit. Any such restriction will be binding on a third party only if he knows of it. If he is unaware of the restriction, the principal will be liable on any contract that the agent enters that falls within the usual authority. It is this aspect of usual authority that has given rise to debate, for this reliance on the way that the agency appears to a third party is very similar to the approach used in apparent authority.

Watteau v *Fenwick* [1893] 1 QB 346 analysed the role of notice in usual authority. Fenwick employed Humble as the manager of his hotel and expressly forbade Humble to buy any cigars on credit. Watteau, unaware of the agency and of the restriction on it, supplied Humble with cigars. Fenwick was held liable for the debt as Humble was deemed to be acting within the usual authority of a hotel manager and Fenwick, the third party, was ignorant of the restrictions.

The case has been subjected to much criticism since it held an undisclosed principal liable for an action that he had expressly forbidden. Nonetheless, while some commentators doubt whether this case will be followed strictly in the future, at the moment it is good law.

Apparent authority

Apparent authority, sometimes called 'ostensible authority', derives not from any agreement between the principal and agent but rather from the appearance of an agreement as seen from the third party's perspective. Hence, it is what appears to exist rather than what actually exists.

Clearly, there must be some reasonable foundation for the third party's belief. Three criteria must be established to prove apparent authority which effectively involve creating an estoppel. These are the existence of a representation, reliance on the representation and the third party altering his position.

(a) **Existence of a representation.** To be effective the principal must have made a representation, whether by words or conduct, that the agent possesses a level of actual authority. The agent is not capable of making such a representation about his authority, it must come from the principal or from someone acting on his behalf who has the actual authority to make such a representation. This means that the existence of the principal must be known to the third party, it following that apparent authority cannot be created where the principal is undisclosed.

The leading case is *Freeman & Lockyer* v *Buckhurst Park Properties (Mangal) Ltd* [1964] 2 QB 480. The defendant company with the acquiescence of its other directors, allowed one of its directors to act as the 'de facto' managing director and undertake the day to day management of the company. He instructed a firm of architects in connection with a property development plan in which the company was involved. Subsequently, the company refused to pay the architects' fee contending that the 'managing director' did not have any authority to engage them. The Court of Appeal held that the board of directors had by their acquiescence represented that the managing director had the authority to act on their behalf. As such, the company was liable.

It is possible for a representation to be made after the agent has agreed the contract with the third party if the principal by his actions has appeared to adopt or affirm it.

In *Spiro* v *Lintern* [1973] 3 All ER 319 the defendant instructed his wife to arrange for the sale of the house although she did not have the authority to enter a binding contract. Acting on her instructions the estate agent arranged a sale to the plaintiffs. Knowing of this supposed contract, the defendant allowed the plaintiffs to make arrangements for alterations to the premises. He subsequently refused to complete the sale relying on his wife's lack of authority. The court held the defendant was bound by the contract as his acquiescence in the plaintiffs' behaviour represented an affirmation of the contract.

(b) **Reliance on the representation.** The existence of reliance is a question of fact in each case. To prove reliance, the third party will need to demonstrate that he had actual knowledge of the representation, constructive knowledge will not suffice. It follows that the third party cannot establish an apparent authority if either he was unaware of the principal's representation or, alternatively, he had actual or constructive knowledge that the agent did not possess any authority.

(c) **Alteration of the third party's position.** Again, this is a question of fact. The third party must demonstrate that, in reliance on the representation, he has altered his legal position. It is generally believed that the third party must have acted to his detriment though there is some debate on this point.

Agency by ratification

If an agent has acted beyond his authority, or a person with no authority has purported to act as an agent, the principal may adopt or ratify any resultant contract and be bound by it. Ratification provides the agent with retrospective actual authority so that he will be deemed to have been acting within his authority at all times and the principal will be bound by the contract *ab initio*.

In order for a valid agency by ratification to be created, certain criteria must be met.

(a) The agent must have contracted as an agent. When negotiating the contract, the agent must have purported to act as an agent for an identifiable principal. It follows that an undisclosed principal cannot ratify a contract as this would necessarily have involved the agency relationship being kept secret.

In *Keighley, Maxted & Co v Durant* [1901] AC 240 an agent exceeded his authority and bought corn at a price higher than that approved by his principal. The agent bought in his own name and did not disclose the agency although his intention was to buy on behalf of his principal. Initially the principal agreed to ratify the contract and accept the wheat but subsequently refused to take delivery. The third party sued the principal who was held not liable by the House of Lords. As an undisclosed principal he was incapable of ratifying the contract.

In a situation such as this, there would be a strong argument for holding that the third party could sue the agent for a breach of warranty of authority. Remedies in agency are discussed later.

(b) The principal can ratify any contract for which he was named. Once the principal has been named by the agent in a contract, the principal has the right to ratify it and receive any contractual benefits even if the agent used his name fraudulently and intended to gain the benefit of the contract for himself.

(c) The principal exists. For ratification to be possible, the principal must have existed at the time that the contract was made. This is of most concern in relation to limited companies and pre-incorporation contracts. As explained previously, a company cannot enter a contract prior to its incorporation as it does not exist at law. For the same reason, it is incapable of ratifying any pre-incorporation contract purportedly made on its behalf.

In *Kelner v Baxter* (1866) LR 2 CP 174 the plaintiff, Kelner, sold some wine to Baxter who purported to act on behalf of a hotel company prior to its incorporation. The wine was consumed but not paid for. It was held that Baxter was personally liable as the company, not being incorporated at the time of the contract, could not ratify it.

This position has now been reinforced by s.36(4) of the Companies Act 1985 as mentioned earlier.

(d) **The principal had the contractual capacity.** The ability of a principal to ratify is limited to those contracts for which he had the contractual capacity at the time that the contract was made. Thus, a minor would only be able to ratify contracts for necessaries.

(e) **The contract must be capable of ratification.** The principal cannot ratify a contract which would be illegal or void *ab initio*. As such contracts would never have any effect, they cannot be ratified. A voidable contract, however, is capable of ratification because it is a valid binding contract until it is avoided.

(f) **The knowledge of the principal.** The principal must have had knowledge of all the material facts prior to ratification if he is to bound by it. The principal can, however, declare an intention to be bound irrespective of the material facts.

(g) **Reasonable time.** Ratification must take place within a reasonable time, this being a question of fact in each individual case.

Agency of necessity

Agency of necessity is seldom used due to the difficulty of establishing the requisite criteria and the attitude of the courts. It is intended to cover those situations where in an emergency or crisis the agent acts on behalf of a principal from whom he does not have the relevant authority. The court will grant the agent appropriate authority but has restricted the application of the doctrine to situations where the agent and the principal have a pre-existing relationship.

(a) **Impossibility of contact.** It must be impossible for the agent to contact his principal to gain instructions. This must be increasingly difficult to prove in this modern age of high-speed telecommunications. Even though it was easier to prove in by-gone days, the burden of proof was still heavy.

In *Arthur v Barton* (1840) 6 M & W 138 the master of a ship validly created an agency of necessity when his ship was badly damaged during a voyage and was forced to put into port for crucial repairs. The master was unable to contact the ship's owners and pledged the ship for the value of the repairs. The owners were held liable for the debt.

In *Springer v Great Western Railway* [1921] 1 KB 257 the railway company failed to establish an agency of necessity because they had not contacted the principal prior to acting. A consignment of tomatoes being sent from Jersey to London arrived in port three days late and was delayed a further two days prior to unloading. As the consignment was bad when unloaded, the railway company sold it locally. The company were held liable to the owner for failing to take instructions and wrongly selling his goods.

(b) Actual and commercial necessity. The agent must demonstrate that there was an actual and commercial necessity for his actions. In the past, this has tended to mean a need to show that his actions were necessary to either preserve or avoid the physical destruction of the principal's goods. Acting to make a profit for the principal is not sufficient. The application of this requirement can be seen by comparing the following decisions.

As seen above, in *Arthur* v *Barton* the undertaking of repairs to a ship to render it seaworthy for the voyage home was a genuine necessity.

In *Great Northern Railway* v *Swaffield* (1874) LR 9 Ex 132 a genuine necessity arose when the plaintiff railway company stabled a horse for the night after no-one arrived at the station to collect it. The railway company were under an obligation to take care of the animal and hence the owner was liable for the costs of the stabling.

Prager v *Blatspiel Stamp & Heacock Ltd* [1924] 1 KB 566 involved the purchase and subsequent sale of some animal skins. The agent purchased some skins for the principal in 1915 but because of the war was unable to send them to the principal or receive instructions. Two years later, the agent sold them at a handsome profit. However, the court held the agent liable to the principal as the sale had not been necessary. The skins would not have deteriorated if stored properly and the opportunity to make a financial gain was not commercial necessity.

(c) The agent acted bona fide. The agent must show that he acted *bona fide* in the best interests of the principal. This is a basic requirement of any agency relationship as it is a relationship *uberrimae fidei* – of the utmost good faith. The existence of good faith is a matter of fact.

DUTIES ARISING FROM AGENCY

There are three distinct relationships in the agency scenario: that between the principal and the agent, that between the principal and the third party and, finally, that between the agent and the third party. Each of these relationships gives rise to rights and liabilities.

THE PRINCIPAL/AGENT RELATIONSHIP

The relationship of the principal and agent is central to the whole concept of agency for it is on this relationship that the whole scenario depends. The relationship is a fiduciary one that creates a variety of rights and obligations on both principal and agent.

Duties owed by the agent

Underlying the duties owed by the agent to the principal is the fact that it is a relationship *uberrimae fidei*. As such, the good faith of the agent is paramount in establishing the nature and extent of his duties with a constant requirement that the agent acts in the best interests of his principal at all times.

The agent is required to act personally, reflecting the fact that the principal, in appointing him, necessarily places a degree of trust in him. The contract is personal in nature. Therefore, the agent is not permitted to delegate his duties to a sub-agent without the agreement of the principal, either expressly or impliedly. Any wrongful delegation of the agent's duties would be actionable as a breach of agency. Delegation in this context would not include the agent employing some other person to undertake a purely menial task.

Implied authority to delegate may arise from the surrounding circumstances. Thus, in *Solley* v *Wood* (1852) 16 Beav 370 it was held that a provincial solicitor had the implied right to delegate his functions regarding High Court attendance to a London solicitor, this being the practice of the profession. By contrast, in *John McCann & Co* v *Pow* [1974] 1 WLR 1643 an estate agent who was appointed as a 'sole agent' had no implied authority to delegate his functions to a sub-agent.

The relationship between the principal and the sub-agent will depend on whether the agent's delegation of his functions was authorised by the principal. If it was, contractual privity would exist between the principal and the sub-agent such as make the sub-agent liable directly to the principal for the performance of his functions. By contrast, if the delegation was not authorised, the agent would remain contractually liable to the principal for both his own actions and those of the sub-agent.

The agent is under a duty to obey the instructions that he receives from his principal for, if he acts outside his express or implied authority, he may be liable to his principal for breach of agency. Should the instructions be ambiguous, he will not be liable if he has acted upon a reasonable interpretation of them, even though that interpretation was wrong.

The agent must exercise reasonable skill and care when performing his functions, the standard of this care depending upon factors such as the expertise of the particular agent, whether or not he was paid and the degree of reliance attached to his duties. Clearly, therefore, a higher standard of care would be expected of a professional agent as opposed to someone acting gratuitously although the decision of *Chaudhry* v *Prabhakar* [1988] 3 All ER 718 held that a gratuitous agent does owe a duty to the principal to exercise reasonable skill and care in all the circumstances. Encompassed within the concept of skill and care is a duty on the agent to tell his principal of all relevant factors, to obtain the best deal possible for his principal if he is buying or selling goods, services or other property and a duty not to disclose his principal's confidential information, be it personal or business. A breach of any of these could attract liability as a breach of agency.

In *Keppel* v *Wheeler* [1927] 1 KB 577 the agent was employed to sell a house. He received an offer of £6150 and the principal subsequently sold the property for this amount. Unknown to the principal, the agent received a second offer of £6750 before the contract for the lower sum was finalised. The court held that the agent was liable to reimburse the principal for the difference between the two bids as he was in breach of his duty.

In *Heath* v *Parkinson* (1926) 42 TLR 693 the agent, Heath, was engaged by Parkinson, to sell the lease of his premises. Parkinson believed that the landlord would not allow the premises to be used for business purposes. However, Heath gained an assurance from the superior landlord that they were prepared to allow the premises to be used for a tailor's business. This affected the desirability of the property and thereby increased the value of the lease. Heath did not disclose this fact to Parkinson and persuaded him to sell the lease for a lower sum than he would have gained otherwise. The court held that Heath was in breach of his agency and was not entitled to receive his commission.

L.S. Harris Trustees Ltd v *Power Packing Services (Hermit Road) Ltd* [1970] 2 Lloyd's Rep 65 addressed the issue of confidentiality. The defendants suffered a fire at their warehouse and instructed the plaintiffs to prepare an insurance claim. In contravention of an express prohibition against disclosing any of the defendants' confidential information during their inquiries, the plaintiffs disclosed such information to one of the defendants' customers. The court held that the defendants were entitled to terminate their contract with the plaintiffs for breach of agency and seek damages.

The general duty to pursue the best interests of his principal and specifically to obtain the best price for him in any deal necessarily requires that an agent must not place himself in the position of conflict with his principal. The difficulty is obvious. If, for example, an agent is selling an item on behalf of his principal and the agent buys the item himself a conflict is created. The principal, as seller, wants to sell for the highest price possible and his agent should work to that end. The agent, as purchaser, however, will want to buy for the lowest sum possible. The two are incompatible. Thus, there is an absolute prohibition against an agent contracting with his principal, a breach of which entitles the principal to rescind the resultant contract.

In *Armstrong* v *Jackson* [1917] 2 KB 822 Armstrong employed Jackson, a stockbroker, to buy some shares for him. In fact, Jackson sold Armstrong his own shares but fraudulently provided contract notes suggesting that they had been bought elsewhere. The court held that Armstrong was entitled to rescind the contract of purchase.

While the decision of *Armstrong* v *Jackson* is clearly justifiable given the agent's fraud, the concept bites much deeper than that. Should the agent get into a position of conflict, he will be liable for breach, and thus liable to account to the principal for any profit that he has made, even if the agent has behaved in good faith and in the best interests of his principal.

In *Boardman* v *Phipps* [1967] 2 AC 46 two agents acting on behalf of the trustees of a trust fund purchased some shares for the fund. On the basis of the information they acquired, the agents also bought some of the shares for themselves, the purchase being made with the consent of the trustees. Both the trust fund and the agents made a profit on the shares. It was accepted that the agents had acted in good faith and that the principal had not suffered by the agents' actions. Nonetheless, the agents were held liable to account to the principal for the profit that they had made on their shares.

The *Boardman* decision may seem draconian given that the agents had acted in good faith and that the principal had not suffered. However, the approach of the English courts to situations of conflict is to construe them very strictly and not to allow the agent, however innocent, to retain any profit. The logic appears to be that if the agent knows that he will not be able to keep the profit under any circumstances, the temptation to place himself in a position of conflict for financial gain will be reduced or even eradicated. Some of the Commonwealth jurisdictions are less stringent in their approach and are prepared to allow an innocent agent to keep the profit in a situation such as *Boardman* provided that his actions have received the genuine consent of the principal. At the moment *Boardman* remains good law in England.

The prevention of a conflict situation presents a real problem if the agent acts in more than one capacity as, for example, in the buying and selling of shares on the Stock Exchange after 'Big Bang'. Under current arrangements, it is possible for one stockbroking company to act as both buyer and seller in respect of an individual share transaction. The Financial Services Act 1986 attempts to control the potential conflicts created by this situation by requiring the different functions to be undertaken by different departments within the organisation these being separated by so-called 'Chinese Walls', the purpose of which is to prevent the transfer of information. While the Stock Exchange presents a pertinent example of such conflict, the same scenario would arise if any agent, e.g. a solicitor, were to act for both the buyer and the seller in any transaction as he could not genuinely serve the interests of both parties.

The duty that attracts most attention is the duty not to make a secret profit, this description covering any unauthorised payment over and above the fee or commission to which the agent is entitled. It does not necessarily connote a bribe although clearly a bribe would be one form of secret profit. Essentially it means that the agent cannot use either the principal's property or any information gained in the course of the agency for the purpose of making a profit. The *Boardman* decision is a good example of this as is the decision of *Regal (Hastings) Ltd* v *Gulliver* [1942] 1 All ER 378.

In the *Regal* decision, the plaintiff company wanted to buy two cinemas and decided to establish a new subsidiary company to undertake the deal. However, the company could not pay up all the share capital for the new company and the defendant directors agreed to purchase the shares themselves to allow the whole deal to go through. The plaintiff company duly bought the cinemas which were sold subsequently at a handsome profit. The defendants made a profit of £2.80 per share but were held liable to account for it to the company.

If the existence of a secret profit is established the principal has a range of remedies available to him. He may choose to do nothing and allow the agent to keep the profit particularly if the agent has acted in good faith and in the interests of the principal. Any suggestion of wrongdoing, however, may encourage the principal to take a far tougher line and exercise some of the other options open to him. These include the summary dismissal of the agent (justified on the grounds that the principal should not be compelled to retain an agent whom he can no longer trust), the recovery of the secret profit from the agent or the third party and a refusal to pay any commission due while recovering any already paid. Further, he can rescind the contract with the third party and sue both the agent and the third party in the tort of deceit for any losses that he has sustained as a result of the bribe. It should be noted that these remedies are available irrespective of the effect, if any, that the bribe had upon the actions of the agent. Thus, an agent whose actions have not been effected by the bribe will still be held liable.

The final duty owed by the agent is to render account to the principal for his affairs whenever he so requests. On the termination of the agency, the agent must give all the books, documents, accounts etc. to the principal.

Duties owed by the principal

The principal owes two duties to the agent namely to pay him his fee or commission when it is due and to reimburse the agent for any expenses incurred legitimately in the course of the agency.

The agent is only entitled to receive payment for work carried out under an express or implied authority and only when the agency task is completed unless the agency agreement specifies otherwise. Further, the agent must have been the effective cause of the contract between the principal and the third party as evidenced by the decision of *Coles* v *Enoch* [1939] 3 All ER 327.

Normally, the contract will specify the level of payment but in the absence of a specific term the court may be prepared to imply a term for payment if the agent was acting in the course of his business. Such an implied term would provide for a *quantum meruit* payment. The court will not intervene however if the contract includes a term providing for payment at a rate to be agreed but no rate has been agreed.

One difficulty facing an agent seeking payment arises if he is prevented by the principal from completing the agency task and is thereby denied the right to his remuneration. The courts have proved unwilling to imply any term into an agency agreement that gives the agent the right to complete his agency function as this interferes with the principal's right to deal with his property as he chooses. However, the courts have been willing to imply such a term where the principal has resorted to a deliberate breach of his contract with the third party as a means of denying the agent his right to payment as in *Alpha Trading Ltd* v *Dunnshaw-Patten Ltd* [1981] QB 290.

When the agent is an employee of the principal, his commission is in the form of his salary which he is entitled to receive for the duration of the contract of employment.

In addition to his fee, the agent has a right to be indemnified for legitimate expenses incurred in the course of the agency. This right is lost if the agent has incurred the expenses negligently or has acted illegally.

The agent has a lien over any of the principal's goods in his possession in respect of any monies owed to him by the principal.

THE PRINCIPAL/THIRD PARTY RELATIONSHIP

When the agent has acted within his actual authority or the principal has ratified his actions, the principal and the third party will have a normal contractual relationship with the ability to sue and be sued upon their contract. As explained earlier, the agent having arranged the contract drops out of the picture.

A more interesting and complex situation arises when the principal is 'undisclosed'. This occurs where neither the existence nor the identity of the principal are made known to the third party who believes that the agent is acting on his own behalf as a contracting party. By contrast, an 'unnamed' principal exists when the agent is known to be acting as an agent but the identity of his principal is unknown. This situation would exist, for example, where an agent, in an auction room, receives his instructions via an anonymous telephone bidder.

When an agent has contracted for an undisclosed principal, the contract is enforceable between the third party and the agent. Should the existence of the principal become known, the third party can elect whether to retain his rights against the agent or enforce the contract against the principal instead. He is free to choose but his election is irrevocable. Alternatively, the principal may choose to make his presence known with the consequent right to enforce the contract although this right is limited to situations where the agent was acting within his actual authority. Where the principal supplants the agent, the former takes the contract subject to any claims that the third party may have against the agent.

There are some restrictions upon the principal's right to adopt the contract if, for example, his intervention is expressly or impliedly prohibited by the contract.

In *Humble* v *Hunter* (1848) 12 QB 310 the agent chartered a ship in his own name describing himself in the contract as her 'owner'. The court held that this implied that there was no other principal and thus the real principal was not liable on the contract.

The intervention of the principal may also be prevented if the third party had genuine reasons for wanting to deal with the agent personally or genuine objections to dealing with the principal. A desire to contract with the agent might arise, for example, if the agent owed money to the third party and the contract was to be used as a means of off-setting the debt. Objections to the identity of the principal are more difficult to substantiate. It must be more than a mere unwillingness by the third party to contract with the principal. He must demonstrate that the identity of the principal is a matter of real importance to him such as to mean that he would never have knowingly consented to contracting with the principal. If this can be established or the agent has misrepresented his position, the principal will lose the right to intervene with the result that the contract will subsist between the agent and the third party.

Financial settlement with the agent

Where agents are used in the commercial context, either party to the contract may wish to settle their contractual debts by paying the agent, particularly if the agent is the only person with whom they have had any actual contact. However, this is not, *prima facie*, an acceptable way of settling contractual debts.

The authority given to an agent by the principal to sell goods on his behalf does not include an authority to receive money on his account. Thus, the payment of a debt by the third party to the agent will not satisfy his liability and he will remain liable if the agent fails to give the money to the principal. Naturally, the principal can give his agent actual authority to receive money on his behalf in which case payment to the agent by the third party will suffice to extinguish the debt. However, the method of such payment must comply with the terms of the authority granted to the agent.

The agent also lacks authority to receive payment on behalf of the third party and thus, the giving of payment to the agent by the principal will not suffice to satisfy the debt. The third party can overrule this general position by indicating that he will accept payment via the agent.

THE AGENT/THIRD PARTY RELATIONSHIP

While the intention in an agency scenario is for the agent to have no liability to the third party, there are some situations in which personal liability will follow the agent.

As seen above, the agent will be personally liable on the contract if he acts on behalf of an undisclosed principal until such time as the principal makes his presence known or the third party elects to be contractually bound to the principal. Also, the agent is personally liable on the contract if he has acted for a non-existent principal or has acted without authority in a situation where the principal cannot ratify the contract.

Liability of a different kind will be visited on the agent if, unknown to the third party, he has acted beyond his authority. In this situation he may be liable to the third party for a breach of warranty of authority. It is argued that such a breach is actionable as a breach of a collateral contract, the terms of the contract being that the agent warrants that he has the authority to act on behalf of the principal in return for the third party entering the main contract with the principal.

Misleading statements made by the agent during the negotiations may result in a tortious action for either misrepresentation or deceit.

TERMINATION OF AGENCY

An agency may be terminated either by the parties themselves or by operation of law.

Termination by the parties

An agency agreement can, like any other contract, be terminated by agreement between the parties. The arrangements for the termination of the agreement may be embodied within the agreement itself. Thus, for example, a fixed term agency agreement will terminate upon the expiration of the period. Similarly, an agreement due to last for the commission of a specified act, e.g. the sale of a piece of property, will terminate when the sale is complete. Otherwise the parties may conclude the agency by agreement. Naturally, at the termination of the agency, the agent is entitled to receive any remuneration or expenses owing to him for work done during the lifetime of the agency agreement.

Termination by operation of law

The law will effect the end of the agency agreement in four situations these being where the principal has died, become insane, been declared bankrupt or become an enemy. In addition, agency agreements may be frustrated in the same way as any other contract.

THE COMMERCIAL AGENTS (DIRECTIVE) REGULATIONS 1993

The common law position described above has been strengthened recently by the passage of the Commercial Agents Council (Directive) Regulations 1993 which implement EEC Directive 86/653 on the coordination of the laws of Member States relating to self-employed commercial agents. These regulations, implemented on 1 January 1994, clarify the position regarding commercial agents who are defined in reg.2(1) as being

> a self employed intermediary who has continuing authority to negotiate the sale or purchase of goods on behalf of another person (the 'principal') or to negotiate and conclude the sale or purchase of goods on behalf of and in the name of that principal.

The definition appears to include limited companies although it continues by excluding from its provisions officers of a company, duly authorised partners and insolvency practitioners.

The first point to note is that the regulations do not apply to commercial agents arranging for services rather than goods and expressly do not apply to agents operating on commodity exchanges in the commodity market. Thus their impact is comparatively limited for they apply only to agents involved in the buying and selling of goods. Further, their impact is limited in that they do not apply to commercial agents whose activities are unpaid or whose activities are to be considered as secondary as defined in the schedule to the regulations.

The regulations apply in their entirety to agency agreements entered into after 1 January 1994 and amended agreements concluded before that date. They do not apply to agency agreements where the parties have agreed that the agency contract is to be governed by the law of another member state.

Part II of the regulations addresses the issue of the duties owed by both the commercial agent and the principal. As seen earlier, duty lies at the centre of the agent/principal relationship and many of the liabilities in agency arise from a breach of the respective duties. Regulation 3(1), which closely echoes the common law position, provides that an agent must look after the interests of his principal and act dutifully and in good faith. Regulation 3(2) which qualifies the general requirement states that he shall:

(a) make proper efforts to negotiate and, where appropriate, conclude the transactions he is instructed to take care of;
(b) communicate to his principal all the necessary information available to him;
(c) comply with reasonable instructions given by his principal.

The duties imposed upon the principal by these regulations exceed those formerly recognised by the common law which relate merely to remuneration and the recovery of expenses. Under the new regulations, the principal is obliged to keep the agent provided with the necessary documentation relating to the goods and the necessary information to enable him to fulfil his duties. Further, the principal must inform the agent within a reasonable period of his acceptance or refusal of any commercial transaction negotiated by the agent and of the principal's failure to perform any transaction agreed upon by the agent.

Regulation 5(1) confirms the status of the aforementioned provisions by stating that the parties cannot derogate from regulations 3 and 4 and that the law applicable to the contract will govern the consequences of breach.

Part III of the regulations, regs. 6–12 deal with the central issue of the agent's right to remuneration. Regulation 6 underlines his right to receive remuneration in the absence of any express term in the agreement. The essential provision (very similar in impact to s.15 of the Supply of Goods and Services Act 1982) is that the agent has a right to receive a level of remuneration that would customarily be received by agents in the same position and, where no such custom exists, that he should receive a reasonable remuneration.

Regulation 7 onwards deals with the agent's entitlement to commission and recognises the right of an agent to receive commission when a transaction has been concluded as a result of his actions (as under common law) or is concluded with a third party whom the agent had acquired previously as a customer for such transactions. Further, it recognises the right of a sole agent to receive commission when the agreement relates to a specific geographic area or a specific group of customers. These rights subsist after the termination of the agreement so that the agent has a right to recover commission if the transaction was attributable mainly to the actions of the agent during the period of the agency. Where a new agent has been appointed, the new agent shall not be entitled to any portion of that commission unless it is equitable that he should be so entitled.

Under reg. 10 commission becomes due when either the principal executes the transaction or when he should have executed the transaction under the terms of the agreement or when the third party executes the transaction. It is payable at the latest when the third party either executes his part of the transaction or should have done so if the principal had complied with the agreement. The right to commission is lost if the major contract between the principal and the third party is not executed for reasons for which the principal is not to blame. If this occurs any commission already received by the agent must be refunded.

Finally, under reg. 12 the agent has the right to receive a statement about the commission due to him not later than the last day of the month following the quarter in which it was earned. The statement must set out the main components used in calculating the commission due, the agent having the right to demand access to the appropriate information to allow him to check the statement. This would include books, papers, accounts, deeds, writings and documents.

Part IV of the regulations deals primarily, though not exclusively, with the conclusion and termination of the agency agreement. Regulation 13 contains an absolute right that cannot be waived whereby either party is entitled to receive from the other upon request a signed document setting out the terms of the agency agreement agreed at the outset of the contract and subsequently. Naturally, this would include any agreed provisions regarding termination of the agreement or, alternatively, rights of extension.

Regulation 14 deals specifically with the position when a fixed term agency agreement (e.g. three years) reaches the end of the specified period and yet the parties continue to act as if the contract was subsisting. The regulation provides that the agency will continue on the same terms but be of an indefinite duration. Thus the agent will continue to exercise the level of authority existing previously and be entitled to remuneration.

Many agreements make suitable provision for the termination of the agreement either because it is for a fixed duration or, alternatively, by stipulating periods of notice. However, the position may arise whereby a commercial agent is employed under an indefinite contract in which no term exists regarding periods of notice. This position is rectified by reg. 15 which stipulates that prescribed minimum periods of notice will apply in that situation, namely one month's notice during the first year of the agreement, two months' notice during the second year and three months' notice during the third or any subsequent year all ending on the last day of the month unless otherwise agreed by the parties. This protection for the agent is reinforced by later provisions within reg. 15 which provide that the parties may agree upon longer periods of notice but subject to the requirement that the period of notice that the agent is entitled to receive must not be shorter than that to which the principal is entitled. These provisions also apply to a fixed term contract which has been rendered indefinite by the operation of reg. 14 as discussed above.

If the agent suffers loss as a result of the termination he is entitled to receive compensation as long as his claim is lodged within one year of termination. While the regulation is sufficiently broad to attract compensation for any termination, the regulation draws attention to two particular situations. The first is where the principal has received a substantial benefit from the agent's activities while depriving the agent of the commission which proper performance of the agency would have earned him and, second, where the agent has not been able to recover any costs or expenses incurred legitimately. The agent's estate can recover compensation if the termination was caused by the agent's death.

Naturally, following the common law approach, compensation is not recoverable if the termination was due to the agent's default. Thus, for example, if the agent had made a secret profit or breached the good faith requirement, the right to compensation would be lost. Further, compensation is not payable if the agent terminated the agreement unless it was due to his age, infirmity or illness rendering further performance unreasonable or was justified by the principal's behaviour. Finally, the right to compensation ceases if the agent assigns his rights and liabilities to a new agent.

Given the *uberrimae fidei* nature of agency and the opportunity it provides for the agent to acquire knowledge of the principal's business, it is perhaps natural that a principal may want to insert a restraint of trade clause into an agency agreement. Such clauses are valid at common law as discussed in chapter 3 subject to certain criteria being satisfied. The proposed Commercial Agents (Directive) Regulations 1993, reg. 20 reinforces this position by stipulating that restraint of trade clauses are valid only and to the extent that two criteria are satisfied, namely, that the clause is written (this puts its scope beyond doubt), and that it relates both to the geographic area or to a group of customers and geographic area in which the agent works and the type of goods covered by the agency. The maximum duration of a restraint of trade clause is two years after termination.

QUESTION

B Ltd employ C Ltd as their agent for the distribution and sale of their cars. The agency agreement provides that the agency will last for a period of two years commencing on 1 January 1993 and that C Ltd will receive a 5% commission on every vehicle sold.

Discuss the rights and liabilities of the parties during the first year of operation of the agency and what alterations will occur after 1 January 1994.

FURTHER READING

Bradgate, R. and Savage, N., *Commercial Law* 1991 (Butterworth)

Dobson, A.P and Schmitthoff, C.M. (eds), *Charlesworth's Business Law* (15th ed) 1991 (Sweet and Maxwell)

Markesinis, B.S and Munday, J.R.C., *An Outline of the Law of Agency* (3rd ed) 1992 (Butterworth)

Richards, P., *Law of Contract* 1992 (Pitman)

Savage, N. and Bradgate, R. *Business Law* (2nd ed) 1992 (Butterworth)

Stone, R.T.H., 'Usual and Ostensible Authority – One Concept or Two?' (1993) *Journal of Business Law* 325

Part II

The supply of goods and services

CHAPTER 7

Implied conditions in the sale of goods

INTRODUCTION

The merchantability and utility of goods is an issue of paramount importance to anyone involved in the regular sale and purchase of goods, whether in a professional capacity or a personal one. The law covering merchantability is derived originally from nineteenth century common law decisions. Indeed, there have only been two statutes governing the merchantability of goods in contracts of sale: the Sale of Goods Act 1983 which codified the pre-existing common law and the Sale of Goods Act 1979 which is a consolidation Act bringing together the previous provisions as amended by the Supply of Goods (Implied Terms) Act 1973 and the Unfair Contract Terms Act 1977.

The 1979 Act (hereafter the Act) seeks to control the relationship between sellers and buyers. Being contractual in nature, the rules of contractual privity apply and thus the manufacturer of a product will not have any direct liability to the ultimate consumer unless he sold the goods to him. Each member of the distributive chain will have privity with the person next to him in the chain whether as seller or buyer and so acquire rights and obligations. A distributive chain might include a variety of persons such as appears in Fig. 2, each of whom will have some contractual responsibilities.

The Act protects the buyer of goods by a collection of implied conditions contained in ss.12–15 that cover title, sales by description, merchantability, fitness for purpose and sale by sample. Being implied conditions any breach, however slight, gives rise to a right to terminate the contract although s.11(2) allows the buyer to treat a breach of condition as merely a breach of warranty. This involves the buyer foregoing his right of termination and electing to continue with the contract while suing for contractual damages for the breach in accordance with s.53. This provides that where the buyer elects or is forced to treat a breach of condition as a breach of warranty, he can either set up the breach as a means of reducing or extinguishing the price or sue for damages. This solution will be forced upon a buyer if he is deemed to have 'accepted' the goods as in *Bernstein* v *Pamson Motors (Golders Green) Ltd* [1987] 2 All ER 220, in which case the buyer will lose his right of termination and be forced to rely on an action for damages.

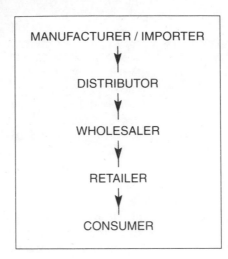

Figure 2   Distributive chain

A 'CONTRACT OF SALE'

The Sale of Goods Act 1979 only applies to contracts for the sale of goods as defined in the Act. It is important to understand the parameters of such contracts for there are many similar contracts involving the transfer of goods which do not attract the protection of ss.12–15. Arguably, the distinction is of less significance today as most of these contracts are now covered by similar provisions contained in other statutes. Nonetheless, it is important to establish the parameters of each classification of contract so as to identify which statute applies to any individual contract.

A 'contract of sale' is defined in s.2(1) as being 'a contract by which the seller transfers or agrees to transfer the property in goods to the buyer for a money consideration called the price'. Section 61 defines 'goods' as 'including all personal chattels other than things in action and money . . . [and] . . . emblements, industrial growing crops, and things attached to or forming part of the land which are agreed to be severed before sale or under the contract of sale'. This latter definition would clearly include things such as timber which can be severed from the land but would not include buildings which cannot.

Analysis of s.2 permits identification of those contracts involving the transfer of goods which would not be covered by the 1979 Act. Hire-purchase contracts are not included for it was held in the case of *Helby* v *Matthews* [1895] AC 471 that the hirer in a hire-purchase agreement has not bought or agreed to buy the goods. (Hire-purchase is considered in depth in chapter 17.)

The requirement for a money consideration necessarily excludes contracts of barter whereby goods are exchanged as in *Esso Petroleum Ltd* v *Customs and Excise Commissioners* [1976] 1 All ER 117 in which World Cup coins were provided as a special offer to customers who purchased four gallons of petrol. The House of Lords held that there was a contract but not a contract of sale. Note however, that the decision of *G.J. Dawson (Clapham) Ltd* v *H & G Dutfield* [1936] 2 All ER 232 decided that a part-exchange agreement in which the goods are paid for partly by exchange goods and partly by money is a contract for the sale of goods. In that decision, two lorries were to be paid for partly by a trade-in of two other lorries with the balance being payable in cash.

The potential inclusion of contracts for the supply of work and materials will depend on the balance between the two elements of the contract. If the contract is primarily for the purchase of the goods, the service element being a mere incidental as, for example, to make a meal in a restaurant, the contract will be covered by the Sale of Goods Act. By contrast, where the primary element of the contract is the provision of the service as in a contract for the repair of a car or the interior decoration of premises, the contract will fall outside the provisions of the Act even though some goods will be transferred in an integral part of the contract. In the above examples, this would be the replacement parts for the car and the paint used for the decoration.

Contracts of bailment likewise fall outside the Act because there is no intention to pass the property in such contracts, merely to pass the temporary possession of the goods. This would include contracts of hire, whether short term or long term, and contracts for the repair of goods whereby the repairer takes temporary possession of the goods but surrenders them to the owner upon completion of the repairs.

The implied conditions of title, description, merchantability etc. for the goods in contracts of barter, contracts for services and contracts of hire are contained in Part I of the Supply of Goods and Services Act 1982.

THE RIGHT TO SELL

When purchasing goods, the buyer naturally wishes to be assured that he is going to acquire good title to them. While this will be of importance to any purchaser, the significance in a commercial context may be overwhelming when any individual contract of purchase may potentially involve thousands or millions of pounds. There is little point in a buyer contracting to buy an extremely expensive piece of precision machinery only to discover that he has not acquired the title to it because the seller did not have the right to sell.

Section 12(1) of the Act addresses this problem and provides

> In a contract of sale, other than one to which subsection (3) below applies, there is an implied condition on the part of the seller that in the case of a sale he has a right to sell the goods, and in the case of an agreement to sell he will have such a right at the time when the property is due to pass.

The requirement is that the seller will have the 'right to sell' at the appropriate time. It does not require that the seller has the title to the goods although this is likely to be so, except in agency situations. The right to sell implies more than a mere ability to pass the property and has been construed to mean the freedom to sell.

In *Niblett Ltd* v *Confectioners' Materials Co* [1921] 3 KB 387 the defendants, an American company, sold 3000 tins of 'Nissly Brand' condensed milk to the plaintiff. Nestlé obtained an injunction preventing the resale of the tins as they infringed Nestlé's copyright. The Court of Appeal held that the defendants had breached s.12 as they did not have the freedom to sell the product in England.

By contrast, in *Microbeads AG* v *Vinehurst Road Markings Ltd* [1975] 1 All ER 529 Microbeads, a Swiss company, sold some road marking machines to Vinehurst who failed to pay. Subsequently, another company unconnected with the sale acquired a patent covering road marking machines. This was enforceable against Vinehurst who argued that this meant Microbeads were in breach of s.12 as they did not have the right to sell the machines in England. The court held that this argument failed as the patent was not effective at the time of sale.

If the buyer can show that there has been a total failure of consideration because the seller does not have the right to sell and cannot get it by the relevant time, then the buyer can terminate the contract and claim a total refund of the contract price. This is one of the few situations in English law where the buyer is provided with a windfall for he is entitled to reclaim the full contract price even though he may have had significant use of the goods meanwhile.

In *Rowland* v *Divall* [1923] 2 KB 500, a case that has been criticised, Divall sold a car to Rowland, a car dealer, for £334. Rowland sold it to a third party for £400. Subsequently, the police took possession of the car which had been stolen. Rowland refunded the £400 to his purchaser and sued Divall to recover his purchase price of £334. The Court of Appeal held that there had been a breach of the equivalent of s.12 of the Sale of Goods Act 1979 and that Rowland was entitled to recover the full £334. This was so despite the fact that Rowland and the third party between them had been using the car for four months and had effectively had this benefit free.

The *Rowland* decision cannot be followed unless the buyer can show a total failure of consideration, partial failure will not suffice. The decision of

Butterworth v *Kingsway Motors* [1954] 2 All ER 694 illustrates the distinction.

Miss A who had a car on hire-purchase sold it to B before she had completed the H.P. payments. As H.P. was owing, she did not have a right to dispose of the vehicle which belonged to the finance company. B sold it to C who sold it to Kingsway Motors who sold it to Butterworth. In practice, every sale of the car involved a breach of the equivalent of s.12 as none of the sellers had a right to sell. Some eleven months later, Butterworth discovered that he did not own the car and purported to terminate the contract with Kingsway Motors suing for a return of the purchase price. At this stage, Miss A completed her H.P. payments and the title fed down the line to Kingsway Motors. The court held that Butterworth could recover the full purchase price even though he had used the car for eleven months as there had been a total failure of consideration. However, B, C and Kingsway Motors could not recover the full purchase price for their respective purchases as they had not suffered a total failure of consideration. Each of them had acquired title to the goods eventually and before they had attempted to terminate their respective contracts. Therefore, they had only suffered a partial failure of consideration for which a claim for damages would suffice.

Section 21 of the Act provides that a seller cannot pass better title than he possesses, summed up in the latin maxim *nemo dat quod non habet*. Where a person who is not the owner of goods purports to sell them, it follows that the buyer cannot generally acquire good title. In such a situation, there has been an actionable breach of s.12 for the seller does not have the right to sell. In fact, there are some exceptions to the basic *nemo dat* rule which provide that in certain situations, the innocent buyer can acquire good title to the goods even though the seller did not have title. One of the statutory exceptions relates to motor vehicles on which there is outstanding hire-purchase. Given the current exception, Butterworth would now have acquired good title to the car. The *nemo dat* exceptions are considered fully in chapter 10.

Section 12(2) provides for the only implied warranty to be found in ss.12–15. Section 12(2) provides

> In a contract of sale, other than one to which subsection (3) below applies, there is also an implied warranty that
> (a) the goods are free, and will remain free until the time when the property is to pass, from any charge or encumbrance not disclosed or known to the buyer before the contract is made, and
> (b) the buyer will enjoy quiet possession of the goods except so far as it may be disturbed by the owner or other person entitled to the benefit of any charge or encumbrance so disclosed or known.

A breach of this warranty would occur if, for instance, the seller did not tell the buyer that he had used the goods as security for a loan he received from a third party. Being a breach of warranty an action would lie for damages.

SALE BY DESCRIPTION

Section 13 of the Act applies to sales by description and provides

(1) Where there is a contract for the sale of goods by description, there is an implied condition that the goods will correspond with the description.
(2) If the sale is by sample as well as by description it is not sufficient that the bulk of the goods corresponds with the sample if the goods do not also correspond with the description.
(3) A sale of goods is not prevented from being a sale by description by reason only that, being exposed for sale or hire, they are selected by the buyer.

It should be noted that this implied condition applies to all sales of goods irrespective of the character of the seller. Thus business sellers and private sellers alike are potentially liable. In this way, this civil law requirement of compliance with description differs from the corresponding criminal law provision contained in s.1 of the Trade Descriptions Act 1968 which only applies where the seller sells in the course of a trade or business.

What constitutes a 'sale by description'

A sale by description for the purposes of s.13 will arise in any sale where the buyer has relied upon a description of the goods when selecting them. Thus, any sale of unascertained or future goods (see chapter 10 for a definition of these terms) such as '10 tons of King Edward potatoes' or a 'cherry red Rover 2000' will necessarily be sales by description for the goods are not to hand at the time of sale and the buyer must rely on the description applied to them by the seller. A prime example is any purchase made from a catalogue where the description applied to the goods is the major selling technique and the seller and buyer may never meet.

Sales by description are not limited though to situations in which the goods are not present. It is equally possible for a sale by description to occur where the purchaser has seen and even handled the goods, a point confirmed in *Grant* v *Australian Knitting Mills* [1936] AC 85 in which the sale of underwear was held to be a sale by description. Similarly in *Beale* v *Taylor* [1967] 2 All ER 253 the sale of a car described as a 'Herald, convertible, white, 1961' was a sale by description even though the buyer subsequently inspected the vehicle prior to purchase. In fact, the car was a 'cut and shut' the back half being from a 1961 car and the front half from an earlier model.

Sales in supermarkets or in trade warehouses would be classed as sales by description if the goods were in any way described by, for example, labels or shelf edge tickets. Further, it is clear from s.13(3) that the self selection of goods by the buyer does not prevent it being a sale by description.

Descriptive words

Not all words that might be classed as descriptive in the normal generic sense of the word will necessarily constitute descriptions for the purposes of s.13. Recently the courts have become more restrictive in their approach and some of the older cases such as *Re Moore and Landauer* [1921] 2 KB 519 are now criticised as being excessively technical.

In *Re Moore* the buyers agreed to buy 3000 tins of fruit to be packed in boxes each containing 30 tins. The correct quantity was delivered but some of the tins were in boxes of 24. The court held that this breached s.13 and that the buyer was entitled to reject the goods.

In *Arcos* v *Ronaasen & Son* [1933] AC 470 the buyer was entitled to reject a consignment of wooden staves which should have been ½ inch thick but some of which were 9/16 inch thick. The House of Lords held that size is an enforceable part of the description.

The modern approach was summed up by Lord Diplock in *Ashington Piggeries Ltd* v *Christopher Hill Ltd* [1972] AC 441, who stated that what really matters

> is whether the buyer could fairly and reasonably refuse to accept the goods on the basis that their failure to correspond with what was said about them makes them goods of a different kind from those he had agreed to buy. The key to section 13 is identification.

Thus it is only those words that identify some essential characteristic of the product that will be classed as descriptions for this purpose. This would include factors such as size (including tolerances where appropriate), constituent elements, capacity, age, manufacturer and performance. This approach accords with that adopted under the Trade Descriptions Act 1968 where the factors subject to criminal control are listed in s.2 and are characteristics of the goods. Liability under s.13 will not arise in respect of general information such as the current location of the goods.

In *Reardon Smith Lines* v *Yngvar Hansen-Tangen* [1976] 3 All ER 570 the buyer ordered a ship described in the contract as being No 354 from Osaka Zosen shipyard. The ship was built in another yard although it conformed with the buyer's specifications. The Privy Council held that the buyer could not reject the ship as the statement about the number and shipyard were not part of the s.13 description.

When drafting commercial contracts of sale close scrutiny must be given to the descriptions applied so that there can be no confusion about the precise details of the goods under contract. Traditionally, the courts have been reluctant to interfere in commercial contracts being of the opinion that businessmen are in the best position to agree terms and decide what significance should be attached to them. It follows that the more precise the terms included, the more precise must be the performance. Thus, for example, if a contract detailing specifications of goods includes details of acceptable tolerances, then those should be enforced and goods failing to comply with such tolerances could be rejected as breaching s.13.

When enforcing s.13, there must also be proof that the description was influential in the sale in that the buyer did rely upon it, for liability will only arise if the sale was by reference to the contractual description. It must be clear that the description must form an essential part of the contract. This position was reaffirmed recently in the decision of *Harlingdon & Leinster Ltd* v *Christopher Hull Fine Art Ltd* [1990] 1 All ER 737, a Court of Appeal decision.

In the *Harlingdon* case, the seller sold a painting described as being by the German expressionist artist, Munter. The seller relied for this description on one previously applied to the painting in an auction catalogue. The seller made clear to the buyer that he was not an expert, unlike the buyer who did specialise in German expressionist paintings. The buyer paid £6000 for the painting which subsequently proved to be a fake worth approximately £100. The Court of Appeal held that the buyer could not reasonably have relied on the description. As such, it was not influential in the sale and was not an essential term of the contract.

Section 13 is often viewed as being closely linked to the s.14 requirement of merchantability. It should be remembered that while the two may go hand in hand on many occasions, this is not necessarily so. It is feasible that goods that comply with their contractual description are not merchantable and *vice versa*. Nonetheless, there are examples where one section has been used when the other was more appropriate, the prime example of this being the decision of *Beale* v *Taylor* in which the courts stretched the use of s.13 to provide the buyer with a remedy because it involved a private sale not amenable to s.14 liability.

MERCHANTABLE QUALITY

Section 14 is often viewed as the central plank of the 1979 Act containing as it does the implied conditions of merchantable quality and fitness for purpose. These two when assessed alongside the price of the product are the standard by which most purchasers would assess value for money.

The term merchantable quality has been much criticised over the years but reflects the rationale of the original section derived from the nineteenth century common law which was to regulate contracts between merchants rather than between trader and consumer. It was a period of economic *laissez faire* when the watchword was *caveat emptor*, let the buyer beware.

The rise of consumerism in the latter half of the twentieth century has given credence to calls for a new term such as 'acceptable quality' but, to date, no such amendment has been passed.

Section 14(2) contains the implied condition of merchantable quality which reads

> Where the seller sells goods in the course of a business, there is an implied condition that the goods supplied under the contract are of merchantable quality, except that there is no such condition—
> (a) as regards defects specifically drawn to the buyer's attention before the contract is made; or
> (b) if the buyer examines the goods before the contract is made, as regards defects which that examination ought to reveal.

Liability under s.14 is strict and thus traders who were not directly responsible for the creation and merchantable quality of the goods will, nonetheless, be held liable for that quality and any direct consequential losses that may be suffered by a purchaser of the product if it should prove faulty. While at face value this appears to be very onerous duty on retailers, the opportunity exists for them to pass liability back up the distributive chain subject, of course, to any valid exclusion clauses that may be contained in their contract of purchase.

In the course of a business

The first significant point to note is that, unlike the other implied terms, s.14 only applies where the seller sells in the course of a business. There is no liability visited upon private sellers and no protection for buyers in that situation. The dividing line between business and private sales is of paramount importance when considering potential liability and, for the business seller, the need to consider insurance against the risk of an item proving defective and causing injury especially given that liability is strict. In practice, the distinction is often easy to draw. A cement company selling bags of cement is clearly acting in the course of a business as is a wholesale greengrocer selling potatoes. Equally clear is the fact that a private individual selling his second-hand lawnmower through the small ads in the local paper is not in the course of a business. But what of a hire-car company selling off their old vehicles or a car enthusiast repairing and selling cars in his spare time. This is a grey area which the courts have sought to clarify to some extent. The bottom line appears to be that if the transaction could be classed as an integral part of the seller's business then it will be a business sale. If the sale is ancillary to the company's main business such as a steel manufacturing company selling off old office furniture as part of a refurbishment plan, the sale will not be classed as a business and will fall outside the strictures of s.14.

The decisive cases are drawn from criminal prosecutions under the Trade Descriptions Act 1968, s.1 which has a similar requirement in that criminal liability under that section is only possible if the defendant was acting 'in the course of a trade or business'.

In *Havering London Borough Council* v *Stevenson* [1970] 3 All ER 609 a car hire company regularly sold off their hire cars after a period of two years. The court held that this was an integral part of the company's business.

In *Davies* v *Sumner* [1984] 3 All ER 831 the House of Lords decided that the sale by a self-employed courier of the car that he used for his business purposes was not a sale in the course of a trade or business. The car was ancillary to his business rather than part of his stock in trade. He could just as easily have used a hire car.

A particular problem is posed where the sale in question is perceived as being the first sale in a series of such sales. In *Abernethie* v *A.M. & J. Kleinman Ltd* [1969] 2 All ER 790 it was suggested that such a sale can be in the course of a trade or business but in the later decision of *Devlin* v *Hall* [1990] Crim LR 879 involving the first sale of a taxi by a taxi proprietor, the Divisional Court held that the first sale could not establish a normal practice. Consequently, there was no liability.

Finally, s.61 of the 1979 Act defines a business as including 'a profession and the activities of any government department (including a Northern Ireland department) or local or public authority'.

The scope of the section

The wording of the section precludes liability in respect of any defects specifically brought to the buyer's attention and any defects which an examination ought to have revealed. The wording of s.14(2)(b) is crucial here. The test is subjective. Before a seller can evade liability, the buyer must actually have examined the goods and it be shown that the defects should have revealed themselves during that particular examination. Arguably, a buyer is wiser not to examine the goods at all as in that way his protection against defects cannot be removed.

The section applies to both new and second-hand goods although the extent of the liability for second-hand items will depend on a variety of factors including the age of the goods and the price paid for them as seen in *Bartlett* v *Sydney Marcus* [1965] 2 All ER 753.

Further, the implied condition applies to 'the goods supplied under the contract'. It follows that this includes packaging and instructions so that absent or faulty instructions could render the product unmerchantable as in *Wormell* v *RHM Agriculture (East) Ltd* [1986] 1 All ER 769 and faulty packaging such as a defective bottle would also breach s.14(2). This would be so even if the bottle is returnable as s.14(2) does not require the goods to have been sold merely 'supplied under the contract'. Hence, a cracked milk bottle leaving splinters of glass in the milk would render the whole item unmerchantable as would a faulty pop bottle which explodes under the pressure of containing the carbonated drink. Similarly, any extraneous matter supplied with the goods will be covered by the section as in *Wilson* v *Rickett, Cockerill & Co* [1954] 1 All ER 168 in which an explosive detonator was included with some coalite. Both the coalite and the detonator were merchantable as individual items but unmerchantable when sold together.

The meaning of merchantable quality

Despite a century of judicial interpretation, the precise meaning of 'merchantable quality' remains unclear. The biggest difficulty in trying to establish a comprehensive definition is the sheer variety of transactions that it must cover, everything from the sale of a cheap toy to a multi-million pound industrial contract.

Prior to 1979, two distinct approaches to merchantable quality developed, first the 'acceptability' test and second the 'usability' test. The 'acceptability' test was summarised by Dixon J in *Grant* v *Australian Knitting Mills* [1936] AC 85, who suggested that goods would be merchantable if they were:

> in such a state that a buyer, fully acquainted with the facts, and therefore knowing what hidden defects exist and not being limited to their apparent condition would buy them without abatement of price obtainable for such goods if in a reasonable sound order and condition and without special terms.

In the *Grant* decision, the plaintiff had purchased some underwear. He contracted dermititis after wearing it because a quantity of excess sulphites had been left in the fabric of the garment after manufacture when they should have been removed.

The 'usability' test provides that goods will be merchantable if they are usable within their contract description.

In *Brown* v *Craiks* [1970] 1 All ER 823 the buyer ordered some cloth to be used for manufacturing dresses. The contract description was sufficiently wide to cover both dress fabric and industrial fabric, the seller believing it was to be used for industrial purposes. The agreed price was marginally higher than the prevailing rate for industrial fabric. When delivered the fabric was suitable for industrial use but not for dressmaking. It was held to be merchantable.

The usability aproach was affirmed in *Kendall (Henry) & Sons* v *William Lillico & Sons Ltd* [1969] 2 AC 31 which held that where the item has more than one common purpose, it will be merchantable if it can satisfy one of them. Thus, in the *Kendall* decision animal feeding stuff that was adulterated with a ground nut extract that proved fatal to pheasants was still merchantable as it could have been fed safely to cattle, one of its other purposes.

The term merchantable does not of itself connote any particular level of quality. To quote Salmond J in *Taylor v Combined Buyers Ltd* [1924] NZLR 627

> The term 'merchantable' does not mean good, or fair, or average quality. Goods may be of inferior or even bad quality but yet fulfil the legal requirement of merchantable quality. For goods may be in the market in any grade, good, bad or indifferent, and yet all equally merchantable.

Section 14(6) of the 1979 Act, originally introduced by the Supply of Goods (Implied Terms) Act 1973, contains a statutory definition that goes some way towards solving the confusion. It states:

> Goods of any kind are of merchantable quality within the meaning of subsection (2) above if they are as fit for the purpose or purposes for which goods of that kind are commonly bought as it is reasonable to expect having regard to any description applied to them, the price (if relevant) and all the other relevant circumstances.

This definition relies heavily on the fitness for purpose of the goods and the first impression must be that little has changed with the usability of the product still being particularly important. The decision of *Aswan Engineering Establishment Co v Lupdine Ltd* [1987] 1 All ER 135 would support this view although the decision has been criticised by the Law Commission among others who feel that the case has followed the *Kendall* decision too closely by holding that goods are merchantable if they are fit for one of their common purposes as opposed to all of them.

In the *Aswan* decision the plaintiff, Aswan Engineering, bought some waterproofing compound from the defendants. It was packed in heavy duty plastic pails which on arrival in Kuwait were stacked five or six high on the dockside in extremely high temperatures. The pails collapsed and the waterproofing compound was lost. On a claim that the pails were unmerchantable, the Court of Appeal held that they were merchantable as they could have been stacked in that way quite safely in many other countries and could have been used in Kuwait if stacked in a different way.

More recently, the court has moved away from such a strict approach and now considers factors such as appearance, minor defects and ease of repair although it is noticeable that these recent decisions are all in respect of 'consumer' cases as opposed to 'commercial' cases. It is possible that different standards may be developing to cater for different categories of contract.

In *Rogers* v *Parish (Scarborough) Ltd* [1987] 2 All ER 232 the plaintiff bought a new Range Rover costing £16 000. It suffered from a variety of faults including faulty oil seals and defects in the engine, gearbox and bodywork. After driving it for 5500 miles in six months the plaintiff sought to reject it as being unmerchantable. The Court of Appeal held that it was unmerchantable as the court should consider not merely the buyer's purpose of driving the car from one place to another but should also take account of other factors such as his ability to do so with the appropriate degree of comfort, ease of handling and pride in the vehicle's outward appearance.

Similarly, in *Bernstein* v *Pamson Motors (Golders Green) Ltd* [1987] 2 All ER 220 a Nissan Laurel was held unmerchantable because some sealant blocked the oil supply causing the car to break down while on a motorway some three weeks and 140 miles after purchase. The plaintiff actually lost the case because the court held that he had accepted the vehicle and so lost his right to terminate. The court felt that three weeks was a reasonable period in which to examine and reject the goods. As he had not done so, acceptance had occurred.

In *Shine* v *General Guarantee Corporation* [1988] 1 All ER 911 this more liberal approach to merchantable quality was extended to cover second-hand goods when the Court of Appeal held that the consumer's expectations as related to the contract description were a relevant factor to consider when assessing merchantable quality. The car sold as 'a nice car, good runner, no problems' was in fact an insurance write-off that had been submerged in water for 24 hours and which 'no member of the public, knowing the facts, would touch with a barge pole unless they could get it at a substantially reduced price'.

The final point that should be mentioned relates to the durability of the goods which is not expressly referred to in the statute but which the Law Commission feels is a relevant factor. At present, merchantable quality is assessed at the time of the contract although a fault that becomes apparent later may be evidence of a defect at the time that the contract was made. Further, goods that are to be transported to the buyer must be capable of surviving the journey, a factor of particular importance if the goods are perishable.

FITNESS FOR PURPOSE

Section 14(3) provides:

> Where the seller sells goods in the course of a business and the buyer, expressly or by implication, makes known:
> (a) to the seller, or
> (b) where the purchase or part of it is payable by instalments and the goods were previously sold by a credit-broker to the seller, to that credit-broker,

any particular purpose for which the goods are being bought, there is an implied condition that the goods supplied under the contract are reasonably fit for that purpose, whether or not that is a purpose for which such goods are commonly supplied, except where the circumstances show that the buyer does not rely, or that it is unreasonable for him to rely, on the skill or judgement of the seller or credit-broker.

This subsection again only applies where the sale is in the course of a business and governs all goods supplied under the contract. Thus, the same arguments considered in respect to s.14(2) would apply here.

The fitness for purpose requirement often overlaps significantly with the requirement of merchantable quality. It is not unusual for a plaintiff to seek to enforce both conditions against a seller.

Particular purpose

For liability to arise under s.14(3) the buyer must demonstrate that the goods were not fit for the particular purpose for which they were bought, whether or not that is a normal usage of the goods. He can assume that the normal purposes of an item are self evident and there is no liability on him to make those expressly known to the seller. Thus, in *Priest* v *Last* [1903] 2 KB 148 it was held that the purpose of a hot water bottle was obvious. Thereafter the buyer may assume that the goods are fit for that purpose. Thus, a local authority buying food for use in school dinners can assume that it is edible, even if the children do not think so. Likewise, a car must be safe to drive, a chair safe to sit on and shampoo safe to apply to the scalp.

The buyer may wish to use the goods for some particular purpose whether or not it is a normal purpose. He is then under an obligation to make this purpose known either to the seller or to his agent. Where goods are purchased on hire-purchase or credit sale, it will suffice to tell the supplier as opposed to the finance company. This obligation will arise between any buyer and seller in the distributive chain, customer and retailer or wholesaler and manufacturer. If the seller knowing of the particular purpose sells the goods to the buyer he is deemed to warrant that they are fit for that purpose or purposes. Thus, in the *Ashington Piggeries* case, the manufacturer was liable under s.14(3) for supplying meal not fit for the specified purpose of being compounded into animal feed. By contrast, in *Griffiths* v *Peter Conway Ltd* [1939] 1 All ER 685 the seller of a Harris Tweed coat was not liable to a buyer who suffered dermatitis resultant upon wearing the coat when the buyer had failed to disclose that she had abnormally sensitive skin.

Reliance

An essential element of s.14(3) liability is that the buyer has relied upon the seller's skill and judgement in selecting the appropriate goods. Lord Wright in *Grant* v *Australian Knitting Mills* made clear that general reliance on the seller's skill is to be assumed from the buyer's decision to do business with that seller. This would be so whether it is a consumer buying from a retail outlet or a business buying from a wholesaler or distributor. Other factors, including the relative expertise of the parties, may play a part in establishing reliance, If the buyer is more experienced than the seller, he may find it difficult to establish either that he did rely or that any reliance was reasonable. In a situation such as occurred in *Harlingdon & Leinster* reliance would be virtually impossible to prove.

Experience may relate equally to the market into which the goods are to be introduced. Thus in *Tehran-Europe Co Ltd* v *S.T. Belton (Tractors) Ltd* [1968] 2 QB 545 the buyer purchased tractors for sale in Persia. The tractors broke Persian criminal regulations and the buyer was convicted and fined. The seller was held not liable under s.14(3) as it was unreasonable for the buyer to rely on the seller's skill given that he knew more about the Persian market.

Partial reliance is possible where the seller is liable for anything left to his discretion but the buyer is responsible for any aspect in which he has relied on his own expertise. Thus, if the buyer supplies a specification for the goods to be manufactured but leaves the seller to decide some details and arrange for the purchase of appropriate components, the seller will be liable if the components are unsuitable, but the buyer will be liable for any deficiency arising from the specification.

In *Cammell Laird* v *Manganese Bronze & Brass* [1934] AC 402 the seller was to provide ship's propellers to be manufactured according to the buyer's specifications. Anything not included in the specification was to be left to the skill of the seller. The propellers were not fit for the purpose because they were not thick enough, a factor not covered by the specifications. The seller was liable.

Taken to its logical conclusion, if the buyer has relied totally on his own opinion, no reliance on the seller will have occurred and no liability will exist under s.14(3). Such lack of reliance might be evidenced by the buyer buying goods by a brand name or buying from a seller who only stocks one make of an item, this fact being known to the buyer.

SALES BY SAMPLE

Section 15 governing sales by sample is applicable both to business and private sales. In practice, of course, it is rare for any private sale to involve the use of samples and, hence, the application of this section is really limited to business sellers.

The mere use of a sample when negotiating a contract of sale does not necessarily make it a contract of sale by sample. Section 15(1) stipulates that a contract of sale by sample occurs where there is an express or implied term to that effect in the contract. If the contract is written, it is easy to establish from the terms whether the parties intended it to be a contract of sale by sample. With an oral contract the court must try to establish the intention of the parties from all the circumstances.

The purpose of a sample was defined in *Drummond* v *Van Ingen* (1887) 12 App Cas 284 as being:

> to present to the eye the real meaning and intention of the parties with regard to the subject-matter of the contract which, owing to the imperfection of language, it may be difficult or impossible to express in words. The sample speaks for itself.

Once it is established that a contract is one of sale by sample s.15(2) provides three implied conditions, namely:

(a) that the bulk will correspond with the sample in quality;
(b) that the buyer will have a reasonable opportunity of comparing the bulk with the sample;
(c) that the goods will be free from any defect, rendering them unmerchantable, which would not be apparent on reasonable examination of the sample.

The first two are self explanatory. First, where the sample is being used as a physical description of the goods, the bulk of the goods supplied must correspond with that description. Second, the buyer must have a chance to compare the bulk with the sample prior to acceptance. This equates very closely with the provisions in s.34 discussed in chapter 9.

The third implied condition relates to freedom from inherent undiscernible defects in the goods. Note that there is no liability for defects that would have been apparent on a reasonable inspection of the goods irrespective of whether an examination actually took place. This test is both objective and more stringent than the equivalent test under s.14(2). Here, it is in the buyer's interests to ensure that he does inspect the goods thoroughly before acceptance.

ACCEPTANCE

Whether the goods have been accepted is of crucial importance because, as can be seen from the *Bernstein* decision, acceptance of the goods will involve the buyer losing his right to terminate the contract. Thereafter, he will only be entitled to recover damages for a breach of ss.12–15. Case law does not provide any firm guidelines about when acceptance occurs as can be seen from contrasting the decisions of *Bernstein* and *Rogers* v *Parish* both of which related to the purchase of cars. In the former decision, acceptance was deemed to have occurred after three weeks and 140 miles, while in

Rogers v *Parish (Scarborough) Ltd* [1987] 2 All ER 232 the buyer was still entitled to reject the goods after six months. Sections 34–35 of the Sale of Goods Act 1979 provide statutory guidance about acceptance and are considered fully in chapter 9.

EXCLUSION OF LIABILITY

As discussed in chapter 4, the seller's ability to exclude the implied conditions in ss.12–15 is governed by s.6 of the Unfair Contract Terms Act 1977. The implied condition of the right to sell cannot be excluded in any contract of sale. However, exclusion of liability under ss.13–15 will depend on the nature of the buyer. If he is 'dealing as a consumer' within the meaning of s.12 of the Unfair Contract Terms Act 1977, liability for the implied conditions contained in ss.13–15 of the Sale of Goods Act 1979 cannot be excluded. If the buyer is dealing otherwise than as a consumer, exclusion is possible to the extent that it is reasonable.

QUESTION

Jeremy was a sales representative for Carpets Ltd. He visited the premises of X Ltd who were interested in refurbishing their reception area. Jeremy spoke to Andrew, the purchasing officer for X Ltd and showed him a sample of a royal blue carpet described as being of 'heavy industrial quality'. Andrew decided to purchase the carpet and placed an order. On delivery, Andrew was certain that the carpet was not of the same colour or quality as the sample that he had been shown. However, he could not check this as he no longer had access to the sample.

Two months after the carpet was laid, Andrew noticed that some of the carpet tufts were coming out and that some faded patches were starting to appear.

Advise Andrew.

FURTHER READING

Atiyah, P.S., *The Sale of Goods* (8th ed) 1990 (Pitman)
Bradgate, R. and Savage, N., *Commercial Law* 1991 (Butterworth)
Dobson, A.P., *Sale of Goods and Consumer Credit* (4th ed) 1989 (Sweet and Maxwell)
Harvey, B.W. and Parry, D.L., *The Law of Consumer Protection and Fair Trading* (4th ed) 1992 (Butterworth)

CHAPTER 8

The supply of goods and services

INTRODUCTION

Prior to 1982, contracts for the supply of services were governed by the common law. In 1982, largely following the recommendations of the report 'Service Please – Services and the Law : a consumer view' published by the National Consumer Council, the Supply of Goods and Services Act 1982 was passed with effect from 4 July 1983.

Contracts for services may be either those for pure services such as hairdressing or insurance and those where the transfer of some goods at the end of the contract forms an integral part of the agreement. The latter would include, for example, the repair of a car, installation of central heating or the painting of a portrait.

PART I – IMPLIED CONDITIONS

Part I deals with the insertion of implied conditions into certain contracts involving the transfer of the property or possession of goods. Thus it goes a long way towards providing protection for people who acquire goods otherwise than by sale.

Sections 2–5 imply conditions of title, compliance with description, merchantable quality, fitness for purpose and compliance with sample. Section 1 stipulates that these conditions will apply to contracts for the transfer of goods other than contracts of sale, hire-purchase, trading stamp exchange, gratuitous transfers by deed and mortgages, pledges and other securities. Thus they would apply, for example, to contracts of barter. The terms of the conditions are identical in effect to ss.12–15 of the Sale of Goods Act 1979.

Sections 7–10 of the 1982 Act imply similar conditions into contracts of hire. The notable difference is in relation to s.7 which corresponds to s.12 of the Sale of Goods Act. Obviously, under a contract of hire there is no intention that the property in the goods will ever transfer to the hirer and consequently a provision confirming the owner's right to sell is inappropriate. Instead, s.7 provides that the bailor of the goods has the right to transfer possession of the goods for the period of the hire and, in the case

Type of contract	Act of Parliament	Title	Description	Merchantable Quality	Fitness for Purpose	Sample
Sale of goods	Sale of Goods Act1979	s. 12	s. 13	s. 14(2)	s. 14(3)	s. 15
Transfer other than sale or H.P.	Supply of Goods and Services Act 1982	s. 2	s. 3	s. 4(2)	s. 4(3)	s. 5
Hire–purchase	Supply of Goods (Implied Terms) Act 1973	s. 8	s. 9	s. 10(2)	s. 10(3)	s. 11
Hire	Supply of Goods and Services Act 1982	s. 7	s. 8	s. 9(2)	s. 9(5)	s. 10

Figure 3   Relationship between the various statutory provisions

of an agreement to hire in the future, that he will have such a right at that time. Sections 8–10, though worded differently, echo the provisions of ss.13–15 of the Sale of Goods Act 1979. A chart showing the relationship between the various provisions appears in Fig. 3.

Given the similarity of these Part I provisions to the corresponding provisions of the 1979 Act, all the relevant case law discussed in the last chapter is equally pertinent here.

Exclusion of these implied conditions is permitted to the extent allowed by the Unfair Contract Terms Act 1977. Section 7 of that Act provides that exclusion is not permitted against anyone 'dealing as a consumer' but is allowed against anyone not dealing as a consumer to the extent that the exclusion is reasonable.

IMPLIED TERMS IN SERVICES

Part II of the 1982 Act provides three implied terms that are to be implied into contracts for the supply of a service. Section 12 defines this to include contracts where the supplier agrees to carry out a service other than contracts of employment or apprenticeship. Further, the fact that some goods may be transferred or bailed as part of the contract does not prevent it being a contract for the supply of a service. Thus a contract to repair and maintain a fleet of vehicles is a contract for the supply of a service even though the vehicles will necessarily be fitted with new parts on occasion.

Sections 13–15 contain the three implied terms. Note that they are implied terms and not implied conditions or warranties. They are effectively statutory implied innominate terms. Consequently, there is no certain remedy for any individual breach. The court has the discretion to stipulate the remedy appropriate to the breach in hand.

Care and skill

Section 13 provides the basic provision regarding the quality of the service. It states

> In a contract for the supply of a service where the supplier is acting in the course of a business, there is an implied term that the supplier will carry out the service with reasonable care and skill.

Note that the section only applies where the supplier of the service is acting in the course of a business. The case law discussed in the previous chapter in respect of s.14 of the Sale of Goods Act 1979 applies here.

Not all providers of services are covered by s.13. The Secretary of State has the power to make orders exempting specified groups of people from its provisions. This he has done in respect of advocates, arbitrators, the directors of building societies, members of the management committees of industrial and provident societies and directors of companies in their capacity as such. In respect of directors, they already owe a duty of care to the company. Section 13 would merely have created an artificial divide between those directors appointed under the articles of a company and those appointed under a contract of service.

Section 13 of the Supply of Goods and Services Act 1982 is the statutory adoption into contract of the tortious concept of care and skill central to negligence. The supplier must act with at least the care and skill to be expected of an ordinary man and, if he claims any particular expertise, then the standard of care and skill expected of him will rise accordingly. (For a full discussion of the standard of care, see chapter 11 *post*.)

The section calls for reasonable care and skill. It does not require the supplier to guarantee the result of the service or to guarantee the safety of his customers, although it does seem that if the purpose of the service is to produce an end product that product should be fit for its purpose. To quote Lord Denning in *Greaves & Co Contractors Ltd* v *Baynham, Meikle & Partners* [1975] 3 All ER 99

The law does not imply a warranty that he will achieve the desired result, but only a term that he will use reasonable care and skill. The surgeon does not warrant that he will cure the patient. Nor does the solicitor warrant that he will win the case. But, when a dentist agrees to make a set of false teeth for a patient, there is an implied warranty that they will fit his gum.

In the *Greaves* decision, the plaintiff, Greaves, contracted to build a factory for a third party for the storage of oil drums. The plaintiff retained the defendants, a firm of structural engineers, to design a factory and floor suitable for the purpose. After relatively short use, the floor cracked. It was held that the plaintiff was liable to the third party and the defendants were liable to indemnify the plaintiff as they had breached their duty of care and skill.

In *Whitehouse* v *Jordan* [1981] 1 All ER 267 a surgeon was held not liable for the brain damage suffered by a baby as a result of a forceps delivery. There had been an error of judgement by the surgeon but not a lack of care and skill sufficient to amount to negligence.

In *Wilson* v *Best Travel Ltd* [1993] 1 All ER 353 a holiday company did not breach the s.13 duty of care and skill when a customer was seriously injured as a result of falling through a glass patio door at a Greek hotel advertised in the defendant's holiday brochure. Their duty of care was satisfied by them inspecting the premises, ensuring that the glass in the doors complied with Greek safety standards and that there were no obvious dangers that would have dissuaded a normal person from booking.

The final issue is whether the plaintiff can sustain both a contractual action and a claim in tort arising out of the same incident. For many years, the presumption was that the plaintiff could only sue in contract. However in *Midland Bank Trust Co Ltd* v *Hett, Stubbs and Kemp* [1979] Ch 384, a case involving a solicitor who negligently failed to register an option for the purchase of land, the court held that the plaintiff could sue in both contract and tort. This decision was followed in *Forsikringsaktieselskapet Vesta* v *Butcher* [1986] 2 All ER 488 and *Thake* v *Maurice* [1986] 1 All ER 497 and most recently in *Lancashire & Cheshire Association of Baptist Churches Inc* v *Howard & Seddon Partnership* [1993] 3 All ER 467. The ability to sue under both contract and tort is potentially significant for the limitation period for contract begins at the time of breach but for a claim in tort it does not begin until the damage is sustained. In practice therefore the limitation period in tort may continue for some period after the contractual limitation period has expired.

Time

Section 14(1) of the Act provides

Where, under a contract for the supply of a service by a supplier acting in the course of a business, the time for the service to be carried out is not fixed by the contract, left to be fixed in a manner agreed by the contract or determined by the course of dealing between the parties, there is an implied term that the supplier will carry out the service within a reasonable time.

Again this provision only applies where the seller is in the course of a business. Thus, the time for performance is not of the essence when the supplier is a private individual unless the parties expressly agree in the contract that it should be.

Section 14 only applies where there is no agreement about the time for contractual performance either made expressly, or by a previous course of dealing or by a method determined by the contract. In brief, the section is effective only where there is a vacuum.

What is a reasonable time is a question of fact dependent upon the circumstances of each individual case.

In *Charnock* v *Liverpool Corpn* [1968] 3 All ER 473 the plaintiff contracted for the repair of his car. The work should have taken five weeks but, because the repairers gave priority to manufacturer's warranty work, the repairs took eight weeks. The Court of Appeal held that the plaintiff could recover damages being the cost of hiring a replacement car for the excess three weeks.

In *Rickards* v *Oppenheim* [1950] 1 All ER 420 the customer was entitled to refuse to take delivery of a car when the supplier failed to deliver at the appropriate time.

Consideration

The last of the three implied terms applies to all contracts for the supply of a service and not merely those where the supplier is in the course of a business. Section 15 relates to the payment of consideration. Section 15(1) reads

Where, under a contract for the supply of a service, the consideration is not determined by the contract, left to be determined in a manner agreed by the contract or determined by the course of dealing between the parties, there is an implied term that the party contracting with the supplier will pay a reasonable charge.

As with s.14, this section only applies where the parties have left a vacuum about the price to be paid for the contract. One would expect that the contract price would be agreed between the parties but this is not always so. For example, in an emergency, the customer may instruct a supplier without giving any thought to the cost. Similarly, in contracts of repair, it may not be possible to accurately assess the cost of the repair until the repairer has inspected the item to assess both the extent of the work needed and which parts will need to be replaced. In this context, the difference between an estimate and a quotation should be acknowledged. An estimate is just that, with it having no binding effect. By contrast, a quotation is a definite offer of a contract price and is binding.

What is a reasonable price is a question of fact in each case. What is clear, though, is that the customer should not pay a price that he believes to be too high but should question it immediately and, if necessary, refuse to pay until a reasonable figure is agreed. If the customer does pay, this will be construed as a contractual agreement and he will not be able to have the contract reopened in the absence of duress.

Exclusion

The parties to a contract for the supply of a service can exclude the implied terms to the extent that this is permissible under the Unfair Contract Terms Act 1977. Under s.2 of that Act it is impossible to exclude liability for death or personal injury caused by negligence but it is permissible to exclude liability for other damage subject to the exclusion being reasonable.

REFORM

The EEC has published a draft Directive on the Liability of Suppliers of Services. It provides that the supplier of a service would be liable for damage to the health of persons and for damage to moveable and immoveable property, including the persons or property which were the object of the service, if the damage was caused by a fault he committed in the provision of the service. The burden of proof would have been on the supplier to show that he was not at fault while on the plaintiff to prove the causal link between the alleged faulty service and his injury. Liability under the Directive could not be excluded.

The damage for which recovery would have been made included death or personal injury and property damage to moveable and immoveable property provided that it is of a type normally used for private use or consumption and that the plaintiff intended to use it principally for his private use or consumption. Financial loss resultant upon property damage would not have been recoverable.

If adopted, the Directive will have a major impact on the law relating to liability for goods and services and require significant amendment to the 1982 Act. However, the draft Directive is on the point of being withdrawn by the Commission.

QUESTION

A Ltd, a small company, decided to have their central heating system overhauled and employed Brian to come and service it. Brian arrived and stated that the job would take two days. He refused to give a quotation for the job stating that apart from the basic charge of £50, the price would depend upon the amount of work to be done and any new parts needed.

Work was started on schedule on Monday morning but it soon became obvious that several new parts were needed. Although the parts were readily available, Brian did not install them and finish the job for five days.

A Ltd were charged £400 for the service which they paid. It later transpired that a reasonable price would have been £250.

Three weeks later the system failed.

Advise A Ltd.

FURTHER READING

Bradgate, R. and Savage, N., *Commercial Law* 1991 (Butterworth)

Geddes, A., *Product and Service Liability in the EEC* 1992 (Sweet and Maxwell)

Harvey, B.W. and Parry, D.L., *The Law of Consumer Protection and Fair Trading* (4th ed) 1992 (Butterworth)

Pitt, G. (ed), *Butterworths Commercial Law Handbook* (Butterworth)

EEC Draft Directive on the Liability of Suppliers of Services

CHAPTER 9

Delivery and payment

INTRODUCTION

When considering the law relating to the delivery of, payment for and passage of title of goods, it is wise to first distinguish between the concepts of transfer of possession and the passage of title or property. There is no requirement that possession and title are vested in the same person.

Possession involves the physical control of the goods by a person who may or may not have any ownership rights. Thus, the hirer in an H.P. agreement gains possession of the goods at the outset of the agreement but does not acquire ownership of them until the option to purchase is exercised at the conclusion of the hire period. Similarly, in a hire agreement, even one with the potential to last for several years, the hirer has possession while the owner retains the title. Likewise, the repairer of goods acquires temporary possession of them during the period of the repair but there is no intention that he will ever acquire ownership rights.

The converse is also true. Title or property speaks to the ownership of the goods and thus passage of title deals with the acquisition of property rights. Again, there is no requirement that the owner has physical possession of the goods or has ever sought to have possession. The finance company in an H.P. agreement has the title to the goods but no intention of seeking possession unless the hirer defaults on the agreement. The buyer in an export or import contract in which the goods are being shipped will acquire title to them when he receives the bill of lading although he will not acquire possession until the goods are unloaded. Likewise, the purchaser of a three piece suite identified at the time that the contract is made in the shop will acquire immediate title to the furniture although he will not acquire possession until it is delivered.

DELIVERY AND PAYMENT

Delivery

Delivery is concerned with the transfer of possession. In the commercial context delivery is arguably more significant than title for it is delivery by the seller that gives rise to a right to payment. Section 28 of the Sale of Goods Act 1979 provides that, unless there is an agreement to the contrary, the delivery of the goods and the payment of the price are concurrent conditions. The seller must be ready and willing to give possession of the goods to the buyer in exchange for the price and the buyer must be ready and willing to pay the price in exchange for possession of the goods. Both parties are under a duty to fulfil their respective obligations in accordance with the terms of the contract.

Delivery is defined in s.61 of the 1979 Act as being 'the voluntary transfer of possession from one person to another'. It may be effected in a variety of ways. The seller may physically hand over the goods or he may give the buyer the means of controlling them, e.g. the keys to a car. If the goods are currently held by a third party, delivery will occur when that person acknowledges that he now holds them on behalf of the buyer as stated in s.29(4).

Delivery may take place via a carrier. Section 32(1) of the Act provides that where the seller is authorised or required to send the goods to the buyer, delivery to the carrier is *prima facie* delivery to the buyer. The responsibility is on the seller to arrange an appropriate contract of carriage unless otherwise authorised by the buyer. Should the seller fail to do so and as a result the goods are lost or damaged in the course of transit the buyer may refuse to treat the delivery to the carrier as effective delivery to himself and hold the seller liable in damages. Subsection (3) states that unless otherwise agreed, where the goods are to be sent by sea and it would be usual to insure them, the seller is under an obligation to inform the buyer so as to allow him to arrange insurance. Should the seller fail to do this, the goods will be at his risk during the transit by sea.

Place of delivery

The parties have the right to decide either expressly or impliedly where delivery will occur and whether the obligation is on the buyer to collect the goods or on the seller to send them to the buyer. In the absence of any agreement the place of delivery is deemed to be the seller's place of business if he has one, or otherwise, his residence. Alternatively, if the contract is for the sale of specific goods (see chapter 10 for definition) which to the knowledge of both parties are at some other place at the time that the contract is made, then delivery will occur at that place.

Section 33 provides that when the goods are to be delivered by the seller at his risk to a place other than that where they are sold, the buyer must take the risk of any deterioration in the goods incidental to the transit unless there is an agreement to the contrary.

Time of delivery

The time of delivery is usually important to the parties particularly in a commercial transaction where the buyer may be buying to resell under another contract, either wholesale or retail, or buying materials for a production process. This would be particularly true if the buyer uses 'just-in-time' stock rotation. It is normally assumed therefore that the time of delivery will be of the essence. Where this is so, the buyer would be entitled to terminate the contract and reject the goods if the seller fails to meet the delivery date. Of course, the buyer may elect to affirm the contract and accept late delivery although he would still have a right to sue for damages.

In *Rickards* v *Oppenheim* [1950] 1 All ER 420 the seller agreed to build a car for the buyer delivery due on 20 March. It was not ready on time but the buyer allowed the seller to continue with the project. At the end of June the buyer announced that if the car was not ready in four weeks he would repudiate the contract. It was not ready. The court held that the buyer was under no obligation to accept it after that date as, although he had waived the original delivery date, he had made time of the essence again by stipulating delivery In four weeks.

Where no delivery date has been agreed and the responsibility is on the seller to send the goods to the buyer, s.29(3) stipulates that he must do so within a reasonable period. Delivery must take place at a reasonable time, this being a question of fact.

Delivery of wrong quantity

The seller is under an obligation to deliver the correct quantity of goods ordered although minimal variations in amount will be tolerated as the law is not concerned with trifles.

In *Shipton, Anderson & Co* v *Weil Bros & Co* [1912] 1 KB 574 the seller contracted to deliver 4950 tons of wheat. He actually delivered 55lb too much, an excess delivery worth 20 pence in a contract worth £40 000. The court held that the excess for which the buyer was not being charged was so slight that it was of no effect.

Commercial contracts are likely to include a clause stipulating an acceptable percentage tolerance in the amount delivered while expecting the price charged for the contract to reflect the amount actually received by the buyer.

Section 30 of the Act regulates the delivery of an incorrect quantity be it too much or too little. It provides

(1) Where the seller delivers to the buyer a quantity of goods less than he contracted to sell, the buyer may reject them, but if the buyer accepts the goods so delivered he must pay for them at the contract rate.
(2) Where the seller delivers to the buyer a quantity of goods larger than he contracted to sell, the buyer may accept the goods included in the contract and reject the rest, or he may reject the whole.

(3) Where the seller delivers to the buyer a quantity of goods larger than he contracted to sell and the buyer accepts the whole of the goods so delivered he must pay for them at the contract rate.

(4) Where the seller delivers to the buyer the goods he contracted to sell mixed with goods of a different description not included in the contract, the buyer may accept the goods which are in accordance with the contract and reject the rest, or he may reject the whole.

(5) This section is subject to any usage of trade, special arrangement, or course of dealing between the parties.

Sub-sections (2) and (4) allow the unusual situation of permitting the buyer to accept some of the goods and reject some of the goods. It should also be remembered that the delivery of a quantity other than that specified in the contract is also likely to be a breach of s.13 sale by description and may constitute an offence against s.1 of the Trade Descriptions Act 1968.

Delivery in instalments

Whether by accident or design, goods may be delivered in instalments. Section 31 acknowledges three possibilities: the parties did not agree to delivery by instalments, the parties did agree to delivery by instalments of a non-severable contract and the parties agreed to delivery by instalments of a severable contract.

Where there is no agreement between the parties about delivery by instalments the buyer is not under any obligation to accept delivery by that method. Where the contract does allow for delivery by instalments it will be a matter of construction whether the contract is severable or non-severable. An indication can usually be gained from whether each instalment carries with it a right for the seller to be paid in respect of it. If so, the contract is likely to be severable. The distinction is important because the remedies available to both seller and buyer will depend on it. If the seller fails to deliver an instalment or the buyer refuses to accept delivery or make payment for an instalment of a severable contract it is likely to give rise to a claim for compensation but not affect the continuance of the contract. If the contract is non-severable a failure would carry a right to repudiate the whole contract.

In *Jackson* v *Rotax Motors* [1910] 2 KB 937 the seller contracted to sell motor horns to the buyer, delivery to be in instalments. About half of the horns were dented and scratched. The Court of Appeal held that the buyer was entitled to reject the whole consignment.

By contrast, in *Maple Flock Co Ltd* v *Universal Furntiure Products (Wembley) Ltd* [1934] 1 KB 148, CA, the buyer was held to have wrongly rejected the whole consignment when one instalment out of twenty (the sixteenth) proved defective. The breach was relatively slight and not likely to recur.

Examination and acceptance

Sections 34 and 35(1) govern acceptance of the goods. As seen in the *Bernstein* decision the fact of acceptance can make a vital difference to the remedies open to the buyer in the event of breach. In that case the buyer was only entitled to damages instead of termination in respect of an unmerchantable car because he was deemed to have accepted it. In situations of conflict between ss.34 and 35, s.35 takes precedence.

Section 34(1) provides that where goods are delivered to the buyer and he has not previously examined them, he is not deemed to have accepted them until he has had a reasonable opportunity of examining them to ensure their compliance with the contract. Similarly, sub-s.(2) states than when the seller tenders delivery he must, on request, afford the buyer a reasonable opportunity of examining the goods for the purpose of establishing their compliance with the contract.

Section 35(1) provides

> The buyer is deemed to have accepted the goods when he intimates to the seller that he has accepted them, or (except where section 34 above otherwise provides) when the goods have been delivered to him and he does any act in relation to them which is inconsistent with the ownership of the seller, or when after the lapse of a reasonable time he retains the goods without intimating to the seller that he has rejected them.

The section admits three possibilities. The first is relatively straightforward: that the buyer has told the seller that he has accepted the goods. The words of acceptance must be clear and unequivocal. Normally the signing of a delivery note merely acknowledges receipt of the goods and does not constitute acceptance. However if the delivery note is phrased in terms of acceptance and the person who signs it has the authority to accept the goods it may be binding.

The second possibility is more demanding requiring two separate elements to constitute acceptance. First, the goods must have been delivered to the buyer and, second, the buyer must then have done something with them that is inconsistent with the continued ownership of the seller. The most obvious example would be that he has sold them or given them to a third party as he is not then in a position to return them to the seller. This may be most pertinent in the commercial context where it is often understood between the parties that the buyer should have the right to sell the goods before contractually accepting them. Indeed, he may need to do so in order to raise the money to pay for them. It is clear that s.34 does apply to this second method of acceptance and thus the doing of the inconsistent act by the buyer will not constitute acceptance unless he has had an opportunity to examine the goods to ensure their compliance with the contract. Thus there is a strong argument that if the buyer resells goods in a sealed container to a sub-buyer without any opportunity for intermediate examination he will be able to reject them if the sub-buyer on examining the goods complains that they are defective. Likewise, in international contracts it would seem that the acceptance of the bill of lading by the buyer does not constitute acceptance of the goods. This will not happen until an opportunity for examination has taken place.

The third method is the lapse of a reasonable time without the buyer intimating rejection of the goods. What constitutes a reasonable time will be a question of fact to be decided on the circumstances of each individual case. The decision of *Bernstein* v *Pamson Motors* made clear that the period is to allow the buyer the opportunity for a reasonable examination of the goods, it is not viewed as being a period to allow any defects to become obvious.

Payment

Unlike delivery, s.10 provides that time is not of the essence as regards payment unless a different intention is evinced by the contract. Thus while payment becomes due when delivery is effected or when the contract stipulates that it is due, a failure by the buyer to provide payment is not a breach that would justify repudiation by the seller although he would have a right to sue for damages for non-payment.

REMEDIES

Both seller and buyer have statutory remedies available to them in respect of breaches arising out of delivery and payment

Seller's remedies

While the primary duty of the seller is to deliver the goods, the primary duty on the buyer is to make payment. If he fails to do so, the seller can seek two sorts of remedies, personal remedies and those against the goods.

Personal remedies

(a) **An action for the price.** Under s.49 the seller has a right to sue for the price in appropriate circumstances. The section provides

(1) Where, under a contract of sale, the property in the goods has passed to the buyer and he wrongfully neglects or refuses to pay for the goods according to the terms of the contract, the seller may maintain an action against him for the price of the goods.
(2) Where, under a contract of sale, the price is payable on a day certain irrespective of delivery and the buyer wrongfully neglects or refuses to pay

such price, the seller may maintain an action for the price, although the property in the goods has not passed and the goods have not been appropriated to the contract.

There are two possibilities for redress, under s.49(1) when the property in the goods has passed to the buyer and under s.49(2) where the price was due to be paid on a 'day certain'. Property in the goods will pass under ss.16–19 of the Act discussed later whereas a 'day certain' will have been agreed upon by the parties. To qualify as a 'day certain' it must be either a fixed date or, under limited circumstances, may be decided by reference to the progress of the work as in *Workman Clark & Co Ltd* v *Lloyd Brazileno* [1908] 1 KB 968 a shipbuilding case in which the seller was able to sue for instalments on the day they became payable, the relevant dates being established by reference to the stages of construction of the vessel.

Both s.49(1) and s.49(2) require that the buyer had 'wrongfully' neglected or refused to pay the price. As the obligation to pay arises concurrently with the seller's duty to deliver, it follows that the buyer's refusal to pay will not be wrongful unless the seller is ready and willing to effect delivery. Further, the refusal to pay will not be wrongful if the 'day certain' has not arrived even though the goods have been delivered. Thus if the contract allows the buyer a period of credit after delivery the seller will not be able to sue the buyer until that period has elapsed. Finally, a refusal to pay will not be wrongful if the buyer is seeking to reject the goods and terminate the contract.

Allied to a claim under s.49 would be a claim under s.37 for any consequential loss that the seller has sustained as a result of the buyer's failure to pay or failure to take delivery. This would include any costs of storage that the seller has incurred.

(b) Damages for non-acceptance. If the seller is unable to sustain an action for the price because, for example, property has not passed or there is no 'day certain', the seller can still maintain an action under s.50 for damages for non-acceptance. The section merely requires that the buyer has wrongfully neglected and refused to accept and pay for the goods. The measure of damages to which the seller is entitled is the loss directly and naturally resulting in the ordinary course of business from the buyer's breach. Subsection (3) provides that where there is an available market for the goods in question the measure of damages is *prima facie* the difference between the contract price and the market or current price at the time when the goods ought to have been accepted, or if no such time was fixed, at the time of the refusal to accept.

Note that this is a *prima facie* level of damages. If the seller can demonstrate that the actual loss suffered was different, he can maintain an action for his actual losses as long as they were foreseeable within the rules of *Hadley* v *Baxendale*. His actual losses will depend to some extent upon the supply and demand for the goods. If supply exceeds demand so that the seller can legitimately say that he has lost a sale he may be able to sue for his lost profit. If demand exceeds supply, he will not have lost a sale but will sell to an alternative buyer. His actual loss will be less.

Remedies against the goods

When the seller is an 'unpaid seller' under s.38 of the Act he may be able to exercise three potential actions against the goods: lien, stoppage in transit and resale.

Section 38 defines a seller as an 'unpaid seller'

(a) when the whole of the price has not been paid or tendered;
(b) when a bill of exchange or other negotiable instrument has been received as conditional payment, and the condition on which it was received has not been fulfilled by reason of the dishonour of the instrument or otherwise.

The remedies of lien, stoppage in transit and resale are all granted to the seller under s.39(1) and take effect even if the property in the goods has passed to the buyer. When the property has not passed the seller will have the additional remedy of withholding delivery.

(a) Lien. The seller has a lien over the goods and is entitled to retain possession of them for any part of the outstanding payment in three situations

(a) where the goods have been sold without any stipulation as to credit;
(b) where the goods have been sold on credit but the term of credit has expired;
(c) where the buyer becomes insolvent.

Where any of these arise the seller can retain possession of the goods as a whole or any part of them still in his possession unless any part delivery that has occurred shows an intention to waive the lien or right of retention. In a severable contract where each instalment carries with it a right to payment he cannot retain one instalment as a lien for the payment of a different instalment. It does not matter whether the seller has possession in his own right or as an agent, bailee or custodian for the buyer.

Being a right in possession, it follows that the right of lien will be lost if the seller loses possession of the goods lawfully. Thus, if the seller gives the goods to the buyer or to a carrier for transmission to the buyer without retaining a right of disposal, or if the buyer or his agent lawfully acquires possession, the lien will cease as it will if the seller chooses to waive it.

(b) Stoppage in transit. If the buyer is insolvent and the goods are in transit, the seller can stop them and reclaim possession of the goods.

Transit starts when the goods are delivered to a carrier or other bailee or custodian for transmission to the buyer and finishes when the buyer or his agent takes delivery from the carrier, bailee or custodian. If the buyer or his agent takes delivery before the goods have reached their appointed destination, the transit will end then. If after arrival the carrier remains in possession of the goods but acknowledges that he is holding them on behalf of the buyer, this will cause the transit to end even if the buyer then instructs that the goods be taken to another place.

Rejection of the goods by the buyer does not cause the transit to end. By contrast, if the carrier wrongfully refuses to make delivery, the transit will end at that time.

Particular arrangements are prescribed for transit involving a sea voyage on a ship chartered by the buyer. Whether the master of the ship accepts the goods as a carrier, meaning that they are still in transit, or as an agent for the buyer, in which case delivery will have taken place and the transit will have ended, is a matter to be determined from the circumstances of the particular case.

The seller effects a stoppage in transit either by taking physical possession of the goods or by giving notice to the carrier or his principal. In the latter instance, the seller must allow reasonable time for the notice to pass from the principal to the person in physical possession of the goods but once notice has been received by the appropriate person he must re-deliver the goods to the instruction of the seller, who must pay any expenses associated with the re-delivery.

In practice, stoppage in transit is of limited use in the commercial world because of the common practice of including a retention of title clause in the contract retaining the property in the goods to the seller until they have been paid for. Where this is the case, the seller will have a right to recover his goods in the event of non-payment even if they are in the possession of the buyer. Retention of title clauses are considered in the next chapter.

Neither the seller's lien nor the right of stoppage in transit are effected by a sub-sale of the goods by the buyer. However s.47(2) provides that where the documents of title have been lawfully transferred to the buyer who has then transferred that same document to a *bona fide* sub-buyer for value then the seller's rights will be destroyed if the sub-purchase was by way of a contract of sale. If the last transfer was by way of pledge the seller can only exercise his lien or right of stoppage subject to the rights of the innocent sub-buyer.

(c) **Right of re-sale.** Section 48 provides the unpaid seller with limited rights of re-sale and makes clear that where the seller exercises such rights the new buyer acquires good title as against the original buyer.

Re-sale is permitted where the goods are of a perishable nature or where the seller informs the buyer of his intention to re-sell and the buyer does not make payment of the outstanding price within a reasonable time. The seller may re-sell the goods and recover from the buyer damages for any loss occassioned by the breach.

It is possible for the seller to reserve a right of re-sale in the contract so that he can re-sell the goods if the buyer defaults. Where a re-sale occurs in this way the original contract is rescinded although the seller may still sue for damages for any consequential loss.

Buyer's remedies

The buyer's remedies fall under three headings, an action for specific performance, damages for non-delivery and remedies for a breach of warranty.

(a) **Specific performance.** An order of specific performance has the effect of requiring the seller to comply with the terms of the contract and deliver the goods to the buyer. As explained in chapter 5 the court will normally only grant specific performance in a contract of sale if the goods are of a unique nature that cannot be purchased elsewhere.

(b) **Damages for non-delivery.** Section 51 of the Act provides that where the seller has wrongfully neglected or refused to deliver the goods, the buyer may sue for damages for non-delivery. The measure of damages is the estimated loss directly and naturally arising, in the ordinary course of events, from the seller's breach of contract. As with the seller's claim for non-acceptance, s.51(3) provides that where there is an available market for the goods in question the measure of damages to be awarded to the buyer for non-delivery is *prima facie* the difference between the contract price and the market or current price at the time that the goods were to be delivered or, if no such date exists, the time when the wrongful refusal to deliver occurred. This is to allow the buyer to recover the difference between the price at which he expected to receive the goods and the price that he actually has to pay to acquire replacement goods. Thus, if the buyer was buying goods at a contract price of £2500 and at the time of the seller's refusal to deliver the market had risen to £2800 the buyer would be able to recover £300 from the seller. If the market price for the goods had fallen however to £2300 the buyer would not have suffered any loss as the replacement goods would not have cost as much as the original goods. In this instance only nominal damages would be recoverable from the seller to acknowledge the breach.

It is possible that the buyer was buying for the purposes of re-sale. The losses arising from the loss of re-sale are not recoverable from the seller unless they were foreseeable within the rules of *Hadley* v *Baxendale*. For this to be the case the buyer will need to demonstrate that to the knowledge of the seller those particular goods were to be used for a sub-sale, that the contract for the sub-sale was in place before delivery by the seller was due and that the contract of sub-sale was not unusual.

(c) **Damages for breach of warranty.** Section 53 provides that where the buyer is suing for a breach of warranty he can claim against the seller either for a reduction or extinction of the price of the goods or alternatively may sue for damages. Section 53(3) provides that the measure of damages will be the loss directly and naturally resulting in the ordinary course of events from the seller's breach. Where the breach is related to a loss of quality, as for example where the goods have been held unmerchantable under s.14, but the right of rejection has been lost through acceptance by the buyer as in the *Bernstein* decision, s.52(3) provides that the damages are *prima facie* the difference in value between the goods at the time of delivery and their value if they had not breached the warranty. However, being a *prima facie* measure of damages the court is free to move away from that rule if the facts of the case so demand as in *Naughton* v *O'Callaghan* [1990] 3 All ER 191.

QUESTION

C Ltd was a construction company. They entered two contracts:

(a) They ordered 20 tons of sand from D Ltd. D Ltd actually delivered 20 tons and 18 cwt. C Ltd want to know whether they are obliged to accept the whole delivery or whether any other options are open to them.

(b) They ordered 5000 feet of timber to be delivered in five instalments of 1000 feet, each instalment to be paid for on delivery. The timber delivered in the third instalment was not properly seasoned and C Ltd want to reject it. They need to know if this is possible.

Advise C Ltd regarding both contracts.

FURTHER READING

Atiyah, P.S., *The Sale of Goods* (8th ed) 1990 (Pitman)
Bradgate, R. and Savage, N., *Commercial Law* 1991 (Butterworth)
Dobson, A.P., *Sale of Goods and Consumer Credit* (4th ed) 1989 (Sweet and Maxwell)
Pitt, G. (ed), *Butterworth's Commercial Law Handbook* (Butterworth)

CHAPTER 10

Passage of title and risk

INTRODUCTION

The passage of title to goods is governed by ss.16–19 of the Sale of Goods Act 1979. Passage of title is significant in establishing who owns the goods and thus who has the risk in them given that s.20 provides that risk passes with title unless there is an agreement to the contrary. Thus it is the owner who should insure them. Further, if the goods are destroyed it is the owner who has the right to sue for damages. Finally and particularly pertinent in recessionary times the ownership of the goods dictates what happens to them if either the buyer or the seller goes into liquidation or is declared bankrupt before contractual performance is complete. Thus, if the buyer goes into liquidation while in possession of the goods the seller will be able to recover the goods if he still has the title in them but only claim the price through the liquidator if title has already passed to the buyer. In the latter situation he would be unlikely to recover the full price, hence the attraction of retention of title clauses. Conversely if the seller goes into liquidation while in possession, the buyer can claim the goods from the liquidator if the title has already passed to him but can only claim a refund of any money he has already paid if title was still in the seller. Again, the chances of recovering the full amount are very slim.

SPECIFIC, ASCERTAINED AND UNASCERTAINED GOODS

To interpret and apply the provisions of ss.16–19, it is necessary to distinguish between specific, unascertained and ascertained goods.

All goods are either specific or unascertained at the time that the contract is made. 'Specific' goods are defined in s.61 of the Act as being 'goods identified and agreed on at the time a contract of sale is made'. This requires that the actual goods that the buyer is to receive under the contract can be identified at the time that the contract is agreed. Thus goods taken to the cash point in a trade warehouse or a supermarket would be specific goods as would a second-hand car chosen off a garage forecourt and sold by reference to its registration number. In each instance the actual goods can be readily identified.

It follows that any goods incapable of identification at the time that the contract is made cannot be specific and therefore must be unascertained. This would include contracts for the sale of a smaller part out of a larger identified whole, e.g. 5 tonnes of sand out of a pile of 20 tonnes stored in a builder's merchants. The part to be sold can be measured in any way, quantity, height, size, location etc.

In *Re Wait* [1927] 1 Ch 606 the seller agreed to sell 500 tons of wheat from a cargo of 1000 tons being carried by the ship Challenger. The Court of Appeal held that this was a sale of unascertained goods because it was impossible to identify the 500 tons out of the bulk of the cargo.

In *Kursell* v *Timber Operators & Contractors Ltd* [1927] 1 KB 298 the buyer agreed to buy timber over a period of fifteen years. The contract covered 'all trunks and branches of trees, but not seedlings and young trees of less than six inches in diameter at a height of four feet from the ground'. The timber that could be felled was unascertained as it could not be identified until the time of felling which could be at any time during the fifteen year period.

Another example of unascertained goods would be goods sold by a purely generic description, e.g. 40 reams of typing paper, with no reference to manufacturer or from where the goods are to be acquired.

Unascertained goods never become specific, they only become ascertained. This normally occurs when the goods are unconditionally appropriated under s.18 of the Act which may not happen until the goods are delivered to the buyer.

The descriptions specific, unascertained and ascertained apply equally to future goods as to goods that are already in existence. Section 5 of the 1979 Act defines future goods as those to be manufactured or acquired by the seller after the contract has been made. The decision of *Varley* v *Whipp* [1900] 1 QB 513 involved the sale of a specified second-hand reaping machine which the seller had not acquired at the time that the contract was made. It was held that the sale was for future specific goods as they were identified at the time of the contract but had yet to be acquired by the seller. Future unascertained goods would include anything yet to be manufactured e.g. a made to measure suit, an item of furniture to be made by the seller or manufacturer and double glazing to be made for a particular building.

PASSAGE OF TITLE

Section 17

The basic section on passage of title is s.17 which reads

(1) Where there is a contract for the sale of specific or unascertained goods the

property in them is transferred to the buyer at such time as the parties to the contract intend it to be transferred.

(2) For the purpose of ascertaining the intention of the parties regard shall be had to the terms of the contract, the conduct of the parties and the circumstances of the case.

This makes clear that the passage of property is a matter between the contracting parties in exactly the same way as most other terms of the contract. Thus they have the ability to decide if property will pass at the time that the contract is made, when delivery takes place, when payment takes place or at any other time agreed upon. Indeed, reservation of title clauses expressly authorised by s.19 are themselves an example of such an agreement.

Agreements about the passage of title must be made at the time that the contract is made. It was held in *Dennant* v *Skinner & Collom* [1948] 2 KB 164 that it is too late for either party to insert a clause about the passage of title after the conclusion of the contract.

The section 18 rules

While the passage of title may be addressed in many commercial contracts, if only by the use of a reservation of title clause, not all contracting parties will make any express agreement. In the average consumer sale the matter is never mentioned and only assumes any importance when things go wrong.

Section 18 is designed to fill this void for it provides five rules dictating when title will pass in any specified situation. Rules 1 to 3 deal with specific goods, rule 4 with goods on approval and rule 5 with unascertained goods and future goods by description.

Rule 1

Rule 1 provides

> Where there is an unconditional contract for the sale of specific goods in a deliverable state the property in the goods passes to the buyer when the contract is made, and it is immaterial whether the time of payment or the time of delivery, or both, be postponed.

For rule 1 to apply the contract must be unconditional and the goods must be 'in a deliverable state'. Unconditional in this context means that there are no pre-conditions that must be satisfied before the contract can take effect or conditions subsequent that must be satisfied afterwards. Thus, for example, a contract for future specific goods could not fall under rule 1 because there is something that remains to be done, e.g. the seller must acquire the goods.

Goods are in a 'deliverable state' for the purposes of rule 1 when they are in such a state that the buyer would be bound to take delivery of them under the terms of the contract. If something remains to be done to put them into a condition whereby the buyer would be contractually bound to accept them, they are not in a deliverable state and property will not pass under rule 1.

In *Underwood Ltd* v *Burgh Castle & Cement Syndicate* [1922] 1 KB 343 the seller agreed to sell a 30 ton condensing machine the contract of carriage being f.o.r. (free on rail). At the time of sale the machine was bolted to the floor and the contract required the seller to arrange for its removal from the building and its delivery onto a train. The machine was damaged during the process of freeing it from the floor. It was held that rule 1 did not apply as the goods were not in a deliverable state as something remained to be done to them and further that the f.o.r. contract implied that the parties had not intended property to pass until the goods were loaded onto the train.

Finally, note that it is immaterial whether the time of payment or delivery or both is postponed. This underlines the distinction between property and possession and makes clear that the passage of title depends on factors other than delivery. Of course, a delay in delivery may be evidence of some agreement by the parties.

Rule 2

Rule 2 is the counterpart of rule 1 and deals with specific goods that are not in a deliverable state. It reads

> Where there is a contract for the sale of specific goods and the seller is bound to do something to the goods for the purpose of putting them into a deliverable state, the property does not pass until the thing is done and the buyer has notice that it has been done.

This is relatively straightforward and would cover situations such as the *Underwood* decision. Note that the rule requires both that the outstanding thing has been done and that the buyer has had notice of the fact. It must be assumed that notice means actual notice and thus it must come to the buyer's attention.

Rule 3

Rule 3 covers the situation where specific goods are to be sold but where the seller must ascertain the price by specified means. It states

> Where there is a contract for the sale of specific goods in a deliverable state but the seller is bound to weigh, measure, test, or do some other act or thing with reference to the goods for the purpose of ascertaining the price, the property does not pass until the act or thing is done and the buyer has notice that it has been done.

Note that this rule only applies if the seller has the responsibility for the measuring etc. If the responsibility is placed on someone else the rule will not apply and property will pass immediately.

In *Nanka-Bruce* v *Commonwealth Trust* [1926] AC 77, PC, the seller agreed to sell cocoa to the buyer at a unit price per 60lb. The buyer contracted to re-sell the cocoa to a sub-buyer who would undertake the weighing of the product to establish the price of the original contract. It was held that rule 3 did not apply and that the property passed to the buyer before the price was agreed.

Rule 4

Rule 4 covers two related yet different scenarios, related in that in both situations the buyer has possession of the goods with the agreement of the seller without there being any firm commitment to purchase. The buyer will have the goods on approval when he wishes to have a period in which to examine and perhaps use the goods in order to establish if they are suitable for his purposes. This is most likely to occur when goods have been purchased through a catalogue with the buyer not having seen the goods prior to ordering them. Sale or return is common in the commercial context. The buyer acquires the goods with the express intention of reselling them but will not be committed to the original purchase until the sub-sale is agreed.

Under rule 4 the title passes to the buyer either

(a) when he signifies his approval or acceptance to the seller or does any other act adopting the transaction;
(b) if he does not signify his approval or acceptance to the seller but retains the goods without giving notice of rejection, then, if a time has been fixed for the return of the goods, on the expiration of that time, and, if no time has been fixed, on the expiration of a reasonable time.

Rule 5

Rule 5 deals with unascertained goods and future goods by description and is the most complex of the s.18 rules. It must be read firstly in the light of s.16 which provides that the title in unascertained goods cannot pass unless and until the goods are ascertained. Further, it is subsidiary to s.17 in that any express agreement about the passage of unascertained goods will take precedence. It reads

> Where there is a contract for the sale of unascertained or future goods by description, and goods of that description and in a deliverable state are unconditionally appropriated to the contract, either by the seller with the assent of the buyer or by the buyer with the assent of the seller, the property in the goods then passes to the buyer; and the assent may be express or implied, and may be given either before or after the appropriation is made.

The key factors are that the goods must be both ascertained and unconditionally appropriated. The two concepts do, to some extent, interweave as when goods are ascertained they may be unconditionally appropriated at the same time. Goods are ascertained when they are identified as the goods that the buyer will receive under the contract. Thus when the buyer is to receive a smaller part of a larger whole as in the *Re Wait* case, they will be ascertained when they are separated out from the remainder of the bulk. This may happen in two ways: either by the goods being separated out from the bulk either prior to delivery or at the latest at the time of delivery, or by exhaustion by virtue of being the only goods left from the bulk capable of fulfilling the contract, the rest having been sold. For example, a seller loads 100 boxes of apples onto his lorry for distribution to three buyers, A who is buying 40 boxes, B who is buying 35 boxes and C who is buying 25 boxes. All the goods are unascertained at that point. A's apples will be ascertained at the time of delivery when they are separated out from the bulk as will B's 35 boxes when they are delivered. C's boxes will be ascertained by exhaustion at the time of the delivery to B for they are the only boxes left on the lorry capable of fulfilling the contract.

In *The Elafi* [1982] 1 All ER 208 the buyer contracted to buy 6500 tons of a bulk cargo of 22 500 tons being carried on board The Elafi. The ship unloaded 16 000 tons in Hamburg leaving only the buyer's goods part of which were damaged thereafter. It was held that the buyer's goods had been ascertained by exhaustion and title had passed such as to enable him to claim compensation.

Similarly, in *Healy* v *Howlett & Sons* [1917] 1 KB 337 the seller despatched 190 boxes of mackerel, 20 of which were for the buyer. The appropriation was to be done by the carrier. Due to a delay, the mackerel deteriorated before it reached the buyer who refused to pay for it. It was held that he had no liability as the goods had not been appropriated and hence the property in the goods had not passed.

The term 'unconditional appropriation' has given rise to much litigation. It occurs when the last act completing the contract has taken place such that the seller is irrevocably committed to using those goods to satisfy the buyer's contract and is incapable of changing his mind.

In *Carlos Federspiel & Co SA* v *Charles Twigg & Co Ltd* [1957] 1 Lloyd's Rep 240 the seller contracted to manufacture and transport f.o.b. (free on board) some bicycles to a buyer in Costa Rica. The bikes were crated up in crates bearing the buyer's name but had not been despatched when the seller went into liquidation. The buyer who had already paid sought possession of the goods. The court held that unconditional appropriation had not taken place, this would have occurred at the time of loading the crates onto the ship.

By contrast, in *Hardy Lennox (Industrial Engines) Ltd* v *Puttick Ltd* [1984] 2 All ER

152 unconditional appropriation of some generators did take place when the seller set them aside and labelled them with the buyer's name but also sent the buyer a delivery note giving details of the serial numbers of the relevant generators. The goods were identified and irrevocably attached to the contract.

The terms of a delivery note may make a crucial difference. If it identifies the actual goods as in the *Hardy Lennox* decision, property passes at that time. If, however, it merely informs the buyer that the correct quantity of goods is awaiting collection, appropriation will not take place until the buyer collects the goods even if they have been labelled as happened in *Wardar's (Import and Export) Co Ltd* v *W Norwood & Sons Ltd* [1968] 2 All ER 602.

Finally, rule 5 requires that the appropriation has been done with the consent of the parties, either express or implied.

Retention of title

It is often in the seller's best interests to retain title to the goods until some condition, usually payment by the buyer, is satisfied. Since the recognition by the Court of Appeal of retention of title clauses in *Aluminium Industrie Vaassen BV* v *Romalpa Aluminium Ltd* [1976] 2 All ER 552 such clauses have become commonplace in commercial contracts as they protect the seller against the liquidation of the buyer and give the seller preferential treatment over other creditors. Section 19 of the Act legitimates such clauses for both specific goods and goods appropriated to a contract and provides that where the passage of title depends upon certain conditions being fulfilled, title will not pass until those conditions are fulfilled.

In the *Romalpa* decision the plaintiff, a Dutch company, sold some aluminium foil to an English company. Clause 13 of the contract was a retention of title clause which retained to the seller the ownership of any unmixed foil in the possession of the buyer until the seller had been paid all that was owing to it. Further, if the foil was used to manufacture any other item, the seller's retention of title should transfer to the manufactured item and the buyer should hold them as 'fiduciary' for the seller as he would the proceeds of sale of such manufactured items. The buyer went into liquidation while in possession of some of the unmixed foil. He had also sold some of the unmixed foil to a sub-buyer. The seller sought to enforce the clause. It was held by the Court of Appeal that the plaintiff seller was able to recover the unmixed foil in the buyer's possession and the proceeds of sales by the buyer.

The *Romalpa* decision was the highspot of the judicial approach to retention of title clauses and later decisions have been less favourable to the seller. While many decisions appear contradictory and are to some extent dependent on their individual facts, the approach of the court appears to differ depending on whether the goods are unaltered or have lost their identity through being subsumed in another product and whether the clause is seeking to recover the goods themselves or the proceeds of sale.

The Court of Appeal in *Clough Mill Ltd* v *Martin* [1984] 3 All ER 982 confirmed that there is no difficulty enforcing a properly worded retention of title clause if the goods in their original form are in the possession of the buyer. However, in practice many goods will change their identity through some manufacturing process, this always having been the intention of both buyer and seller. In this situation, the court has construed retention of title clauses as really being a form of security for payment and, as such, should be registered as a charge under s.395 of the Companies Act 1985. In that situation, the assumption is that the property has passed to the buyer despite the retention of title clause.

In *Borden (UK) Ltd* v *Scottish Timber Products Ltd* [1981] Ch 25 the seller supplied resin to the buyer for incorporation into chipboard. It was held that the seller's retention clause under which he tried to claim a portion of the chipboard must fail as the resin had lost its identity.

Further, in *Re Peachdart* [1983] 3 All ER 204 the buyer had incorporated leather supplied to him by the seller into handbags. The court held that although the individual pieces of leather could be recognised they had lost their identity in that they had become a new product. As such the retention clause was of no effect and merely created a registrable charge. As the seller had not registered the charge, it was unenforceable. Title had passed to the buyer.

A retention clause covering goods would seem to be effective even if it is an 'all monies' clause whereby the seller seeks to retain title to any of his goods still in the buyer's possession until the buyer has settled all the debts that he owes to the seller. This approach, accepted by the House of Lords in *Armour* v *Thyssen Edelstahlwerke AG* [1990] 3 All ER 481 is significantly broader in its effect as it permits goods from one contract to be used as security for debts owing to the seller from other contracts. It further prevents the need for the seller to have to identify which batch of goods were delivered in respect of each contract.

The courts are noticeably less supportive in respect of retention clauses that attempt to hold the buyer liable to the seller for the proceeds of any resale to a sub-buyer. While a clause of this nature was successful in the *Romalpa* decision the buyer in that case did acknowledge that he was holding the proceeds as a fiduciary for the seller. In the average seller/buyer relationship it would be very difficult to establish that a fiduciary relationship exists and hence such clauses are unlikely to be upheld.

THE PASSAGE OF RISK

Section 20 of the Act raises the presumption that the risk in the goods will pass with the property, although this presumption can be rebutted by an agreement between the parties or by their conduct.

Thus in *Sterns Ltd* v *Vickers Ltd* [1923] 1 KB 78 the buyer of some white spirit received a delivery note from the seller asking him to arrange for the collection of his goods by a particular date and make his own arrangements for storage thereafter. The buyer neglected to collect the goods for several months during which time they had deteriorated. The Court of Appeal held that it was implied that the risk should pass to the buyer when he received the delivery note. This was so despite the fact that the goods were unascertained being 120 000 gallons out of a storage tank containing 200 000 gallons and thus the property in them had not passed.

The close relationship between property and risk is significant for it follows that the buyer should arrange for appropriate insurance cover for the goods from the moment that title passes even though the goods may not have been delivered. Indeed, rule 1 of s.18 specifically mentions that where that rule applies property passes, it being irrelevant whether delivery or payment or both are delayed. The converse is also true. If the buyer has possession of the goods in a situation where property has not passed the goods are at the seller's risk. Obvious examples would include goods sent to a buyer on approval or on a sale or return basis. Equally, this would apply where goods have been supplied to a buyer subject to a retention of title clause though clearly in this situation one would expect that the contract would stipulate that the buyer must insure the goods while they are in his possession.

Section 20(3) reinforces the normal duties of a bailee to take care of any goods in his possession while sub-s.(2) provides that if delivery has been delayed through the fault of either seller or buyer then the risk is with that person for any loss which would not have occurred but for their fault.

SALE BY A NON-OWNER

In dealing with the passage of title, the assumption has been made that the seller had the right to sell in accordance with the implied condition contained in s.12. Of course, this is not necessarily the case and situations may arise where the seller has no right to sell. The problem then posed to the law is who should be protected: the innocent buyer who has bought in good faith or the true owner who has been deprived of his goods.

The basic presumption is to be found in s.21 of the 1979 Act and is that a seller cannot pass better title than he has, often expressed in the latin maxim *nemo dat quod non habet*. However, the law has developed a selection of exceptions to this basic rule, five of which are to be found in the Sale of Goods Act itself.

Estoppel

Section 21 provides the first such exception, namely estoppel. Section 21(1) reads

> Subject to this Act, where goods are sold by a person who is not their owner, and who does not sell them under the authority or with the consent of the owner, the buyer acquires no better title to the goods than the seller had, unless the owner of the goods is by his conduct precluded from denying the seller's authority to sell.

An estoppel under this section would be effective to protect an innocent purchaser if certain criteria are satisfied

a)   the seller has by word or conduct made a representation that the seller has his authority to sell,
b)   the representation was made intentionally or negligently, and
c)   the innocent purchaser has relied on that representation.

The representation must have been made either intentionally or negligently. Intentionally would also include fraudulently as in *Eastern Distributors Ltd v Goldring* [1957] 2 All ER 252.

In the *Goldring* decision, the owner of a van wanted to use his van to raise some money. He conspired with a trader to raise the money by deceiving a hire-purchase company. The owner, pretending that the car was owned by the trader and that he was a customer, completed an H.P. application form on the vehicle. The trader also completed the requisite form inviting the finance company to buy the car from him and sell it on H.P. to the owner. The finance company agreed. They discovered the fraud when the owner/customer defaulted on the loan and sold the car to an innocent third party. The question arose as to whether the finance company owned the car or whether the innocent third party owned it. The answer hinged on whether the original owner still had ownership such as to be able to pass it on to the third party or whether, because of the fraud, the finance company had acquired the title.

The court held that by signing the H.P. proposal form the owner had represented that the trader had the authority to sell it to the finance company and was estopped from denying the representation. The car belonged to the finance company who could recover it from the third party.

This case should be contrasted with the decision of *Mercantile Credit Co v Hamblin* [1965] 2 QB 242, a case with strikingly similar facts to the *Goldring* decision. The significant exception is that the customer was induced to sign the H.P. proposal form by a fraudulent trader who led her to believe that it was a loan application form. The court held that she had not made any intentional representation that the trader owned the car nor had she been negligent in relying on the trader's advice. As such there was no representation and no estoppel. The car was still owned by her.

Merely allowing a person to have possession of the goods is not a representation by the owner as evidenced by yet another car-related H.P. case *Central Newbury Car Auctions* v *Unity Finance* [1956] 3 All ER 905.

In that case, a trader allowed a customer to take possession of a car together with the registration document before the finance company had replied to the H.P. proposal. The customer sold the car to an innocent third party. It was held that the trader was entitled to recover the car as he had not made any representation and thus could not be estopped from recovering his property. Note that the registration document of a car is not a document of title and thus even the possession of that was not sufficient to raise an estoppel.

It is clear that for an estoppel to be effective it must have misled the innocent third party and that the falsity of the representation was not known to the third party at the time that the property in the goods was due to pass. It follows that if the third party became aware of the falsity before the property passed he cannot rely on the estoppel and the true owner will have the right to sue the third party in conversion with a view to recovering either the goods or monetary compensation.

Market overt

Section 22 encompasses the exception of market overt which though historically quaint is of little significance in the commercial context. Indeed there have been recent calls for its abolition. Section 22(1) reads

> Where goods are sold in market overt, according to the usage of the market, the buyer acquires a good title to the goods, provided that he buys them in good faith and without notice of any defect or want of title on the part of the seller.

The requirements for the market overt exception are straightforward. Naturally, the market must be a properly constituted market overt established by royal charter or statute or long usage. The City of London is a market overt together with various markets in England. There are none in Wales or Scotland. Given the antiquity and novelty of the concept it is unlikely that any new ones will be created. Indeed the recent decision of *Long* v *Jones* [1991] TLR 113, QBD confirmed that the exception is confined to sales occurring within the boundaries of the market. It was held that where the market had spilled over onto adjoining land, stalls in that part of the market did not attract market overt protection.

The goods on sale must be openly displayed to the public with the sale taking place according to the normal usages of the market (*Bishopsgate Motor Finance Corpn Ltd* v *Transport Brakes Ltd* [1949] 1 All ER 37, CA) and between the hours of sunrise and sunset (*Reid* v *Metropolitan Police Commissioner* [1973] 2 All ER 97, CA).

The main concern over market overt is that it permits markets to be used as a means of disposing of stolen goods.

Voidable title

Section 23 provides a specific statutory application of the law of misrepresentation as to identity discussed in chapter 3. Section 23 provides

> When the seller of goods has a voidable title to them, but his title has not been avoided at the time of sale, the buyer acquires a good title to the goods, provided that he buys them in good faith and without notice of the seller's defect of title.

While the section is wide enough to cover any situation in which the innocent third party acquires goods from someone with voidable title, the most common example will be where the buyer has misrepresented his identity to the original seller. To recap briefly, a seller is presumed to want to contract with the person with whom he is actually dealing. If that person misrepresents his identity the contract will be voidable, i.e. a perfectly valid contract under which the fraudulent buyer acquires good title to the goods until such time as the contract is avoided. The buyer is capable of passing good title to an innocent third party provided he does so before his own title is avoided. Thereafter the third party would not get good title. If, however, the supposed identity of the fraudulent buyer was crucial to the contract with the seller the contract will be void, the fraudulent buyer will not acquire any title and neither can the third party.

Seller in possession

We have already recognised that there may be situations in which the seller of goods retains possession of them after sale. This might occur, for instance, where the goods are physically too big for the buyer to remove them at the time of sale or, alternatively, where the seller retains them in order do some necessary repair or alteration to the goods. Section 24 allows for the possibility that when in such possession the seller might resell the goods to an innocent second buyer as in Fig. 4.

The question arises as to which of the two buyers, both of whom are innocent, should be able to claim ownership of the goods. Section 24 provides

> Where a person having sold goods continues or is in possession of the goods, or of the documents of title to goods, the delivery or transfer by that person, or by a mercantile agent acting for him, of the goods or documents of title under any sale, pledge, or other disposition thereof, to any person receiving the same in good

faith and without notice of the previous sale, has the same effect as if the person making the delivery or transfer were expressly authorised by the owner of the goods to make the same.

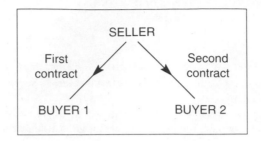

Figure 4   Seller in possession

This section is markedly similar to s.8 of the Factors Act 1889 which provides essentially the same protection although s.8 extends to goods under an 'agreement for sale, pledge or other disposition'.

Provided that the provisions of the section can be satisfied the second buyer will acquire good title leaving the first buyer to sue the seller for conversion. The requisite criteria are manifold. The seller must have continued in physical possession of the goods after the first sale, although it does not matter in what capacity he retained possession, whether as seller, repairer or some other capacity.

Thus in *Worcester Works Finance Ltd* v *Cooden Engineering Ltd* [1972] 1 QB 210 the seller wrongfully remained in possession after selling the goods to a finance company as part of a fraudulent H.P. application. His subsequent return of the vehicle to the person from whom he had acquired it originally was a disposition within the meaning of s.24 and did attract protection for that person.

It is clear though that once the seller has lost possession the *nemo dat* exception expires and will not be revived by the seller regaining possession at some future point.

The section requires that there must be a delivery or transfer of the goods to the third party. Thus in *Nicholson* v *Harper* [1895] 2 Ch 415 it was held that where the seller of the goods remained in possession via a warehouseman with whom the goods were stored he did not transfer or deliver them for the purposes of the section when he pledged them a second time to the warehouseman. There was no physical delivery. Although this case has been heavily criticised it is, at present, good law in England.

In these situations where the seller has wrongly resold goods belonging to the buyer, the latter will be able to sue the seller for conversion and recover damages. However, s.24 does not affect the right of the unpaid seller to resell the goods under s.48 of the Act as discussed in the previous chapter. Where such a resale does occur, the second buyer acquires good title to the goods as against the original buyer but the seller is not liable for a breach of contract.

Buyer in possession

The buyer may acquire possession before property. We have already seen how, in a commercial context the buyer often acquires the goods with the express purpose of resale with the possibility of the resale happening before property passes. This could occur where the buyer needs to resell the goods to raise the money to pay the seller for them while the goods are subject to a retention of title whereby the buyer does not acquire title until after full payment has been made. Clearly it would be very disruptive to trade if the innocent sub-buyer was not sufficiently certain of acquiring title in this situation such as to give him the confidence to purchase.

Section 25(1) of the 1979 Act provides appropriate protection and reads

> Where a person having bought or agreed to buy goods obtains, with the consent of the seller, possession of the goods or the documents of title to the goods, the delivery or transfer by that person, or by a mercantile agent acting for him, of the goods or documents of title, under any sale, pledge or other disposition thereof, to any person receiving the same in good faith and without notice of any lien or other right of the original seller in respect of the goods, has the same effect as if the person making the delivery or transfer were a mercantile agent in possession of the goods or documents of title with the consent of the owner.

Again this section is very similar to a section of the Factors Act 1889, s.9, although again that section is slightly wider than the Sale of Goods Act 1979 as it extends to anyone who receives the goods under any 'agreement for sale, pledge or other disposition'.

The provision only takes effect where the first buyer has 'bought or agreed to buy' the goods. The case of *Helby* v *Matthews* [1895] AC 471 confirms that the hirer in a hire-purchase contract has not bought or agreed to buy the goods and thus a sub-buyer acquiring goods subject to a hire-purchase contract could not acquire title (but see the following section on the hire-purchase of motor vehicles). Section 25(2) confirms the same position in respect of conditional sales.

Possession must have taken place with the consent of the seller. However, the House of Lords in *National Employers Mutual General Insurance Association Ltd* v *Jones* [1990] 1 AC 24 adopted a restrictive approach to the meaning of the word 'seller'. Rejecting the literal interpretation and seeking one that was more attuned to the problem at hand, the court held that in this context seller should mean owner. Thus if the seller is anyone other than the owner, e.g. a thief, s.25 will not protect an innocent sub-buyer who will not get title. Having gained possession with consent, it does not matter if the owner's consent is later withdrawn as long as the sub-buyer is not aware of this as otherwise he would not be in good faith.

The court has been more liberal in its interpretation of the requirement that the buyer has possession and has been prepared to accept that constructive possession may occur where the seller delivers the goods direct to a sub-buyer at the request of the original buyer. Such constructive notice does satisfy the requirements of s.25.

A last difficulty posed by the wording of the section was exposed in the decision of *Newtons of Wembley Ltd* v *Williams* [1964] 3 All ER 532, CA. The section states that the disposal by the buyer will have the same effect as if it were made by a mercantile agent. A mercantile agent is in business selling from business premises and thus a private buyer reselling the goods would be unlikely to satisfy this provision. Consequently, it may be that an innocent sub-buyer buying from such a private buyer would not be protected against a claim by the seller.

Mercantile agent

Of real interest to the commercial buyer is the position regarding sales by mercantile agents. A mercantile agent is an independent agent acting in the course of a business who buys and sells goods or raises money on the security of goods on behalf of one or more principals. Under s.2 of the Factors Act 1889 special protection is given to *bona fide* purchasers acquiring goods from mercantile agents on condition that certain criteria are met. Section 2(1) reads

> Where a mercantile agent is, with the consent of the owner, in possession of goods or of the documents of title to goods, any sale, pledge, or other disposition of the goods, made by him when acting in the ordinary course of business of a mercantile agent, shall, subject to the provisions of this Act, be as valid as if he were expressly authorised by the owner of the goods to make the same; provided that the person taking under the disposition acts in good faith, and has not at the time of the disposition notice that the person making the disposition has not authority to make the same.

For the disposition in question to be covered, the mercantile agent must have had possession of the goods in his capacity as a mercantile agent as opposed to any other capacity. Further, possession must have been with the consent of the owner, whether obtained legitimately or by deception, and possession must have been for a purpose related to the sale of the item. This would include, for example, displaying the item for sale and receiving offers.

Finally, the disposition must have been undertaken by the agent when acting in the normal course of his business and in the manner that one would expect an agent to act. This will be a question of fact in each individual instance.

In *Stadium Finance Ltd* v *Robbins* [1962] 2 All ER 633, CA, the owner gave a car to a trader to get offers for it prior to sale. While the owner left the registration document in the car, he retained the keys. The trader subsequently obtained a spare key and sold the car to an innocent third party. It was held that this was not a sale in the ordinary course of business as a mercantile agent and title did not pass to the innocent purchaser.

Hire Purchase Act 1964

Part III of the Hire Purchase Act 1964 provides one specific exception in respect of certain hire-purchase agreements. As already explained, the hirer in an H.P. agreement does not have ownership of the goods during the lifetime of the agreement and has no right to dispose of them. Where such a disposal occurs the finance company still owns the goods and has the right to recover them.

The Hire Purchase Act 1964 provides an exception to this rule for motor vehicles. Section 27 provides that where the hirer of a motor vehicle under an H.P. agreement disposes of it before the property is vested in him, the first private purchaser to acquire the vehicle in good faith will acquire good title. This is so whether that private purchaser acquires the car directly from the hirer or obtains it through an intermediate trader or financier.

This provision clearly is of real benefit to the private purchaser who acquires good title and is able to pass it on to subsequent purchasers. However, the Act is restricted in that it only applies to goods subject to H.P. or conditional sale agreements and does not apply, for example, where the car was subject to a lease or was a company car. Further, it only applies to private purchasers and thus business purchasers acting in good faith are not protected.

QUESTION

F Ltd, an agricultural merchant, made the following contracts with Angus, a farmer:

(a) to supply Angus with 30 bags of chemical fertilizer. F Ltd had 90 bags of the relevant fertilizer in stock at the time that the contract was made. They put 30 bags to one side and labelled each bag with Angus's name before sending a delivery note to him. The bags were destroyed in a fire at F Ltd's warehouse before Angus had collected them.

(b) to sell Angus a rotovator for £350. The contract was subject to a clause stating that property in the goods would not pass until Angus had paid for it. The rotivator was stolen from Angus's farm before he had paid.

(c) to sell 30 immature trees to Angus for replanting. The trees were to be delivered by F Ltd and were part of a consignment of 100 trees intended for several purchasers. The trees were not labelled. Due to poor care by the carrier, the 65 trees remaining on the lorry at the time it reached Angus's farm had perished and Angus refused to accept delivery.

Advise F Ltd about who must bear the risk in each of the three situations.

FURTHER READING

Atiyah, P.S., *The Sale of Goods* (8th ed) 1990 (Pitman)

Bradgate, R. and Savage, N., *Commercial Law* (Butterworth)

Dobson, A.P., *Sale of Goods and Consumer Credit* (4th ed) 1989 (Sweet and Maxwell)

Hicks, 'Retention of Title – Latest Developments' (1992) *Journal of Business Law* 398

Pitt, G. (ed), *Butterworth's Commercial Law Handbook* (Butterworth)

Part III

The law of tort

CHAPTER 11

Negligence

INTRODUCTION

Contract law, as discussed in Parts I and II, is only of any real benefit to those persons who have contractual privity. Legal action is limited to immediate buyers and sellers. This restriction creates two real problems in the present context. First, it denies the purchaser of the product the opportunity to sue anyone other than his immediate supplier, this being so even if his supplier has gone into liquidation or somebody further up the distributive chain may be better able to satisfy his claim. Second, contract ignores the needs of non-purchasers who suffer damage because of faulty goods or services but lack privity totally.

DUTY OF CARE

This void is filled by the law of tort and, in particular, by the tort of negligence. The modern law of negligence is founded on the decision of *Donoghue* v *Stevenson* [1932] AC 562.

The plaintiff, Mrs Donoghue, went to a cafe with a friend. While there, the friend bought a bottle of ginger beer for consumption by the plaintiff. The drink was contained in an opaque bottle. After consuming half of it, the remainder of the drink was being poured out of the bottle when the alleged remains of a decomposed snail floated out. Mrs Donoghue suffered from shock and gastro-entiritis as a result of the experience and wished to sue for compensation. She could not sue in contract as she lacked privity and thus tried to sue the manufacturer of the drink for her injuries. The case was remitted to the House of Lords to decide whether, as a matter of law, the manufacturer of a product owed any duty of care to the ultimate user or consumer of his product. The court held that such a duty does exist.

Lord Atkin in giving judgment spelt out the duty laid upon manufacturers. He stated

A manufacturer of products, which he sells in such a form as to show that he intends them to reach the ultimate consumer in the form in which they left him with no reasonable possibility of intermediate examination, and with the knowledge that the absence of reasonable care in the preparation or putting up of the products will result in an injury to the consumer's life or property, owes a duty to that consumer to take reasonable care.

This statement has been analysed and applied in numerous cases over the last sixty years. Consequently, the term manufacturer would now be interpreted to include wholesalers, distributors, repairers, assemblers, indeed anyone who has played a part in the construction or packaging of the final product. The phrase ultimate consumer includes any user of the product as opposed to a contractual purchaser. Reference is made to the potential lack of the opportunity for an intermediate examination, a factor of particular pertinence nowadays given the extent to which products, particularly foodstuffs, are pre-packed and sealed with no opportunity for intermediate examination at any stage of the distribution process. Heuston and Buckley in their text *The Law of Torts* suggest that the manufacturer may remain liable for a defect in an item if the goods are examined but the defect remains undisclosed. Naturally, if an examination reveals the defect but the consumer knowingly continues to use the goods, the manufacturer will be free from liability.

While specifically setting out the liability of manufacturers *Donoghue* v *Stevenson* also laid the foundations for a much wider use of the concept of duty of care. Consequently, actionable negligence exists if the plaintiff can establish that the defendant owed him a duty of care, that there was a breach of that duty and that the plaintiff suffered damage as a result of the defendant's breach.

The traditional approach to establishing the existence of a duty of care was laid out by Lord Atkin in *Donoghue* v *Stevenson* in his much quoted 'neighbour principle'.

> The rule that you are to love your neighbour becomes in law, you must not injure your neighbour; and the lawyer's question, Who is my neighbour? receives a restricted reply. You must take reasonable care to avoid acts or omissions which you can reasonably foresee would be likely to injure your neighbour. Who then, in law, is my neighbour? The answer seems to be – persons who are so closely and directly affected by my act that I ought reasonably to have them in contemplation as being so affected when I am directing my mind to the acts or omissions which are called in question.

This quote begs the leading question as to who is reasonably foreseeable as a person likely to be affected by the defendant's actions. Arguably, in the context of faulty goods and services, it is possible to identify certain categories of people who would fall naturally into that grouping. Thus the user or consumer of the product, whether a businessman or a private individual, is foreseeable as is anyone likely to be in the vicinity when the product is being used. However the boundaries are not necessarily as clear cut as that. Supposing the brakes on a car are defective as a result of which an accident occurs. The driver of the car together with his passengers are clearly foreseeable as, arguably, are other motorists or pedestrians who might become embroiled in the accident. But what of an innocent bystander watching from an office window who happens to witness the accident and suffers nervous shock. He is probably not foreseeable.

The law is littered with cases in which the courts have tried to decide whether an individual plaintiff was foreseeable and to establish a satisfactory test for deciding foreseeability. More recently the courts have shifted the emphasis away from foreseeability and towards an analysis of whether the plaintiff was sufficiently proximate to the defendant for it to be reasonable to impose a duty of care on him.

Potential defendants who might be held to owe a duty of care in the context of the supply of goods and services, would naturally include the manufacturer of the product but would also include anyone else involved in the distribution or supply of the product. Thus wholesalers, retailers etc. are under a duty to store goods correctly so as to prevent them becoming damaged and thereby posing a threat to potential plaintiffs. For example, distributors of chilled foodstuffs that need to be stored below a given temperature would be under a duty to ensure the correct storage of the products as a failure to store correctly could result in a deterioration of the product causing food poisoning to the ultimate user. As well as founding an action in negligence, these facts would also constitute a criminal offence contrary to the Food Safety Act 1990.

STANDARD OF CARE

Having established the existence of a duty of care, the level or standard of that duty must be settled. The basic requirement is that the defendant must exercise the same standard of care when going about his affairs as would be exercised by an ordinary reasonable man, the so-called 'man on the Clapham omnibus'. However, if the defendant professes some expertise in the matter complained of, then his actions will be judged in accordance with the standard to be expected of someone with that level of expertise. The higher the level of professed expertise, the higher the standard of care demanded. If no expertise is professed, the normal standard will apply.

In *Luxmoore-May* v *Messenger May Baverstock* [1990] 1 All ER 1067 a firm of provincial auctioneers were employed to attribute two foxhound paintings and then auction them. They took the paintings to London for examination at Christies but neither Christies nor the defendants correctly attributed the paintings to Stubbs, a noted eighteenth century artist. The defendants sold the paintings at auction for £840 but they were subsequently sold at Sothebys for £88 000. The defendants were not liable for negligence as they had acted reasonably and satisfied the standard of care demanded of provincial auctioneers.

It should be noted though that even where a higher standard of care exists it does not guarantee results but merely requires that the defendant will exercise the appropriate level of care and skill when attempting to achieve the desired results. Hence, in *Whitehouse* v *Jordan* [1981] 1 All ER 267 a surgeon was not held liable for the brain damage caused to an infant at birth by a forceps delivery, when the surgeon's decision was held to be an error of judgement rather than negligence.

Naturally, there is a requirement that a professional person will be up to date in his field and employ the skills and knowledge available at the time as held in the decision of *Roe* v *Minister of Health* [1954] 2 All ER 131. The issue of prevailing knowledge has assumed a new significance since 1987 with the introduction of the state-of-the-art defence in strict liability. This will be considered in depth in the next chapter.

Breach of the duty

A breach of the duty occurs when the defendant is shown not to have satisfied the duty placed on him. Where goods and services are concerned, a breach is likely to take one of three forms, either that the manufacturer has produced goods that are defective and his quality control systems are not sufficiently good to have prevented the circulation of the faulty item, or the design of the goods is defective or appropriate instructions for use and warnings were not given such as to allow the plaintiff to use the product safely.

In assessing whether there has been a breach, the defendant has the right to assume that the plaintiff will use the product properly and in accordance with any instructions provided.

CAUSATION

Liability will only arise if the plaintiff can establish that the defendant's breach of duty caused his injuries. There is no need to show that the defendant's breach was the only cause of the damage but it must be established that it was one of the causes and that the court should consider it so when deciding liability. The chain of causation between the defendant's breach and the plaintiff's damage must be unbroken and thus the defendant's liability will cease if there has been an intervening act either by the plaintiff or by a third party.

DEFENCES

When considering causation, the court will assess the extent, if any, to which the plaintiff is responsible for his own injuries. This does not deny the liability of the defendant but permits the court to state that the plaintiff was also culpable and partly responsible for the incident that injured him. Where this is so, the court can hold that the plaintiff has been contributorily negligent and, by virtue of the Law Reform (Contributory Negligence) Act 1945, this will impact on the amount of damages that the plaintiff will receive. His damages will be reduced by a percentage equivalent to his share of the blame. Thus, if the court finds that the plaintiff was 40% contributorily negligent and that the total value of the claim is £1000 the plaintiff will receive £1000 minus 40%, i.e. £600. It may be, of course, that the court will find the plaintiff 100% contributorily negligent in which case the defendant has a total defence.

In addition to being able to show that the plaintiff was contributorily negligent, the defendant may be able to show that the plaintiff has failed to establish one or more of the essential elements of the tort. Thus, it may be that the plaintiff had failed to show that he was a foreseeable plaintiff to whom there was any duty owed.

The other possible defence lies in the concept *volenti non fit injuria* – the law will not aid a volunteer. This simply means that if the plaintiff has consented to run the risk he cannot complain of any injury that he suffers. Consent is a complete defence. To be valid, the consent must be genuine as opposed to a situation in which the plaintiff really had no choice but to agree to run the risk.

In *Smith* v *Baker & Sons* [1891] AC 325, HL, the plaintiff employee who worked in a quarry complained to his employer on numerous occasions about the danger posed by a a crane working overhead. When the plaintiff was injured by a load falling from the crane, the House of Lords held that his decision to continue working despite the risk did not constitute consent.

RECOVERABLE DAMAGE

To be recoverable, the damage suffered must have been of a type that was foreseeable. The leading authority on the point is *Overseas Tankship (UK) Ltd* v *Morts Dock and Engineering Co Ltd, The Wagon Mound* [1961] 1 All ER 404, PC (*The Wagon Mound*).

In *The Wagon Mound* the defendants negligently spilt some oil into the water at a harbour causing an oil slick. The slick spread to a nearby jetty belonging to the plaintiffs. Some welding work was under way on two ships moored at the jetty but, believing that the oil posed a fire risk, the plaintiffs stopped work. However, work was restarted when an expert confirmed that there was no fire risk from oil on water. Subsequently the two ships and the jetty were damaged when the oil caught fire. The Privy Council held that the defendants were not liable for the damage caused by the fire as damage by fire was unforeseeable. By contrast, damage due to oil pollution would have been foreseeable and provided grounds for recovery.

Once it is established that the type of damage suffered was foreseeable, the defendant is liable for all the damage of that type suffered by the plaintiff even though its extent may be far greater than would have been expected. This is the so-called eggshell skull rule which says that you must take your plaintiff as you find him and are responsible for whatever level of damage he has actually suffered even though it might be more than would have been suffered by a normal person.

The plaintiff can claim for death and personal injury together with property damage both for personal property and business property. The remaining two heads of damage, nervous shock and economic loss are both more restrictive and less clear cut.

Nervous shock

Anybody witnessing an accident may suffer from some degree of shock. In the example of the car accident mentioned earlier there is no doubt that the witness watching from the window did suffer shock. But that alone is not sufficient to found an action in nervous shock. If it were, the defendant in any action would be liable potentially to a very large number of plaintiffs. By the same token, anyone bereaved by an accident is likely to suffer grief but this is not sufficient to found a nervous shock case. Nervous shock is provable psychiatric damage caused by the defendant's negligence.

The leading case now is *Alcock* v *Chief Constable of South Yorkshire* [1991] 4 All ER 907, HL, a case based on the Hillsborough disaster. The House of Lords stipulated the three criteria to be used when assessing whether any individual plaintiff could recover for nervous shock as a result of being bereaved in an accident as being

(i)   whether the relationship between the plaintiff and the deceased was sufficiently close for it to be foreseeable that the plaintiff would suffer nervous shock,
(ii) whether the proximity between the plaintiff and the accident or its immediate aftermath was sufficiently close in both time and space, and
(iii) whether the plaintiff suffered nervous shock through seeing or hearing the accident or its immediate aftermath.

Clearly, the combination of these factors means that the scope for successful claims in nervous shock is restricted. For example, while a spouse or parent might have a strong claim if witnessing an accident or its immediate aftermath, a colleague in that situation would be unlikely to succeed.

Economic loss

Of more concern in the commercial context is the limited opportunity to recover for economic loss, i.e. to recover for monetary loss such as profit. The law has always taken a restrictive approach to the recovery of damages for economic loss and recent decisions have confirmed this general stance.

One must differentiate between financial loss consequent upon physical injury or property damage and pure economic loss that is not connected to other damage. The distinction is crucial for the first is recoverable while in most instances the second is not.

The decision of *Spartan Steel & Alloys Ltd* v *Martin & Co (Contractors) Ltd* [1973] 1 QB 27 demonstrates the distinction. The defendants cut through a power cable to the plaintiffs' factory thereby interrupting the electricity supply. The plaintiffs claimed for damage to the metal in their furnace at the time of the power cut and for the lost profit on that metal. They further claimed for the lost profit on another four melts that were planned but could not take place because of the power cut. The court allowed the plaintiffs to recover for the physical damage to the metal in the furnace and the lost profit attached to that damage. However, the plaintiffs could not recover for the lost profit on the other four melts as that was pure economic loss not attributable to any physical damage.

This would mean that, for example, lost earnings due to being hospitalised following injury by a faulty product would be recoverable as being economic loss resultant upon physical injury.

Pure economic loss can seldom be recovered for the rules are very restrictive and firmly applied. Pure economic loss falls basically into three types: that suffered because of an inherent defect in the quality of a product or service, a loss of profit or business of the type seen in *Spartan Steel* caused by the defendant's negligent act and, finally, that suffered through reliance on negligent advice.

It is clear from the decisions of *D & F Estates Ltd* v *Church Commissioners for England* [1988] 2 All ER 992, HL and *Department of the Environment* v *Thomas Bates & Sons* [1990] 2 All ER 943, HL, that the court will not allow a negligence action to recover the cost of repairing a defect in an item. Such a claim should really be made in contract under s.14 of the Sale of Goods Act 1979 (or other equivalent relevant section) by the purchaser of the defective item. As a claim in tort, it would be for pure economic loss and is not permissible.

In the *D & F Estates* decision the plaintiff was the lessee and occupier of a flat. The defendant was the builder of the premises who had employed a sub-contractor to do the plastering in the building. The claim arose because the plastering was sub-standard and the plaster was coming off the walls. The House of Lords held that the defendant builder was not liable because the cost of repairing a defect in a chattel or structure before it had caused any personal injury or physical damage was pure economic loss and not recoverable in tort.

A similar approach was adopted in the *Department of the Environment* case when the House of Lords refused to allow a claim for the cost of remedial work to a building necessary to render the building safe for its design purpose when the defect had not caused any damage to person or property. The House of Lords adopted that approach again in *Murphy* v *Brentwood DC* [1990] 2 All ER 908 when holding that a local authority was not liable for the cost of remedying a defect in a property caused by the authority's negligent failure to ensure that the property was designed and built in accordance with building regulations. However, the court did express the opinion that while a complex structure such as a building manufactured and equipped by one contractor must be treated as a single unit for this purpose, ordinary liability in negligence would arise in respect of damage done to the structure by defective ancillary equipment such as central heating or electrical installations.

A potential exception to the general rule that you cannot recover for a defect in the item may arise in product liability cases if it can be shown that the plaintiff relied on the manufacturer, an idea explored in the decision of *Junior Books Ltd* v *Veitchi Co Ltd* [1982] 3 All ER 201, a case that has been heavily criticised and is now seen as an exceptional case. Two later cases in which this idea was considered were *Muirhead* v *Industrial Tank Specialities* [1986] QB 507 and *Simaan General Contracting* Co v *Pilkington Glass Ltd (No 2)* [1988] QB 758 although in both cases the plaintiffs lost the case as they were unable to establish a sufficiently close relationship with the manufacturer.

Pure economic loss such as lost business or loss of profit caused by the negligent act of the defendant is not recoverable as evidenced in *Spartan Steel*.

The third cause of pure economic loss is likely to be reliance upon negligent advice. The extent to which damage can be recovered in this situation will be considered in the next section.

NEGLIGENT MISSTATEMENT

Prior to 1963, the law of tort did not recognise any liability for negligent misstatements, only for the fraud-based tort of deceit. However, a new avenue of liability was opened up that year by the unanimous decision of the House of Lords in the case of *Hedley Byrne & Co Ltd* v *Heller & Partners Ltd* [1964] AC 465. Their Lordships decided that liability would arise in respect of a statement made by a defendant to someone with whom he had a special relationship if he had not validly disclaimed his liability.

Hedley Byrne were a firm of advertising agents retained to do some work for Easipower Ltd. Wanting to ensure that Easipower were creditworthy, Hedley Byrne asked their bankers to make some inquiries. Heller & Partners, Easipower's bankers, confirmed in a statement headed 'without responsibility' that Easipower were good for their normal business commitments. Relying on this, Hedley Byrne did business with Easipower and lost £17 000 when Easipower went into liquidation. The House of Lords held that there was a duty owed in this situation and that the defendants could be liable for their negligent misstatement. However, on the facts they escaped liability because of the exclusion clause.

Certain factors are relevant when analysing the *Hedley Byrne* decision. It is clear that there must be a relationship between the person making the statement and the person receiving it. This is necessary to set reasonable boundaries to the potential liability of the makers of statements who might otherwise face an open-ended liability to an infinite number of people. The relationship is the means of establishing to whom a duty is owed. Further, the maker of the statement should know the purpose for which it is to be used and that the recipient will rely on the statement and act upon it without making any other inquiries. The importance attached to the purpose for which the statement was made is evident from two recent decisions, *Smith* v *Eric S. Bush* [1990] 1 AC 831 and *Caparo Industries plc* v *Dickman* [1990] 2 AC 605.

Smith v *Eric S. Bush* investigated the liability of a surveyor for a valuation carried out on a house. While it was undertaken on behalf of a building society, the surveyor knew that it would be shown to the customer who would rely on it when considering whether to purchase the property. It was held that the surveyor owed a duty of care to the purchaser.

However, in *Caparo Industries plc* v *Dickman* the duties of auditors were analysed. The auditors in auditing the accounts of a company called Fidelity plc for the year ended 31 March 1984 negligently concluded that the company had made a pre-tax profit of £1.3m whereas in fact they had made a loss of £400 000. In reliance on these accounts, Caparo Industries bought shares in the company and mounted a successful take-over bid. On discovering the real state of the company, Caparo Industries sued the auditors. The House of Lords held that the auditors did not owe any duty of care to potential investors in general or to individual shareholders who might rely on the accounts when considering further share purchases. The purpose of accounts is to allow the shareholders of a company as a body to exercise informed control over the company and not to provide information for potential investors.

In practice, the majority of advice received by any business will be from paid advisors such as solicitors, accountants, marketing agencies etc. In these situations, there will be a contract for the provision of the advisory service governed by the Supply of Goods and Services Act 1982. As s.13 of the Act requires that the provider of a service acts with appropriate skill and care, an action for breach of contract would exist if the advice were negligent. This would permit the recovery of all direct consequential loss, including economic loss, under the normal contractual rules. A tort action would be unnecessary.

The provision of references for employees is a normal part of business life and can have a significant effect on a prospective new employer. However the Court of Appeal recently held in the decision of *Spring* v *Guardian Assurance plc* [1993] 2 All ER 273 that the giver of a reference owes no duty of care in negligence to the person who is the subject of the reference either in giving or compiling it. Any duty to the subject of a reference and any remedy in respect of it lie in the tort of defamation.

VICARIOUS LIABILITY

Any business acts through its personnel from the Managing Director at the top to the newest joined junior clerk at the bottom. Vicarious liability addresses the extent to which a business may be held liable for the negligent acts of its employees while they are working for the business.

Two criteria must be satisfied if the employer is to be held liable, first it must be shown that the person committing the tortious act is an employee and not an independent contractor and, second, the tortious incident must have occurred during the course of the person's employment.

The distinction between employees and independent contractors is vital for the employer will have vicarious liability for his employees but not his contractors. The original test was the so-called 'control' test whereby if the employer had the power to dictate both what the worker did and how he did it, the worker would be an employee. However, with increasingly sophisticated machinery and skills, this test has proved too simplistic and has been replaced with a multiple test involving factors such as who pays the worker's wages, who provides any necessary equipment and whether the worker must undertake the work personally or can delegate it to another person. In practice, an independent contractor is likely to be in business for himself.

Liability only attaches in respect of tasks done by the employee in the course of his business. Anything falling outside the course of his business remains the personal liability of the individual employee. Thus if he undertakes an activity for which he was not employed the employer may reject liability for his actions. Similarly, no vicarious liability arises in respect of acts that the employer has expressly forbidden although liability will arise if the employee does an authorised act in an unauthorised manner. Thus in *Limpus* v *London General Omnibus* (1862) 1 H & C 526 the defendant bus company was held liable for an accident caused by one of their drivers while he was 'racing' in the bus. While the defendant had forbidden drivers to race, they had employed the individual employee to drive buses which is what he was doing. It was an authorised act in an unauthorised manner.

An employer may even be liable for the fraudulent acts of his employees if they were committed in the course of the employment. Thus in *Lloyd* v *Grace Smith & Co* [1912] AC 716, HL, a firm of solicitors were held liable for the fraudulent act of their managing clerk when he defrauded a client.

Under vicarious liability the employer can be held liable to any foreseeable plaintiff under the normal rules of negligence. In particular, this includes other employees who may be affected by the tortious act.

Vicarious liability has the effect of providing the plaintiff with an additional defendant for, naturally, the employee remains liable for his own tortious actions as well. In practice, one would expect most plaintiffs to opt to sue the employer on the basis that he is more likely to be in a financial position to satisfy the claim. If the employer is sued, he assumes the rights and liabilities of the employee and thus would be able to claim the benefit of any defences that would have been open to him.

QUESTION

Y Ltd is a wholesaler storing large quantities of goods in a warehouse. Bill was an employee employed to drive a fork lift truck. He received appropriate training and the company had stressed to him the importance of driving the truck carefully and safely with due regard for other people on the premises. One afternoon, Bill was hurrying to finish a job and backed the truck too quickly through a plastic dividing screen without checking whether anyone was standing on the other side. He knocked over Fred, the stores manager, and David, a visiting surveyor who had come to inspect the premises. Both were injured.

Advise Y Ltd and Bill about their potential liability, if any, as a result of this incident.

FURTHER READING

Jones, M.A., *Textbook on Torts* (4th ed) 1993 (Blackstone Press)

Harvey, B.W. and Parry, D.L., *The Law of Consumer Protection and Fair Trading* (4th ed) 1992 (Butterworth)

Heuston, R.F.V. and Buckley, R.A., *Salmond & Heuston on The Law of Torts* (20th ed) 1992 (Butterworth)

Savage, N. and Bradgate, R., *Business Law* (2nd ed) 1993 (Butterworth)

CHAPTER 12

Product liability

INTRODUCTION

There has been increasing concern over the ability of the law of negligence to cope with liability for injuries caused by defective products since the late 1960s and early 1970s, a concern made more real by the apparent inability of the negligence system to provide a remedy for the victims of the Thalidomide tragedy. In 1973 a Royal Commission was set up under the chairmanship of Lord Pearson to consider and make proposals on Civil Liability and Compensation for Personal Injury. This Commission which reported in 1978 (Cmnd 7054 (1978)) came out strongly in favour of the adoption of a system of strict liability for the producers of defective products. This accorded with the conclusions of the joint Law Commission and Scottish Law Commission report Liability for Defective Products (Law Comm No 82, Scot Law Comm No 45, Cmnd 6831 (1977)) published in 1977 which likewise wished to see the implementation of a system of strict liability in Britain.

Strict liability negates the need for the plaintiff to show that anyone is to blame for his injuries. The emphasis is switched away from the blameworthiness of the tortfeasor as occurs in negligence and concentrates instead on the defective condition of the product. To found a claim, therefore, the plaintiff must demonstrate that the product in question was faulty and that there was a causal link between the defect and the injuries suffered. Whether the defect arose through negligence is not relevant.

THE AMERICAN EXPERIENCE

Strict liability for defective products is not a totally new concept; it was already in place in America where it had been expounded in 1963 by Justice Trayner in the decision of *Greenman* v *Yuba Power Products* 59 Cal 2d 57 (1963), who declared on behalf of a unanimous court

> A manufacturer is strictly liable in tort when an article he places on the market knowing that it is to be used without inspection for defects, proves to have a defect which causes injury to a human being . . .

This strict liability duty is intended to protect the same people to whom a duty of negligence would be owed in Britain by virtue of *Donoghue* v *Stevenson*. The *Green Man* case was followed only two years later by the statutory Restatement of Torts, 2d, section 402A of which stipulates that 'one who sells any product in a defective condition unreasonably dangerous . . . is subject to liability for physical harm caused to the ultimate user or consumer'. This statutory statement of strict liability for products has now been adopted in 45 out of 50 states.

Unfortunately, the American experience of strict product liability has been far from happy although the difficulties are more to do with the American legal system than with the concept of strict liability. The problems are threefold: pro-plaintiff juries, punitive damages and the contingency fee system.

America, unlike Britain, uses juries to decide liability in product liability cases and it is suggested that juries tend to be pro-plaintiff in that they are biased in favour of the injured plaintiff rather than the defendant producer and that this may influence their decision in the case. This would certainly explain some of the more extreme decisions such as *Luque* v *McLean* 8 Cal 3d 136 (1972) a Californian decision which effectively required manufacturers to make their products idiotproof. In that case the plaintiff had put his hand through an unguarded hole in the cover of a rotary lawn mower when the machine was switched on.

The second problem is the use of punitive damages, the purpose of which is to punish the defendant producer rather than compensate the injured plaintiff. These punitive damages come to the plaintiff as a windfall in addition to any award of compensatory damages. The example quoted most often is the case of *Grimshaw* v *Ford Motor Co* 119 Cal App 3d 757 (1981) in which the plaintiff received 90% burns when his Ford Pinto car burst into flames after being hit from the rear. The plaintiff received $2 842 000 in compensatory damages and a further $125 000 000 in punitive damages. While the punitive damages were reduced to $3 500 000 on appeal, the case still demonstrates the willingness of American courts to award significant sums in damages.

The third recognised problem is the existence of the contingency fee system. Under this system, the advocate receives as his fee a percentage of the damages awarded to the plaintiff with the obvious risk that if the case is lost he does not earn anything. The effect of this system has been twofold. First, plaintiffs have become more litigious for they have nothing at risk, if they win they get the damages, if they lose they owe nothing to their lawyer. Second, where the plaintiff wins his action, it may lead to an award of artificially inflated damages by the jury to allow for the lawyer claiming his percentage.

In addition to these three acknowledged features of the American legal system, none of which exists in Britain, other developments have put further strain on the American system and consequently on people producing for the American market. The decision of the Californian Supreme Court in *Sindell* v *Abbott Laboratories* 26 Cal 3d 588 (1980) developed the concept of 'market share liability' under which liability was imposed upon the producers of a defective drug without proof of causation, their individual liability being for a percentage of the damages equivalent to their percentage share of the market for the drug at the time of distribution. The *Sindell* case revolved around the so-called 'DES Daughters' who developed vaginal and cervical cancers as a result of being exposed to the drug Diethylstilbestrol (DES) while *in utero*. These side effects did not become apparent until approximately 10–12 years after birth and sometimes not until the plaintiff was in her twenties. After that period it was impossible to prove which company (of approximately 200–300 producers) had manufactured the particular pill that had caused the damage to any individual plaintiff. The court apportioned the liability between the five defendant companies to the action who, together, accounted for approximately 90% of production.

The application of strict product liability in America caused a crisis within the production sector as producers found it increasingly difficult to obtain insurance to cover their potential liability. Producers in some industries, notably the high risk industries such as drug production, found it impossible to get insurance cover and were forced to 'go bare' and run the risk of liquidation if faced with a successful product liability action. Producers from other countries likewise found it difficult to get insurance cover for products being exported to America because of the potential legal exposure in that jurisdiction.

THE CONSUMER PROTECTION ACT 1987

Reform in Britain arose out of the implementation of the EC Directive on Product Liability 85/374/EEC. This Directive was first proposed in 1976 with the intention of harmonising European law on product liability and increasing protection for users of defective products. However, because of deep-rooted divisions of opinion among the Member States, the Directive in its final form contains three derogations which allow Member States to assert their own preferences. These derogations, which have seriously undermined any question of European harmonisation, relate to the inclusion of agricultural products, global financial limits for liability under the Directive and the inclusion of a development risk defence. All of these derogations will be discussed later but have the combined effect of encouraging 'forum shopping' where the plaintiff in an action if faced with the possibility of suing in more than one jurisdiction will opt for that most beneficial to his claim. Given the movement of components and finished products between Member States and the increased mobility of purchasers within the Community it is entirely feasible that a British tourist on holiday in France might purchase a product manufactured in Germany containing a defective component manufactured in Italy. The scope for forum shopping is obvious. The position regarding these derogations will be reconsidered by the Commission in 1995.

The Directive was given force in Britain by Part I of the Consumer Protection Act 1987 which came into force on 1 March 1988.

'Producer' and 'product'

Section 1 of the Act defines some of the key terms used in the Act. A 'producer' in relation to a product means

(a) the person who manufactured it;

(b) in the case of a substance which has not been manufactured but has been won or abstracted, the person who has won or abstracted it;

(c) in the case of a product which has not been manufactured, won or abstracted but essential characteristics of which are attributable to an industrial or other process having been carried out (for example, in relation to agricultural produce), the person who carried out that process.

This definition recognises that there is a variety of ways in which a person may be responsible for the production of a product. Apart from the manufacture of a product, it acknowledges that some products such as coal exist already but need to be abstracted from the earth before they are in a usable form. Finally, it acknowledges the potential significance of other processes that may be needed to bring the product to fruition. Thus a firm involved in assembling products from components bought in for that purpose would be classed as a producer with the consequent liability as such. Likewise, in respect of agricultural produce, some processes sufficiently change the character of the goods to mean that production of a new product has taken place. For example, the production of apple juice by squeezing apples would fall into this category and the person producing the juice would be a 'producer'.

'Product' for the purposes of Part I of the Act means any goods or electricity including any component part or raw material comprised in another product. However, there is an express exclusion in respect of 'any game or agricultural produce . . . at a time when it had not undergone an industrial process'. This is the first of the three derogations referred to earlier and one which the UK decided to adopt. The definition poses problems for it can be very difficult to establish what is or is not an industrial process. In the example of the apples given above, the producer of the unprocessed apples would not be liable while the producer of the juice would be. The process is clearly industrial. By contrast, however, suppose that the only process undertaken was to wash the apples and prepack them in labelled plastic bags each containing 2 lb weight of fruit. Is the packing process an 'industrial process'? If it is, the producer of the packs will be liable, if it is not, he will not be. The distinction is very fine but extremely important. As yet, the courts have not provided any guidance. As regards the wording of the exception, it should be noted that the Directive talks of an 'initial' process rather than an industrial one. As s.1(1) of the 1987 Act states that Part I is to be construed to comply with the Directive, the court may apply the phrase 'initial process' if asked to rule on the matter.

An unresolved issue is whether computer software is classed as a product for this purpose. Clearly, computer hardware is a product and poses no difficulty of interpretation but computer software is a different proposition. The true value of a piece of software is not the actual disk which may be worth only a few pounds but the intellectual property stored on it. The loss of this could have far-reaching consequences within any business as could the introduction of a computer virus via a piece of software.

Who is liable

One of the advantages to an injured user of a defective product is that the Act has broadened the range and number of potential defendants, all of whom are jointly and severally liable. This means that the plaintiff can decide which defendant he wishes to sue and is most unlikely to ever face the situation where there is no accessible defendant as can happen under both contract and negligence. Under contract the plaintiff is limited by privity and may discover that his supplier has either ceased to exist or, in a non-consumer sale, has validly excluded his liability. Similarly in negligence, he can only sue the negligent defendant, the identity of any other party involved in the production or distribution process being irrelevant.

Section 2(2) places liability for any damage caused wholly or partly by any defect in a product upon

(a) the producer of the product;
(b) any person who, by putting his name on the product or using a trade mark or other distinguishing mark in relation to the product, has held himself out to be the producer of the product;
(c) any person who has imported the product into a member State from a place outside the member States in order, in the course of any business of his, to supply it to another.

The first and third are straightforward, for the first includes anyone who falls within the definition of producer while the third places liability on the initial importer into the Community. The latter means that, with at least one identifiable defendant within the Community subject to Community legislation, the injured defendant is not faced with enforcing unknown product liability laws in a foreign jurisdiction.

The second relates to the use of 'own-branding' whereby one person passes off goods manufactured by another person as his own. It is most common at retail level with department stores and, more latterly, supermarkets indulging in the practice. Clearly, it has marketing advantages because it develops and encourages a store's identity in the public mind but it does leave the own-brander exposed to legal liability. The wording used on the packaging will be crucial in deciding whether the own-brander had 'held himself out to be the producer of the product'. If the only name that appears on the product is that of the own-brander, then he has done so. If however, the packaging reads to the effect 'specially prepared for X' there is a clear implication that another person actually produced the product and the own-brander may be nothing more than a supplier able to evade liability by revealing the name of his supplier. Lastly, if the producer's name appears on the pack along with the own-brander's, the own-brander will be merely a supplier.

Section 2(3) fixes secondary liability on anyone who supplied the defective product, whether to the injured person or to someone else. Such a supplier will only be liable however, if he fails to identify his own supplier (whether still in existence or not) within a reasonable period of being so requested by the injured person.

Defective

Defects fall into three main categories, manufacturing defects, design defects and duty to warn defects. The first, manufacturing defects, occur when the product deviates from the manufacturer's specification. It is a rogue product and however good a manufacturing system the producer may employ, it is a statistical certainty that rogue products will occur. If the producer's quality control system fails to recognise the rogue item, a defective product will reach the market. The cost of damage done by such products can be covered by insurance with the risk spread among purchasers of the item through a few extra pence on the price. The second type of defect, design defects, has a far greater potential for harm. In this situation the product accords with the specification but the specification itself is defective and poses a risk. This has very serious economic ramifications for a business as it means that whole production runs, as opposed to isolated items, will be faulty. This may involve scrapping whole batches prior to distribution or removing them from sale or even mounting a product recall with the attendant publicity that causes. At its most extreme a design defect may cause catastrophic damage such as occurred with Thalidomide with consequent heavy liability. The final type of defect is the duty to warn defect where the accident has occurred because the producer failed to warn the user about dangers posed by the product and how to use the product safely.

The meaning of defective within Part I of the 1987 Act is crucial to establishing liability, for liability only arises in respect of defective products. The term is considered in s.3(1) which states that a product is defective for the purposes of Part I if the safety of the product is not such as persons generally are entitled to expect; and for those purposes 'safety' in relation to a product, shall include safety with respect to products comprised in that product and safety in the context of risks of damage to property, as well as in the context of risks of death or personal injury.

The test is an objective one being based on the expectations of consumers generally rather than the plaintiff in particular. In applying the test the court must consider all the circumstances including three factors specifically mentioned in s.3(2). The first is 'the manner in which, and purposes for which, the product has been marketed, its get-up, the use of any mark in relation to the product and any instructions for, or warnings with respect to, doing or refraining from doing anything with or in relation to the product'. This covers a variety of factors such as whether the product was aimed at children or adults, whether appropriate safety features were included to take account of the likely product users, the quality and relevance of instructions for use and, of course, whether appropriate warnings of potential dangers were provided. As we have already seen in a previous chapter, a failure to provide appropriate warnings is considered to be a defect.

In assessing defectiveness the utility of the product can be crucial. For example, it is widely accepted that many drugs have side effects but the risk posed by them is tolerated as long as they are less serious than the illness being treated. In a risk-benefit analysis, the product is not defective.

The second specific factor drawn to the court's attention is 'what might reasonably be expected to be done with or in relation to the product'. It is reasonable to impose liability for defects that occur while the product is being used for one of its usual purposes but would be unreasonable to expect producers to be liable for injuries caused through product misuse if that use was not reasonably foreseeable. However it may be reasonable to expect producers to issue appropriate warnings in respect of foreseeable misuse.

The last of the three specific factors mentioned in s.3(3) is 'the time when the product was supplied by its producer to another'. The section also states that a product shall not be deemed defective merely because a later product is safer. This requires the court to consider the safety of the product and therefore its defectiveness in the context of the time when it was produced. Products move on with newer, safer versions being developed and it would be unrealistic to judge one product by comparison with a later version. This idea of judging situations in their own context was overtly considered as far back as 1954 in the decision of *Roe v Minister of Health* [1954] 2 All ER 131 when the court ruled in a medical negligence case that 'we must not look at the 1947 accident with 1954 spectacles'. Further, this protection must be afforded to producers if we are to encourage product development, for, if producers were to be penalised for improving their products, improvements would never take place and innovation would be non-existent.

Defences

The Act imposes strict liability not absolute liability. Consequently s.4 provides six defences that are open to anyone sued under Part I of the Act.

The first is that the defect is attributable to compliance with any requirement imposed by or under any enactment or with any Community obligation. Note that the defence only applies if compliance with the requirement is mandatory and the compliance is the cause of the defect. Even though standards agreed by a group of people with vested interests often reflect the lowest common denominator rather than the highest common factor, it still seems unlikely that compliance with a regulation would itself be the cause of a defect.

Section 4(1)(b) provides a defence if the defendant did not at any time supply the product to another. This will provide protection in two possible situations where the defendant has acted innocently. The first is where the product has been stolen from him and put into circulation by the thief. The producer may be able to show that the product had failed his own quality control systems and was due to be discarded or destroyed at the time that it was stolen. Clearly accurate production and quality control records would be helpful in establishing this. The second situation is where the goods were not even manufactured by the producer but are counterfeit. Given the quality of some of the counterfeit goods currently in the market it may be virtually impossible for the purchaser to recognise that they are imitation. For the producer however it is the perfect defence. Further, while the supply of counterfeit goods is no longer a criminal offence under s.1 of the Trade Descriptions Act 1968 as long as the supplier makes clear that the goods are counterfeit, as held in *Kent County Council* v *Price* [1993] 8 CL 102, such a supply would still constitute the tort of 'passing off' such as to enable the real producer to sue for damages.

The defence contained in s.4(1)(c) is designed to protect private sellers. It requires both that the supply by the defendant was not in the course of a business and also that the defendant is either not a producer within the meaning of s.2(2) or that while it is a producer it acted otherwise than with a view to a profit. This defence will protect voluntary organisations such as the Guide movement or the Boys Brigade who produce and supply goods for sale to raise funds.

The fourth defence is that the defect did not exist at the relevant time. The relevant time for a defendant under s.2(2) (i.e. producer, own-brander or importer) is the time at which they supplied the product to another person. For any other defendant (i.e. a supplier under s.2(3)) the relevant time is the last occasion on which a producer, own-brander or importer supplied the product. Thus no liability under this Act exists in respect of any defect that was introduced to the product after it last left the control of a s.2(2) defendant. Damages in respect of defects introduced later remain recoverable under the law of negligence.

The fifth and most controversial of the defences is the so-called 'development risk' defence found in s.4(1)(e). This states that it is a defence to show

that the state of scientific and technical knowledge at the relevant time was not such that a producer of products of the same description as the product in question might be expected to have discovered the defect if it had existed in his products while they were under his control.

This defence is the second of the optional derogations included in the Directive, disagreement about the inclusion of such a defence being one of the major causes of the delay in its implementation. Approximately half of the Member States have opted to include the defence to some extent in their national legislation. Britain opted to include the defence, as producers argued that it would be unfair to hold them responsible for unknowable defects and that to expose them to such liability would affect, adversely, future developments in industries at the forefront of scientific and technical knowledge. By contrast, the consumer lobby argued that it is not unreasonable to expect producers to accept such liability as they both take the profit from the resultant goods and also are in the best position to spread the risk through insurance.

The defence seeks to protect producers against damage caused by defects that were unknowable at the time that the product was put into circulation. The acid test is whether the producer might be expected to have discovered the defect. This places a burden on the producer to be up to date with developments in his field and to implement new knowledge as it becomes available. Of particular concern is the extent to which knowledge may be transferable within industries such as to mean that it is available to a producer in a different industry from that in which the research and development has been made. The Directive takes a hard line limiting the defence to situations where

the state of scientific and technical knowledge at the time when he put the product into circulation was not such as to enable the existence of the defect to be discovered. . . .

There is no mention in the Directive of there being any limitation based on individual industries. By contrast, s.4(1)(e) of the 1987 Act, in a provision which does not comply with the Directive, seeks to extend the defence to a producer unless the scientific and technical knowledge was available to other producers of the same product. This is a far more liberal defence and places a less onerous burden on the producer.

The relevant time for assessing whether the risk was unknowable is at the time that the product was put into circulation for that is the moment that it passes beyond the control of the producer. Therefore, it is incumbent upon the producer to ensure that there have not been any developments between the date of manufacture of the goods and the time that they leave his control. Clearly, the stockpiling of products by a producer presents a potential risk of liability. Further, any producer would be wise to keep good stock control records so as to establish beyond doubt when any individual item passed out of his control. This could be crucial given that products cannot be declared unsafe and therefore defective purely because a later product is safer.

The existence of a development risk defence will be reconsidered by the Commission in 1995 when further decisions will be made about the continued existence of the defence.

The final defence, which has two potential strands, is aimed at the producers of component parts. The first is that the defect in the component is wholly attributable to the design of the product in which it was subsequently used. It may be, for example, that the component was expected to withstand far greater stresses than those for which it was designed. Products such as screws, which may be used for everything from car manufacture to kitchen shelves, are particularly susceptible to this problem. The second strand is that the component producer can demonstrate that he manufactured the component in accordance with a specification provided by the producer of the finished product and that the defect is in the specification rather than in the physical production of the item. Component producers would be well advised to keep copies of all such specifications for future reference.

Recoverable damage

Section 5 prescribes the heads of damage for which compensation can be claimed under Part I of the Act. Recovery is permitted in respect of death, personal injury and certain property damage. Economic loss is not recoverable.

There are three restrictions on the plaintiff's ability to recover for property damage. First, only damage to private property can be recovered. The property concerned must be of a type ordinarily intended for private use, occupation or consumption and, further, the plaintiff must have intended to use it mainly for his own private use, occupation or consumption. Note that there is no need for it to have been exclusively for the plaintiff's private use. Thus, for example, a private car that is occasionally used for business would be covered. Second, a claim for property damage must exceed £275. The intention of this provision is to prevent a multiplicity of very small claims by restricting such claims to a negligence action. Such an arbitrary rule may, of course, create some apparent unfairness in that a claim for £276 is subject to strict liability while a claim for for £274 must be founded in negligence. Finally, no claim can be made for damage to the defective item itself. As the *Murphy* decision prevents such recovery in negligence as well, the onus is on the purchaser of the item to make a contractual claim under s.14 of the Sale of Goods Act (or other equivalent relevant section).

In assessing damages the court must consider the extent, if any, to which the plaintiff was responsible for his own injuries as the statutory provisions relating to the reduction of damages for contributory negligence apply to claims under Part I.

Time limits

Two time limits are of interest here. The Limitation Act 1980 as amended by s.6(6) and Schedule 1 of the Consumer Protection Act 1987 provides that claims for personal injury or property damage must be commenced within three years of the date on which the cause of action accrued or the date of knowledge of the injured party, whichever is the later. In respect of property damage the date of knowledge of the plaintiff includes, if earlier, the date of knowledge of any person in whom the claim was vested previously.

Under s.14(1A) of the Limitation Act the plaintiff's date of knowledge is determined by when he first had knowledge of the following

(a) such facts about the damage caused by the defect as would lead a reasonable person who had suffered such damage to consider it sufficiently serious to justify his instituting proceedings for damages against a defendant who did not dispute liability and was able to satisfy a judgement; and
(b) that the damage was wholly or partly attributable to the facts and circumstances alleged to constitute the defect; and
(c) the identity of the defendant.

More controversial is the ten year cut-off period found in s.11A of the Limitation Act which provides that a claim under Part I of the 1987 Act cannot be brought after the expiration of ten years from the relevant time i.e. the time when the product last left the control of a producer, own-brander or importer. This cut-off period applies even though the cause of action may not yet have accrued. This is most likely to be of import in cases for drug-related injuries where the damage may not become obvious for fifteen or twenty years after the relevant time. *Sindell* v *Abbott Laboratories*, discussed earlier, is a prime example of where the plaintiffs would have been deprived of their right of action under Part I before they were even aware of their injuries. Clearly, this is contrary to the individual consumer's best interests. However, the rationale behind the adoption of such a cut-off period is that it permits a definite end to a producer's liability in respect of any individual product and this eases both the availability of insurance cover and general corporate planning.

Global limits

The last of the three derogations permitted under the Directive relates to the imposition of global financial limits. Article 16 of the Directive provides that Member States may restrict the total liability of any producer to not less than 70 million ECU (approximately £40 million) in respect of death or personal injury caused by identical items with the same defect. The potential problem with such global limits is to find an equitable scheme of payment. One method is to pay compensation to plaintiffs on a first-come first-served basis in which case those who claim towards the end of the ten year cut-off period may find that there is no money left to satisfy their claim. An alternative method is that no claims are paid until the expiration of the ten year period and then all plaintiffs are paid on the same pro rata basis. This is fairer but involves making all plaintiffs wait ten years. In the event, Britain has not adopted this derogation with the result that producers subject to English law have unlimited liability.

Exclusion

Section 7 of the 1987 Act prohibits the limitation or exclusion of Part I liability whether by contract term, notice or any other provision.

QUESTION

Screen Ltd is a manufacturer of television sets which include component parts manufactured by Components Unlimited. While in use, one of these sets caught fire because of a faulty component produced and supplied by Components Unlimited. In the ensuing blaze, a video costing £300 was damaged and the nearby curtains valued at £175 caught alight. Elsie who was watching the television at the time burnt her hand while fighting the blaze.

Advise Elsie about any claim she may have under Part I of the Consumer Protection Act 1987.

FURTHER READING

Clark, A.M., *Product Liability* 1989 (Sweet and Maxwell)

Geddes, A., *Product and Service Liability in the EEC* 1992 (Sweet and Maxwell)

Harvey, B.W. and Parry, D. L., *The Law of Consumer Protection and Fair Trading* (4th ed) 1992 (Butterworth)

Pitt, G. (ed), *Butterworth's Commercial Law Handbook* (Butterworth)

Wright, C.J., *Product Liability – The Law and its Implications for Risk Management* 1989 (Blackstone Press)

preventing the offence from ever taking place. Thus a disclaimer is preventative rather than curative.

Disclaimers are only relevant to charges under s.1(1)(b), those of supplying or offering to supply. They cannot be used by a defendant charged with an offence of 'applying' under s.1(1)(a) as held in the Court of Appeal decision of *R v Southwood*. The logic is straightforward. It would be contrary to public policy to allow a person to wilfully apply a description and then escape liability for his criminal act by disclaiming it. This would place a premium on criminal actions.

The validity of disclaimers was acknowledged by the Divisional Court in the decision of *Tarleton Engineering Co Ltd v Nattrass* [1973] 3 All ER 699. However two basic requirements must be satisfied if the disclaimer is to be effective, these being the prominence of the disclaimer and the time at which it was drawn to the customer's attention.

In the decision of *Norman v Bennett* [1974] 3 All ER 351, a car clocking case in which the mileage of the vehicle had been reduced from 68 000 miles to 23 000 miles, the court held that for a disclaimer to be effective it

> must be *as bold, precise and compelling* as the trade description itself and must effectively be brought to the attention of any person to whom the goods may be supplied. In other words the disclaimer must equal the trade description in the extent to which it is likely to get home to anyone interested in receiving the goods.

The requirement of prominence means that, in practice, the disclaimer will need to be closely associated physically with the description, hence the practice in the car trade of affixing disclaimers over the mileage reading on the mileometer. Subsequent cases have established that notices on office walls or desks will not be effective if they are not proximate to the description. Similarly documentary disclaimers may not be effective as held in *R v Hammerton Cars Ltd* [1976] 3 All ER 758 and in the 1990 decision of *May v Vincent* (1990) 154 JP 997 in which it was held that a disclaimer in an auctioneer's catalogue was not effective.

As well as the prominence of the description, the time of its application is also crucial. The cases of *Doble v David Greig* [1972] 1 WLR 703 (a case under the now defunct s.11 of the Trade Descriptions Act), *Zawadski v Sleigh* [1975] RTR 113 and *Norman v Bennett* itself all confirm that the disclaimer must be given no later than the time at which the description is applied. Once the description has taken effect, it is too late to disclaim it.

Services

Section 14(1) provides that

> It shall be an offence for any person in the course of a trade or business —
>
> (a) to make a statement which he knows to be false; or

PART IV

Consumer protection

CHAPTER 13

Criminal liability for false statements

INTRODUCTION

Parts I to III of this book have dealt exclusively with the civil law governing the rights and liabilities between individuals arising out of contract or tort. Such rights are enforced by the two parties to the action with no involvement by the State. The only way that a central government department or local authority would be involved in such an action is as a plaintiff or defendant enforcing its own contractual and tortious rights and obligations.

This part of the book turns to the criminal law aspect of consumer protection. In this context, criminal law comprises those statutes establishing the basic standards of trading to be enforced by the State. It stipulates the level of behaviour to be expected from traders and the basic level of protection afforded to consumers generally. In most instances enforcement of consumer protection law is the responsibility of local authorities, primarily consumer protection departments, although government departments and the Office of Fair Trading also play a part. Ultimately, enforcement is by means of criminal prosecution.

THE TRADE DESCRIPTIONS ACT 1968

The Trade Descriptions Act 1968 controls the application of false trade descriptions to goods and services. While the primary purpose of criminal prosecution under this Act is to punish the offender, typically by means of a fine or custodial sentence, it is possible for the victim of the crime to receive compensation as well. Section 35 of the Powers of Criminal Courts Act 1973 provides that the court has the power to make a compensation order against anyone convicted of an offence for up to a maximum of £5000 per offence. The compensation is to compensate the victim of the crime for any personal injury, loss or damage resulting from the offence.

Goods

Section 1(1) of the Trade Descriptions Act 1968 provides the basic offence prohibiting the application of false trade descriptions to goods. It reads

> Any person who, in the course of a trade or business,
> (a) applies a false trade description to any goods; or
> (b) supplies or offers to supply any goods to which a false trade description is applied:
> shall, subject to the provisions of this Act, be guilty of an offence.

The section creates two distinct offences, the first 'applies' being aimed at the primary offender responsible for the creation of the false trade description while the second 'supplies or offers to supply' is aimed primarily at traders further down the distributive chain who, while not responsible for the creation of the false trade description, have nonetheless supplied goods to which the description attached. For example, a manufacturer of an electrical item who includes a false trade description on the outer packaging would be guilty of the 'applying' offence while a retailer who merely bought in the item and resold it would be guilty of the 'supplying' offence.

Note that s.1 does not include any words such as knowingly, intentionally or recklessly and thus creates strict liability offences. There is no need to prove *mens rea* (a guilty mind) as the state of mind of the defendant is irrelevant.

'Goods' are defined for this purpose in s.39 as including ships and aircraft, things attached to land and growing crops. It follows that land and houses are not covered by the Act. However, after much criticism of that fact, misdescriptions of property are now governed by the Property Misdescriptions Act 1991.

In the course of a trade or business

The Act is aimed at preventing false statements by traders. Hence, s.1 only applies if the offence has occurred in the course of a trade or business. This concept was considered at length in chapter 7 in the context of liability under s.14 of the Sale of Goods Act 1979. The same cases apply here. Thus applying *Havering London Borough* v *Stevenson* and *Davies* v *Sumner* the prosecution will need to show that the application of the false trade description or the supply or offer to supply the relevant goods occured as an integral part of the defendant's business.

There is no requirement that the person applying the false trade description is the seller or supplier of the goods. It is clear from the decision of *Fletcher* v *Budgen* [1974] 2 All ER 1243 that an offence can be committed by a trader buying goods in the course of a business.

In *Fletcher* v *Budgen*, a car trader told a customer that his car was irreparable and had only scrap value. Having bought the car for £2, the dealer spent some money repairing it before offering it for sale for £135. The trader was convicted of an offence against the Trade Descriptions Act 1968.

Trade description

The meaning of the phrase trade description is central to the provisions and enforcement of the Act. Section 2 provides that a trade description is an indication, direct or indirect, and by whatever means given, with respect to the goods or parts of them or any of a variety of factors. The factors are listed in s.2(1) and are:

(a) *quantity, size or gauge* This would include length, width, height, area, capacity, volume, e.g. 2 litres, 4 tons, 72 inches wide, 20 denier,

(b) *method of manufacture, production, processing, or reconditioning* This would include descriptions such as hand-made, organically grown,

(c) *composition,* e.g. plastic, stainless steel, oak, Harris tweed,

(d) *fitness for purpose, strength, performance, behaviour or accuracy* This might include a wide range of descriptions, e.g. child resistant, rustproof,

(e) *any physical characteristics not included in the preceding paragraphs* Colour and shape would be included here,

(f) *testing by any person and results thereof,* e.g. MOT

(g) *approval by any person or conformity with a type approved by any person* This would include use of the B.S.I. Kitemark. Note that there is a specific offence under s.12 of falsely claiming approval by a member of the Royal Family or using without authority any device or emblem signifying the Queen's Award to Industry.

(h) *place or date of manufacture, production, processing or reconditioning* e.g. Made in England, 1989 car, locally grown,

(i) person who manufactured, produced, processed or reconditioned, e.g. Rolls Royce,

(j) *any other history, including previous ownership or use* The most common example here is that applied by the mileometer on a car, i.e. 39 000 miles. Other examples would include one owner.

Any description that does not fit into one of the categories listed is not a trade description for the purposes of the Act. Thus in *Cadbury Ltd* v *Halliday* [1975] 2 All ER 226 a bar of chocolate bore the legend 'Extra Value' on the outer wrapper. The Divisional Court held that this did not constitute a trade description. All the factors in s.2 are for definite identifiable characteristics of the item whereas 'value' is an imprecise term and 'extra' merely added further uncertainty.

False trade description

To be actionable the trade description complained of must be 'false' within the meaning given to that term by the Act. Section 3(1) stipulates the basic requirement that a trade description is false for the purposes of the Act if it is false to a material degree. This confirms that the falsity must be substantial and that the law is not concerned with trivialities. Each case will be dependent on its facts but it would be reasonable to assume that the section is concerned with criminal liability arising from descriptions that would mislead a potential purchaser rather than with advertising puffs that an average person would not treat seriously.

In *R v Ford Motor Company* [1974] 3 All ER 489 a car was described as a 'new Ford Cortina'. In fact, the car had received slight damage while in a compound and had been repaired at a cost of £50 to be as good as new. The Court of Appeal held that the car had not been misdescribed.

In *Kent County Council* v *Price* [1993] 8 CL 102 the court held that there was no offence when goods which were counterfeit were described as such. The defendant sold T-shirts bearing recognised logos. Adjacent to the T-shirts was a sign stating 'Brand copy'. A further disclaimer was made at the time of sale. This decision of the Divisional Court contrasts with the previous case of *Lewin* v *Fuell* [1990] Crim LR 658 when a market stallholder was convicted of an offence against s.1 when he affixed expensive brand names to cheap watches.

Section 3(2) further states that where a trade description which, though not false, is misleading to a material degree, it shall be deemed to be a false trade description. This covers both those statements which though strictly true are nonetheless misleading and those where only half the truth has been told.

In *R v Inner London Justices ex parte Another* [1983] RTR 425 a car was described as having had one previous owner. This was strictly true but the one owner had been a car leasing company and the car had been used by five different clients.

Section 3(3) provides that anything which, though not a trade description, is likely to be taken for an indication of any of those matters and, as such an indication, would be false to a material degree, shall be deemed to be a false trade description. This catch-all provision would have the effect of covering an indication given by some other means than those expected. A prime example would be where the goods have effectively lied about themselves.

In *Cottee* v *Douglas Seaton (Used Cars) Ltd* [1972] 3 All ER 750 the owner of a rusty car had repaired it with plastic filler without seeking to disguise the fact. He sold it to the defendant garage who smoothed down the filler and painted over it to disguise its existence. The defendant then sold it to another garage who, in turn, sold it to a customer who was involved in an accident. While the defendant escaped liability on a technicality, the court was satisfied that the deliberate concealment of the repair constituted a false trade description.

In the decision of *R v A.F. Pears Ltd* (1982) 90 *ITSA Monthly Review* 142 the company packed moisturising cream in double-skinned containers which had false bottoms. While the correct weight of the cream was shown on the container, the volume of the container was approximately 30% larger than the volume of the cream it contained. The court held that the container was capable of being construed as a description within s.3(3) as to the volume of the product, one of the factors listed in s.2.

Section 2(4) makes it an offence to suggest approval by a non-existent person or compliance with a non-existent standard.

Applying

The offence under s.1(1)(a) requires that the defendant applied the false trade description. Section 4(1) states that a person applies a trade description to goods if he

(a) affixes or annexes it to or in a manner marks it on or incorporates it with
    (i)   the goods themselves, or
    (ii) anything in, on or with which the goods are supplied; or
(b) places the goods in, on or with anything which the trade description has been affixed or annexed to, marked on or incorporated with, or places any such thing with the goods; or
(c) uses the trade description in any manner likely to be taken as referring to the goods.

This subsection covers a wide range of methods by which a trade description may be applied. Clearly it includes labels on the goods or on packaging but it has a much greater impact than that. Shelf edge tickets such as appear in most trade warehouses and self-service retail premises would be covered as would posters in shops or warehouses and point of sale literature placed near the goods.

In *Roberts v Severn Petroleum and Trading Co Ltd* [1981] RTR 312 the defendants were found guilty of an offence of applying a false trade description contrary to s.1(1)(a) when a petrol station displayed Esso signs on the premises when not supplying Esso petrol.

Application of a false trade description may also occur by omission of relevant information.

In *R v Haesler* [1973] RTR 486 a car which had been registered first in the Channel Islands was re-registered when it was brought to England. The registration book was stamped with the words 'Ex Channel Islands' to indicate that the car was re-registered and thus older than its registration number suggested. The defendant car dealer erased the words 'Ex Channel Islands' from the registration document. It was held that this amounted to the application of a false trade description and an offence against s.1(1) had been committed.

Further the case of *Cavendish Woodhouse Ltd* v *Wright* (1985) 149 JP 497 held that it is possible to use a comparison with other goods as a means of description. In that decision the defendant was found guilty of an offence for failing to supply goods identical with those on display, having promised to do so.

Application not only relates to documentary or written descriptions but by virtue of s.4(2) expressly includes oral descriptions. The difficulty of oral descriptions is the same as that with oral contracts, namely proof. Evidence of oral descriptions may be difficult to establish unless a witness was present, particularly given that the burden of proof is higher for a criminal prosecution than for a civil law claim. In criminal cases, it is 'beyond reasonable doubt' instead of 'on the balance of probabilities' as is the case in civil law actions.

It is not always the case that the supplier applies the description but rather that he responds to a description applied by the recipient of the goods. Section 4(3) provides that where goods are supplied in pursuance of a request in which a trade description was applied and it is reasonable to assume that the goods supplied corresponded to the description, the supplier will be deemed to have applied the trade description to the goods.

As the s.1 offences are strict liability offences there is no need to prove that the defendant knew that the description was false although he will need to be aware that there was a description. Further, there is no requirement that the description actually misled anyone. Thus descriptions that are obviously false are capable of giving rise to liability under s.1(1) if they were applied deliberately. A particular example of the problem relates to the one-time practice of zeroising the mileometers on cars, a practice that had received judicial approval in the case of *K. Lill (Holdings) Ltd* v *White* [1979] JP 534 on the basis that a mileage reading of zero on a second-hand car would not mislead anyone. However, in *R* v *Southwood* [1987] 3 All ER 556 the Court of Appeal held that the practice was illegal as it is as much the application of a false description to zeroise the mileometer as it is to merely reduce the mileage reading. Either practice results in an inaccurate reading.

While the actual supply of the misdescribed item is not essential to create an offence of application under s.1(1)(a) there must be an ability to supply the goods at some point.

In *Wycombe Marsh Garages Ltd* v *Fowler* [1972] 3 All ER 248 the defendant garage wrongly refused an MOT certificate stating that the tyres on the car were faulty. In fact, they were all right. It was held that the garage had not committed an offence against s.1 as there was no intention to supply the goods at any stage. The garage was undertaking the MOT on behalf of the owner.

Supplies or offers to supply

The s.1(1)(b) offence relates to the supply or offer to supply goods to which a false trade description has been applied. Thus there is the potential for any subsequent supplier to be charged under this subsection.

It should be noted that there is no requirement that the goods have been sold, merely offered for supply. This broadens the ambit of the offence considerably for it would cover goods supplied on H.P., barter, promotional free gifts, hire etc. under which the possession of goods changes hands by means other than a contract of sale.

Section 6 defines 'offer to supply' thus

> A person exposing goods for supply or having goods in his possession for supply shall be deemed to offer to supply them.

The section has two interesting phrases. The first 'exposing for supply' means that any goods displayed in a business premises on shelves, or in bins, or in the window would be classed as being offered for supply even though no subsequent supply takes place. There is a presumption that they are intended for supply. Similarly goods on display at an auction would be deemed to be offered for supply. This differs significantly from the contractual position where goods on display would merely constitute an invitation to treat and not create any civil liability or any obligation to sell as was held in *Fisher* v *Bell* [1961] 1 QB 394.

The second phrase is 'having goods in his possession for supply'. This does not require that the goods are visible. Thus goods stored in a back room or a warehouse would be caught by this provision. This is reasonable given the modern trading practice, notably with larger items, whereby a demonstration model is on display in the seller's premises but the buyer actually receives an item from the stores. Further, there is no requirement that the goods in the seller's possession must necessarily be held at his business premises. In the case of *Stainethorpe* v *Bailey* [1980] RTR 7 the defendant car dealer advertised a car with a false mileage reading. The car was parked at his private address rather than at his business premises. The Divisional Court held that the car was in his possession for supply.

Disclaimers

The innocent businessman involved in the supply of goods will wish to protect himself against criminal liability in respect of goods to which someone else has affixed a false trade description. To deal with this situation the courts have recognised the validity of disclaimers. A disclaimer is very different in effect from a defence. A defence is an acceptable reason why a defendant should be excused from liability for an offence that has occurred. By contrast, the purpose of a disclaimer is to avoid liability arising by preventing the offence from ever taking place. Thus a disclaimer is preventative rather than curative.

Disclaimers are only relevant to charges under s.1(1)(b), those of supplying or offering to supply. They cannot be used by a defendant charged with an offence of 'applying' under s.1(1)(a) as held in the Court of Appeal decision of *R* v *Southwood*. The logic is straightforward. It would be contrary to public policy to allow a person to wilfully apply a description and then escape liability for his criminal act by disclaiming it. This would place a premium on criminal actions.

The validity of disclaimers was acknowledged by the Divisional Court in the decision of *Tarleton Engineering Co Ltd* v *Nattrass* [1973] 3 All ER 699. However two basic requirements must be satisfied if the disclaimer is to be effective, these being the prominence of the disclaimer and the time at which it was drawn to the customer's attention.

In the decision of *Norman* v *Bennett* [1974] 3 All ER 351, a car clocking case in which the mileage of the vehicle had been reduced from 68 000 miles to 23 000 miles, the court held that for a disclaimer to be effective it

> must be *as bold, precise and compelling* as the trade description itself and must effectively be brought to the attention of any person to whom the goods may be supplied. In other words the disclaimer must equal the trade description in the extent to which it is likely to get home to anyone interested in receiving the goods.

The requirement of prominence means that, in practice, the disclaimer will need to be closely associated physically with the description, hence the practice in the car trade of affixing disclaimers over the mileage reading on the mileometer. Subsequent cases have established that notices on office walls or desks will not be effective if they are not proximate to the description. Similarly documentary disclaimers may not be effective as held in *R* v *Hammerton Cars Ltd* [1976] 3 All ER 758 and in the 1990 decision of *May* v *Vincent* (1990) 154 JP 997 in which it was held that a disclaimer in an auctioneer's catalogue was not effective.

As well as the prominence of the description, the time of its application is also crucial. The cases of *Doble* v *David Greig* [1972] 1 WLR 703 (a case under the now defunct s.11 of the Trade Descriptions Act), *Zawadski* v *Sleigh* [1975] RTR 113 and *Norman* v *Bennett* itself all confirm that the disclaimer must be given no later than the time at which the description is applied. Once the description has taken effect, it is too late to disclaim it.

Services

Section 14(1) provides that

> It shall be an offence for any person in the course of a trade or business —
>
> (a) to make a statement which he knows to be false; or

(b)   recklessly to make a statement which is false;
as to any of the following

   (i)   the provision in the course of a trade or business of any services, accommodation or facilities;

  (ii)   the nature of any services, accommodation or facilities provided in the course of a trade or business;

 (iii)   the time at which, manner in which or persons by whom any services, accommodation or facilities are provided;

 (iv)   the examination, approval or evaluation by any person of any of the services, accommodation or facilities so provided; or

  (v)   the location or amenities of any accommodation so provided.

As with s.1 offences, false means false to a material degree.

Many of the cases relating to s.14 involve package holidays. However, the law is equally applicable to other services such as building, repair work and insurance. Thus it essentially covers the same area as the Supply of Goods and Services Act 1982.

A major difference between the s.1 and s.14 offences is that s.14 requires *mens rea* as actual knowledge is required for the 14(1)(a) offence and a degree of recklessness is needed for the s.14(1)(b) offence. However, in respect of the requirement for recklessness it is perhaps fairer to say that it is a half *mens rea* offence for the court in *MFI Warehouses Ltd* v *Nattrass* [1973] 1 All ER 762 held that 'recklessly' in this context does not imply dishonesty merely that the defendant did not pay due regard to whether the statement was true or false. Further, a statement will not be reckless if it was true at the time that it was made but was rendered untrue subsequently by something beyond the defendant's control, as long as the defendant was unaware of its falsity.

In *Sunair Holidays Ltd* v *Dodd* [1970] 2 All ER 410 the defendant company advertised holiday accommodation as 'all rooms with terrace overlooking the harbour'. Such accommodation had always been provided previously. However, on the occasion in question, the hotel allocated different accommodation to the defendant's clients. It was held that the defendant had not been reckless.

Of course, if the defendant knew that the statement had become false, it would be reckless not to correct it. Further, the decision of *Best Travel Co* v *Patterson* (1986) 151 JP 619 held that an advertiser was reckless when he failed to check the truth of a statement when he had cause to doubt its accuracy.

The leading decision of *Wings Ltd* v *Ellis* [1984] 3 All ER 577 considered the time at which the defendant must know of the falsity of a statement if he is to be convicted of making 'a statement which he knows to be false' contrary to s.14(1)(a). Again, it is a holiday case but the decision would be equally relevant to any situation in which services are described in a brochure or leaflet.

In *Wings Ltd* the company advertised a holiday in a hotel in Sri Lanka stating that the hotel had air-conditioning. This was not so, a fact which was brought to the defendant's attention. Despite their attempts to remedy the situation, a customer subsequently booked a holiday relying on an unamended brochure. The House of Lords held the company liable on the basis that the statement was false and the company knew of its falsity at the time that the client relied upon it. Their belief in its truth at the time of publication of the brochure was irrelevant.

Thus there is an obligation on those supplying services to ensure that any brochure, leaflet or other advertising material is accurate at all times for liability will arise as soon as the defendant is aware of any falsity. Further, the decision of *R v Thomsom Holidays Ltd* [1971] 1 All ER 823 confirms that a new offence occurs every time the brochure is read and thus one misdescription may give rise to many offences.

In determining what is covered by s.14, it is important to examine what constitutes a 'service, accommodation or facility'. In *R v Breeze* [1973] 2 All ER 1141 it was held to be an offence to falsely describe one's qualifications, as this relates to the provision of professional services. 'Facility' has posed greater difficulty. Thus the provision of a 'closing down sale' was held not to be a facility in *Westminster City Council v Ray Allan (Manshops) Ltd* [1982] 1 All ER 177. In *Newell v Hicks* (1983) 148 JP 308 the promise of a free video cassette recorder with every X-registered Renault bought at a specific time was not a facility as it related to the acquisition of goods. By contrast, in *Kinchin v Ashton Park Scooters Ltd* (1984) 148 JP 540 the offer of free insurance with the purchase of a motor cycle was the provision of a facility.

Section 14 is limited further by the fact that it relates only to statements about present or past facts and does not cover promises as to the future.

Thus in *Beckett v Cohen* [1973] 1 All ER 120 the defendant builder contracted to build a garage in ten days identical to one on adjacent premises. The garage was not completed within the ten day period and differed from the neighbouring garage. The court held that the defendant was not liable under s.14 as it does not extend to future promises only statements about past or existing facts. The breach was a breach of contract not a breach of the criminal law.

However, if the promise as to the future also contains some element of present fact, liability will arise.

In *British Airways Board v Taylor* [1975] 3 All ER 307 the defendants practised a policy of overbooking on planes to take account of 'no-shows'. As a result of this policy there was no seat available for a customer on his flight. The court held that liability was possible as a letter confirming that a seat had been reserved for the customer made a statement about the present availability of his seat as well as its future availability. On the facts, the defendants escaped liability on the basis that the statement had been made by their predecessor BOAC for which they could not be held liable.

Finally, it should be noted that s.14 does not cover statements about price as held in *Dixons Ltd* v *Roberts* (1984) 148 JP 513.

In *Dixons Ltd* v *Roberts* the defendant company issued an advertisement promising to 'refund the difference if you buy Dixon's Deal products cheaper locally at the time of purchase and call within seven days'. The defendant intended that the offer would apply only to selected goods but the advertisement was ambiguous. A refund was refused to two customers who had bought goods to which the advertisement was not intended to apply. The defendant was acquitted as the court held that a statement relating to a refund of part of the price was not a service within s.14 of the Trade Descriptions Act.

Misleading price indications are covered now by Part III of the Consumer Protection Act 1987 to which reference will be made later in this chapter.

Defences

Section 24 provides the main statutory defences in the Trade Descriptions Act. It provides that it shall be a defence for the person charged to prove

(a) that the commission of the offence was due to a mistake or to reliance on information supplied to him or to the act or default of another person, an accident or some other cause beyond his control; and

(b) that he took all reasonable precautions and exercised all due diligence to avoid the commission of such an offence by himself or any person under his control.

For the defence to succeed the defendant must be able to satisfy both strands of the defence.

Part (a) of the defence permits of five different options. Case law has established that the mistake must have been that of the person charged as held in *Birkenhead & District Cooperative Society* v *Roberts* [1970] 3 All ER 391. By contrast, reliance on information supplied or the act or default of another necessarily implies the presence of a third party. It was held in *Tesco Supermarkets Ltd* v *Nattrass* [1972] AC 153 that in a corporate structure an employee or manager can be 'another person' for this purpose and that a company may escape liability by alleging an employee's act or default. Only those persons, typically the directors and company secretary, who constitute the *alter ego* of the company would not be classed as another person in this context. Of course, the directors, managers, secretary and other corporate officers can be charged with an offence under s.20 if the company has committed an offence with their consent, connivance or neglect.

In the *Tesco* decision, the supermarket company were running a 'flash' offer on washing powder whereby customers obtained the product at a specially reduced price. An advertising poster to this effect appeared in the store. The store in question ran out of the special packs of washing powder and a shop assistant put ordinary packets on the shelf without removing the advertising poster. The manager of the store who was responsible for checking that everything was in order did not notice this. A customer was charged the full price for a packet of washing powder. The House of Lords held that the offence had been committed by the shop manager who was another person for the purposes of the s.24 defence.

If the defendant wishes to plead reliance on information or the act or default of another he must give the prosecutor seven days' clear notice of this fact and provide the prosecutor with information identifying or assisting with the identification of that other person.

The second strand of the defence requires that the defendant show that he took all reasonable precautions and exercised all due diligence. In the *Tesco* decision the court held that all reasonable precautions involved the establishment of a suitable system and due diligence involved ensuring that it worked. It has yet to be seen whether the setting up and operation of a quality control system under BS 5750 will *prima facie* constitute due diligence although certainly it would appear to be good evidence of such. The parameters of the due diligence defence are extremely important as it appears regularly in consumer protection legislation including weights and measures and food safety both of which are discussed later.

One aspect of reasonable precautions and due diligence involves the question of sampling and the extent to which the supplier of goods should sample them to ensure compliance with any description. This question was addressed in *Garrett* v *Boots Chemists Ltd* (16 July 1980, unreported, DC).

In the *Garrett* decision the defendant company were found guilty of an offence against the Pencil and Graphic Instrument Regulations 1974 (S.I. 1974/226) for having for sale pencils that exceeded the permitted levels of lead and/or chromium. The Divisional Court held, overruling the magistrates' court, that the defendant had not exercised reasonable precautions as, even though it was a condition in the contract with their supplier that all goods must conform to regulatory standards, they had not taken any random samples to ensure compliance.

The court in the *Garrett* decision acknowledged that the level of sampling to be required will depend to some extent upon the nature of the defendant. Thus it would be unreasonable to expect a small corner shop to undertake the same level of testing as a major national retailer, particularly if the tests are of a technical nature or very expensive. However, simple tests can be undertaken by anybody as seen in *Sherratt* v *Gerald's The American Jewellers Ltd* (1970) 114 Sol Jo 147.

In the *Sherratt* case, the defendant was charged under s.1(1)(b) with supplying a diver's watch which was falsely described as 'waterproof' when, in fact, the watch stopped after being submerged in water for one hour. The Divisional Court held that the retailer had not exercised all reasonable precautions and due diligence in relying on a manufacturer's statement. It would have been a simple matter to test a watch by placing it in water. The defendant was convicted.

Section 24(3) provides a further defence to those charged with offences of supplying or offering to supply contrary to s.1(1)(b). It provides that it shall be a defence for the person charged to show that he did not know, and could not with reasonable diligence have ascertained, that the goods did not conform to the description or that the description had been applied to the goods.

Section 25 provides a separate defence for the innocent publisher of an advertisement containing a false trade description. It is a defence for him to show that he is a person whose business is to publish or arrange for the publication of advertisements, that he received the offending advertisement in the ordinary course of his business and that he did not know and had no reason to suspect that the advertisement would amount to an offence under the Act.

Section 23, while not strictly a defence, dovetails with s.24. It provides that where an offence committed by one person is due to the act or default of another, that other person shall be guilty of an offence and can be proceeded against irrespective of whether proceedings are taken against the first person. Thus, in the situations discussed above where a company claims that the offence was due to the act or default of an employee, the enforcement authorities could charge the employee irrespective of whether they prosecute the company. The only requirement for the section, confirmed in the case of *Coupe v Guyett* [1973] 2 All ER 1058 is that a *prima facie* case can be made against the main offender. If no case could be made because, for example, the main offender is not in the course of a business, no action under s.23 is permitted. The fact that the main offender would be able to make out a s.24 defence is not relevant. The second, and rather surprising, point is that s.23 can be used to prosecute a private individual as the section does not contain a requirement that the defendant be in the course of a trade or business. This was confirmed in the decision of *Olgeirsson v Kitching* [1986] 1 All ER 746. However, this decision has been much criticised and it seems likely that the law will be changed at some point.

PRICES

Misleading price indications are controlled by Part III of the Consumer Protection Act 1987, s.20(1) of which provides that

a person shall be guilty of an offence if, in the course of any business of his, he gives (by any means whatever) to any consumers an indication which is misleading as to the price at which any goods, services, accommodation or facilities are available (whether generally or from particular persons).

Further, s.20(2) provides that if a price indication becomes misleading after it was given to any consumers and that some or all of those consumers were likely to rely on it after it became misleading, the defendant will be guilty of an offence if he fails to take all such steps as are reasonable to prevent the consumers from relying on it. This might be true if, for example, a trader published a brochure or other advertising material which became inaccurate after publication because of a change in the rate of VAT increasing prices.

The s.20 offence is broader than the now defunct s.11 of the Trade Descriptions Act which it replaced in that the new offence covers both goods and services while the old provision only covered goods. Services are defined as including the provision of credit, insurance and banking services together with ancillary services, the purchase or sale of foreign currency, the supply of electricity, the provision of a place (other than on a highway) for the parking of a motor vehicle and the making of arrangements for a person to site a caravan other than for use as his main residence. It expressly does not include the carrying on of an investment business or any services provided to an employer under a contract of employment. The 'price' is the aggregate of the sums payable by the consumer for the supply of goods or the provision of services, accommodation or facilities.

In construing the s.20 offence it is important to note that it only applies where the person making the indication was acting in the course of a business of his. The House of Lords in *Warwickshire County Council* v *Johnson* [1993] 1 All ER 299 held that the section only applies where the defendant is the owner of the business or has a controlling interest in it. Thus, where the offending statement had been made by a branch manager, a mere employee of the company, there was no liability.

A further restriction on the impact of s.20 is that it only applies where the indication is given to consumers, who are defined in s.20(6) as being

(a) in relation to any goods, means any person who might wish to be supplied with the goods for his own private use or consumption;
(b) in relation to any services or facilities, means any person who might wish to be provided with the services or facilities otherwise than for the purposes of any business of his; and
(c) in relation to any accommodation, means any person who might wish to occupy the accommodation otherwise than for the purposes of any business of his.

Thus these provisions do not apply in business to business sales, and companies compiling brochures for use by business purchasers or, for example, the supply departments of local authorities would not be governed by the Act. Nonetheless, great care should be taken for if it is possible that personnel within such a business or local authority might buy an item from the catalogue in their personal capacity, s.20 would apply in relation to that purchase. Thus, for example, suppose an office equipment catalogue is available in the offices of a company or local authority and that a member of staff ordered a word-processor for their private use at home, the purchase would be subject to s.20 and if the price indication was misleading an offence would have occurred. Further, note that the s.20(6) definition does not require that the item purchased was of a type ordinarily acquired for private use or consumption, merely that that particular consumer was buying it for his private use or consumption. The test is subjective.

For the purposes of the Act a price indication is misleading if it would imply:

(a) that the price is lower than it is;
(b) that the price does not depend on facts on which it does depend, e.g. cash sales only;
(c) that the price includes matters for which an additional charge will be made, e.g. service extra;
(d) that the person expects the price to increased, reduced or maintained when this is not the case;
(e) that a price comparison is accurate when it is not so.

The understanding of the pricing provisions of the Act has been enhanced greatly by the publication of the Code of Practice for Traders on Price Indications published by the Department of Trade in November 1988. The Code of Practice seeks to explain the provisions clearly and provides many examples of how they would apply in practice. Compliance with the Code can be used as defence evidence in a prosecution but it is not an absolute defence.

Section 24 provides for some specific defences including that the Act or omission was authorised under regulations made under s.26 (to date no such regulations have been made), that the indication was not contained in an advertisement, that an advertisement was published innocently by a professional publisher and that the price indication related to a recommended price which did not apply to the availability of the goods or services from the defendant, that it was reasonable for the defendant to assume that the price recommendation was being followed and that the offence arose because of the failure of a person to follow the recommendation.

PROPERTY MISDESCRIPTIONS

As stated earlier, the Trade Descriptions Act 1968 does not cover land or buildings. Most specifically, therefore, it does not cover the supply of houses or commercial buildings. This omission has been addressed by the passage of the Property Misdescriptions Act 1991. Section 1 of the Act provides the main offence which is that where a false or misleading statement about a prescribed matter is made in the course of an estate agency business or a property development business, otherwise than in providing conveyancing services, the person by whom the business is carried on shall be guilty of an offence under this section.

A property development business for this purpose means a business wholly or substantially concerned with the development of land. A statement is made in the course of such a business if it is made for the purpose of, or with a view to, disposing of an interest in land consisting of or including a building, or part of a building, constructed or renovated in the course of the business.

To be an offence under s.1 the statement must relate to a 'prescribed matter' it being the function of the Secretary of State to stipulate by Order which matters are to be covered. To date, no such Orders have been made.

Section 2(1) of the Act provides a statutory due diligence defence available to the defendant if he can show that he 'took all reasonable steps and exercised all due diligence to avoid committing the offence'. However, it is qualified by s.2(2) which provides that if the defendant wishes to rely on information provided to him as part of his defence, he must demonstrate that it was reasonable for him to have relied on the information particularly having regard to what steps he took to verify it and whether he had any reason to disbelieve it.

QUESTION

Downshire County Council ordered some outdoor jackets from Clothes Ltd, a clothing wholesaler, for use by employees in the authority's direct labour organisation. The jackets were described as 'waterproof' and bought on that basis. In fact, they were only showerproof and not suitable for their intended usage. Clothes Ltd had relied for the description on information supplied to them by Koats Ltd, the manufacturer. The jackets were packed in sealed boxes which Clothes Ltd had not opened but merely passed on to Downshire County Council.

Consider whether any offences have been committed contrary to the Trade Descriptions Act 1968.

FURTHER READING

Dobson, A.P., *Sale of Goods and Consumer Credit* (4th ed) 1989 (Sweet and Maxwell)

Harvey, B.W. and Parry, D.L., *The Law of Consumer Protection and Fair Trading* (4th ed) 1993 (Butterworth)

Miller, C.J. and Harvey, B.W., *Consumer Trading Law Cases and Materials* 1985 (Butterworth)

Pitt, G. (ed), *Butterworth's Commercial Law Handbook* (Butterworth)

Ramsay, I., *Consumer Protection – Texts and Materials* 1989 (Weidenfeld and Nicolson)

CHAPTER 14

Product safety

CONSUMER PROTECTION ACT 1987

The safety of products is extremely important in both civil and criminal law. As we have seen already, defectiveness in Part I of the 1987 Act is determined by whether the product provides the safety that persons generally are entitled to expect.

Part II of the Act, which is the criminal law counterpart of Part I, continues the safety theme and is the latest criminal legislation relating to the safety of goods following on from the Consumer Protection Act 1961 and the Consumer Safety Act 1978. While continuing the established practice of providing the framework for regulations governing safety aspects of specified products, it has also introduced a new concept in 'the general safety requirement'.

The general safety requirement

Section 10(1) of the Consumer Protection Act 1987 reads

A person shall be guilty of an offence if he—
(a) supplies any consumer goods which fail to comply with the general safety requirement;
(b) offers or agrees to supply any such goods; or
(c) exposes or possesses any such goods for supply.

Three points are immediately obvious from this subsection. First, it refers only to the supply of goods, not to their sale. Thus the Act applies to goods supplied by any means including hire-purchase, barter, hire, promotional offers etc.

Second, its application is limited to 'consumer goods' which are defined in s.10(7) as being 'any goods ordinarily intended for private use or consumption, not being:

(a) growing crops or things comprised in land by virtue of being attached to it;
(b) water, food, feeding stuff or fertiliser;
(c) gas which is, is to be or has been supplied by a person authorised to supply it by or under section 6, 7 or 8 of the Gas Act 1986 (authorisation of supply of gas through pipes);

    (d)   aircraft (other than hang gliders) or motor vehicles;
    (e)   controlled drugs or licensed medicinal products;
    (f)   tobacco.'

In practice, (b) to (e) are controlled through other Acts and regulations such as the Food Safety Act 1990 and the Agriculture Act 1970 as amended. Thus local authority supplies departments negotiating contracts for the supply of food for school canteens or fertilisers for use in public parks would be more concerned with the protection offered by those other Acts. What is equally clear from s.10(1) is that goods intended for business or industrial use are not included in Part II of the 1987 Act although in practice they will be covered by the Health and Safety at Work etc. Act 1974 instead.

Third, s.10(1) reads such that liability is placed on 'any person' who undertakes the prohibited acts. Therefore, liability is not limited to producers, importers and own-branders but can be used against anyone involved in the production, importation or distribution process right down to retailers. As such, it has greater impact than Part I where suppliers can evade civil liability through identifying their own supplier. In Part II criminal liability is imposed on all parties involved subject, of course, to the statutory defences.

In deciding whether consumer goods conform to the general safety requirement, consideration must be given first to the definition of 'safe' contained in s.19 and then the provisions contained in s.10(2).

Section 19 states that goods are safe for this purpose when there is no risk, or no risk apart from one reduced to a minimum, that the goods will cause death or personal injury. Note that it refers only to death and personal injury and does not include property damage. Thus in this respect, it is narrower in effect than Part I and any goods that are only likely to cause property damage will not offend against the general safety requirement.

Section 10(2) stipulates the factors that the court must consider when deciding whether the goods are reasonably safe. They are

    (a)   the manner in which, and purposes for which, the goods are being or would have been marketed, the get-up of the goods, the use of any mark in relation to the goods and any instructions or warnings which are given or would be given with respect to the keeping, use or consumption of the goods;
    (b)   any standards of safety published by any person either for goods of a description which applies to the goods in question or for matters relating to goods of that description; and
    (c)   the existence of any means by which it would have been reasonable (taking into account the cost, likelihood and extent of any improvement) for the goods to have been made safer.

Paragraph (a) is very similar to the matters to be considered in deciding whether a product is defective under Part I and thus goods that fail the general safety requirement are likely to be defective for the purposes of civil action under Part I. However, one distinction is crucial. Civil liability under Part I arises only if someone has been injured or suffered recoverable loss caused by a defective product, whereas Part II, being regulatory in nature, is enforced regardless of whether anyone has been injured. Indeed, one of the main effects of good enforcement is that with a reduced number of unsafe products on the market, the likelihood of injuries to product users should be reduced together with the resultant civil claims for compensation.

Section 10(3) provides that goods will not fail the general safety requirement in respect of any aspect attributable to compliance with any regulation imposed by or under any enactment or Community obligation. This echoes one of the Part I defences. Further, a failure to do more than is required by any safety regulations, approved standards of safety or the provisions of any enactment or subordinate legislation will not cause the goods to fail the general safety requirement. This means that the minimum standard required by such regulations or standards has effectively become the maximum to be demanded when applying the general safety requirement. This is a lower standard than under Part I where it would be reasonable to expect a producer to incorporate the latest safety features in his product even though they exceed any regulatory requirement.

Section 10(4) provides the statutory defences to anyone charged with a s.10(1) offence. The first defence is that the defendant reasonably believed that the goods would not be used or consumed in the UK. This acknowledges the realities of manufacturing in that manufacturers may be producing goods for export and, as such, producing them in conformity with regulatory standards applicable in the recipient country. The defendant would need to demonstrate that none of the goods were intended to reach the UK market and have done so by methods beyond his control, e.g. theft.

The second defence is available only to retailers and applies if the retailer can show that at the time that he supplied the goods or offered or agreed to supply them or exposed or possessed them for supply, he neither knew nor had reasonable grounds for believing that the goods failed to comply with the general safety requirement. This defence is very similar to that provided in s.24(3) of the Trade Descriptions Act 1968.

The third defence is that the goods supplied were second-hand goods for sale. Note that it does not cover goods on hire so companies involved in the hire of second-hand goods cannot claim protection from the defence.

Section 39 provides a due diligence defence applicable to specified offences including s.10. It provides, in terms very similar to those found in the defence under the Trade Descriptions Act, that it shall be a defence for the defendant to show that he took all reasonable steps and exercised all due diligence to avoid the commission of the offence. Unlike the Trade Descriptions Act defence, the due diligence defence contained in the 1987 Act is a single strand defence.

Safety regulations

Section 11(1) provides the Secretary of State with the authority to make regulations to ensure that goods are safe or that their availability is restricted to particular groups of people or that appropriate information is provided and inappropriate information not provided in relation to goods. Subsection (2) provides a comprehensive list of those factors that the Secretary of State may seek to control through the use of such regulations. It includes, among other things, composition, design, packaging, the granting of approvals, the testing or inspection of goods and the requirement that marks, warnings or instructions be included with the goods.

The section applies to goods other than growing crops and things comprised in land by virtue of being attached to it, water, food, feeding stuffs and fertilisers, gas, and controlled drugs and licensed medicinal products. Note, first, that tobacco is not excluded and thus is subject to control under this section and that, second, the section is not restricted to consumer goods and thus is applicable to industrial goods.

When drafting safety regulations, the Secretary of State must consult such organisations as appear to him to be representative of interests substantially affected by the proposals, such other persons as he considers appropriate and finally, in respect of goods suitable for use at work, the Health and Safety Commission. The duty to consult was confirmed in the decision of *R v Secretary of State for Health ex parte US Tobacco International Inc.* [1992] 3 All ER 212.

In the *US Tobacco* case the plaintiff sought judicial review of a decision by the Secretary of State to introduce the Oral Snuff (Safety) Regulations 1989 without undertaking appropriate consultation with the plaintiff who was the only manufacturer of oral snuff in the UK and had been encouraged by the government to establish a factory in Scotland. The decision to ban oral snuff was based on a report and recommendation to which the plaintiff was denied access. The plaintiff sought to have the regulations quashed on the basis that due consultation had not occurred. The Court of Appeal found in favour of the plaintiff and granted an order of *certiorari* to quash the regulations. A side issue in the case was whether, as the plaintiff suggested, the Secretary of State's powers to make regulations under s.11 is limited to matters governing consumer protection and safety and that the regulations in question were *ultra vires* as they purported to deal with health. The court held that regulations to protect the health of the consumer do fall within the general aim of consumer protection.

Several safety regulations have been made under this section including the Furniture and Furnishings (Fire) (Safety) Regulations 1988 (S.I. 1988/1324) as amended, the Low Voltage Electrical Equipment (Safety) Regulations 1989 (S.I. 1989/728), the Toys (Safety) Regulations 1989 (S.I. 1989/1275)the All-Terrain Motor Vehicles (Safety) Regulations 1989 (S.I. 1989/2288), the Gas Cooking Appliances (Safety) Regulations 1989 (S.I. 1989/149) and the

Heating Appliances (Fireguards) (Safety) Regulations 1991 (S.I. 1991/2693). In addition, the Act has adopted the numerous safety regulations formulated under the Consumer Protection Act 1961 and the Consumer Safety Act 1978.

Section 12 creates a number of offences dependent upon the terms of individual safety regulations. Thus s.12(1) makes it an offence to supply or offer or agree to supply, or expose or possess any goods for supply where any safety regulations prohibit such action. Further s.12(2) provides that where a safety regulation requires that a particular test or process is to be adopted in connection with goods, or where the goods must be dealt with in a particular way when the whole or part of them does not satisfy a test, it is an offence not to act in the correct way. Section 12(3) and (4) create offences relating to the non-compliance with any requirement imposed by safety regulations with regard to use of marks or the provision of information. Offences against s.12 are punishable on summary conviction by up to six months' imprisonment or a fine not exceeeding level 5 (currently £5000) or both.

It is recognised that someone may be injured by a product which does not comply with an appropriate safety regulation. Where that is so, s.41 of the Act permits the injured user to sue for compensation for breach of statutory duty.

Prohibition notices

Section 13 re-enacts provisions first introduced by the Consumer Safety Act 1978. Section 13(1)(a) permits the Secretary of State to serve a prohibition notice on any person prohibiting that person, except with the consent of the Secretary of State, from supplying, or from offering to supply, agreeing to supply, exposing for supply or possessing for supply, any relevant goods which the Secretary of State considers are unsafe and which are described in the notice.

A prohibition notice may be made against any individual involved in the manufacture or supply of the unsafe goods. Thus it would include manufacturers, wholesalers, retailers etc. It relates to the prohibition of relevant goods which are defined as being goods to which s.11 applies. The object of such notices is to prevent any individual from introducing unsafe goods into the market or selling them to vulnerable groups, e.g. small toys to children aged under three. A prohibition notice must state that the Secretary of State considers the goods to be unsafe together with the reasons for that decision, the date on which the prohibition notice is to come into effect and the ability of the trader to make representations in writing to the Secretary of State to establish that the goods are safe. If the trader wishes to challenge the prohibition notice, he should compile a full written report with all the relevant details, expert opinions etc. to establish the safety of the product. The Secretary of State must either revoke the notice or appoint somebody to consider further representations from the trader and to examine any relevant witnesses according to the procedure laid down in Schedule 2 to the Act. Ultimately, the Secretary of State can confirm the order or revoke or vary it although it cannot be varied to be more restrictive on the trader.

Section 13(1)(b) permits the Secretary of State to serve a notice on any person requiring him to publish at his own expense, in a form and manner and on occasions specified in the notice, a warning about any relevant goods which the Secretary of State considers are unsafe, which that person supplies or has supplied and which are described in the notice. Relevant goods mean any goods to which s.11 applies together with growing crops or things comprised in the land by virtue of being attached to it. To date, this provision has never been used.

Offences against s.13 are punishable in the same way as those under s.12.

Suspension notices

Speed is of the essence when seeking to prevent dangerous goods from being sold in the market. Therefore, s.14 provides the enforcement authority, i.e. trading standards departments, with the ability to act quickly to remove unsafe goods from supply. It provides that where the authority has reasonable grounds for believing that any safety provision has been contravened in relation to any goods, it can serve a suspension notice on any person prohibiting them from supplying, offering to supply, agreeing to supply or exposing for supply the goods for a period not exceeding six months. Note that it only requires 'reasonable grounds' for belief and not absolute proof of the contravention of a safety provision. This approach is necessary to encourage effective enforcement. The suspension notice must describe the goods sufficiently, set out the reasons for believing that a safety provision has been contravened and explain the person's right of appeal under s.15. Breach of a safety provision in this context includes breach of the general safety requirement, a safety regulation, a prohibition notice or a suspension notice. A suspension notice can only be served once, unless either criminal proceedings are pending against the person for breach of a safety provision or the goods are in the process of being forfeited under ss.16 or 17. During the period of the suspension notice the enforcement authority has the right to be kept informed about the whereabouts of the goods. If it is established that there had not been any contravention of a safety provision in respect of those goods and that the notice was not served as a result of the neglect or default of the person, then the person upon whom the notice was served is entitled to compensation.

Appeals against a suspension notice must be taken under s.15, decisions not being subject to judicial review as established in *R v Birmingham City Council ex parte Ferrero Ltd* [1993] 1 All ER 544.

In the *Ferrero Ltd* decision, the plaintiffs were the manufacturer of a chocolate novelty called a 'Kinder Surprise Egg'. This comprised a small chocolate egg in which was placed a plastic capsule containing the pieces to construct a child's toy, some of which were a model of the Pink Panther. A three year old child died after swallowing a foot from one of these toys. Birmingham City Council issued a suspension notice which, despite offers of undertakings from the plaintiffs, they refused to withdraw. Ferrero Ltd sought judicial review to have the council's decision quashed. The Court of Appeal refused the application judging that the purpose of the suspension notice as issued was to remove dangerous goods from the market as envisaged by the Act and that the statutory appeal procedure under s.15 was adequate to allow the plaintiffs to put their case.

It was made clear in the *Ferrero Ltd* case that an enforcement authority is not under any duty to consult a trader either before or after the service of a suspension notice as that would frustrate the purpose of permitting the immediate withdrawal of unsafe goods. The statutory appeal system combined with the right to compensation if a suspension notice has been served wrongly is adequate to achieve justice.

Forfeiture

Under s.16 (s.17 in Scotland) an enforcement authority may apply to the court for an order for the forfeiture of any goods if there has been a breach of a safety provision in respect of those goods. This will apply also if goods from the same consignment or batch, or goods of the same design have been the subject of a contravention. The court has the authority to order that the goods be destroyed or that they be given to a specified person for repair or reconditioning or for use as scrap. Under s.16(5) anybody aggrieved by such a decision may appeal to the Crown Court with the order for destruction or disposition of the goods being suspended until after the decision of the appeal.

Enforcement

Part IV of the Act (ss.27–35) contains details of the enforcement powers given to local authority enforcement officers enforcing Parts II and III of the Act (no enforcement powers are needed in respect of Part I as it relates only to civil law rights and compensation). The powers contained in ss.27–35 are typical of those contained in most criminal consumer legislation including the Trade Descriptions Act 1968, the Food Safety Act 1990 and the Weights and Measures Act 1985. Indeed, standard wording is often used.

The powers given under the Consumer Protection Act 1987 include the power to make test purchases, to search premises and to seize goods and records. The obstruction of an authorised officer acting in pursuance of the Act is an offence punishable by a fine not exceeding level 5 on the standard scale. Naturally, the Act provides an appeal procedure against the detention of goods together with provisions for compensation if there has not been any contravention of any safety provision in relation to the seized goods.

EEC developments

The EEC Directive on General Product Safety, 92/59/EEC was adopted on 29 June 1992 with Member States being required to promulgate appropriate national legislation to take effect no later than 29 June 1994. Regulations are currently being drafted by the Department of Trade and Industry with the intent of achieving this aim. These regulations will replace Part II of the Consumer Protection Act 1987 as the major mechanism for controlling the safety of goods to which they apply with any conflicting provisions in Part II being overruled or replaced. Part II will still have a role in that it will continue to apply in any situation not covered by the new regulations.

The ambit of the new regulations is dictated by Art.2 of the Directive which provides that it applies to 'products', defined as being 'any manufactured, processed or agricultural product supplied whether for consideration or not in the course of a business, and whether new, used or reconditioned'.

This definition means that the new regulations will apply to a wider range of products than either Part I or Part II of the Consumer Protection Act 1987 as Part I of the Act (governing civil liability) does not include agricultural products while Part II expressly excludes liability for food. Under this new regime, food will be subject to the same general safety requirement as other products rather than the very specific food safety requirement currently contained in the Food Safety Act 1990 (*see* next chapter).

The new regulations revolve around the concepts of the 'safe product' and the 'dangerous product', the basic obligation being that suppliers should only place safe products on the market. A product is to be deemed dangerous if it does not satisfy the definition of 'safe product' contained in Art.2. This is one which 'during its foreseeable time of use, does not present any risk or only one reduced to such a level taking account of the product's use, considered as acceptable and consistent with a high standard of protection for the health and safety of persons'. This statement declares both the standard of safety to be demanded, i.e. one consistent with a high level of protection, and the period during which the product must be safe, i.e. during its foreseable time of use. The length of this period will vary from product to product and hence can only be evaluated in context. Also worthy of note is the fact that the definition specifically refers to the protection of the health of persons. Thus the issues discussed in *R* v *Secretary of Sate for Health ex parte US Tobacco International Inc* are put beyond doubt. The protection of health is a relevant factor in determining the safety of a product.

When evaluating product safety, Art.3 requires that consideration must be given to a variety of factors including its composition, execution, wrapping, presentation and labelling, conditions of assembly, maintenance or disposal, instructions for handling or use and its direct and indirect effect upon or in combination with other products. This provides a very broad range of factors to be assessed.

The regulations further require that the safety of a product should be viewed against its intended use or reasonably foreseeable use having regard to any specific statement made by the supplier. This places a reasonable limitation on the liability of suppliers in that they will not be criminally liable in respect of any product proving unsafe when misused. The regulations demand that particular regard must be paid to the 'normal behaviour' of children which presumably might involve foreseeable misuse of the product.

The test of safety is not absolute. If it were, no product would ever be classed as safe. Article 2 provides an approach very similar to Part I of the Consumer Protection Act 1987, that a product will not be classed as 'not safe' or 'dangerous' purely because it is feasible to obtain higher levels of safety or to obtain other products that present a lesser degree of risk. A product may still be safe even though it is not the safest on the market.

Potential defendants proliferate for 'supplier' in this context includes the manufacturer of the product, own-branders, the manufacturer's agent (if the manufacturer is not established in the EEC), the importer in the absence of an agent, distributors and other professionals in the supply chain and the commercial supplier of used and/or reconditioned products. However the distributors of other supply chain professionals are liable only to the extent that their activities affect the safety of a marketed product. This includes packaging, assembly, labelling, storage etc. Commercial suppliers are equally liable with other distributors and, unlike Part I of the Consumer Protection Act 1987, cannot escape liability merely by identifying their own supplier. This criminal safety provision imposes a far more stringent liability upon them than does the comparable civil legislation.

Article 3 stipulates the general safety requirement imposed on suppliers, namely to place only safe goods on the market. Article 3(2) clarifies and qualifies this requirement by drawing particular attention to the obligation placed on suppliers to provide potential users or consumers with relevant information. The expressed purpose of this information is to allow the potential user or consumer to assess any significant risk presented by the product which though acceptable is not immediately obvious and take appropriate precautions against those risks throughout the foreseeable use of the product. The provision of such information or warnings, while obviously an important factor in deciding whether a product meets the general safety requirement, does not avoid liability under the requirement or provide a defence if the product proves to be dangerous.

In addition to providing information about the product, suppliers are also under a duty to continue to monitor the safety of a product with a view to being properly informed about any risks that the product might pose. Armed with any such information, the supplier must take any appropriate action including if necessary withdrawing the product from sale or arranging for a product recall. The mechanics of product monitoring might include batch marking to aid subsequent identification of unsafe batches, the sampling of marketed products to ensure compliance with safety standards and the maintenance of an effective system for handling and investigating complaints. Distributors and other professionals in the supply chain must participate as appropriate in the monitoring process by passing on information and cooperating in any necessary actions including, for example, the withdrawal of products from the shelves and using sales records to help identify purchasers for a product recall.

As is usual with regulatory controls in this general area, the Directive provides some defences, even though they are rather limited. Essentially a supplier will be deemed to have complied with the general safety requirement if the product conforms with any Community rules stipulating health and safety requirements with which the product must comply before it can be marketed. In the absence of such EEC rules, compliance with national safety standards will suffice provided those standards conform with EEC requirements. However conformity with such rules does not prevent competent authorities within Member States from imposing restrictions either preventing the product being marketed or requiring its withdrawal from sale.

The state-of-the-art concept (as discussed in chapter 12) is adopted here in that when assessing conformity with the general safety requirement the state-of-the-art allied to practical feasibility is to be assessed along with codes of practice covering health and safety in the relevant sector. Finally, the safety which consumers may reasonably expect is to be considered.

HEALTH AND SAFETY AT WORK ETC. ACT 1974

Businesses and public authorities are equally, if not more, concerned about the safety of goods intended for use in business or public service. This issue is addressed by the Health and Safety at Work etc. Act 1974, s.6(1) of which, as amended by Schedule 3 of the Consumer Protection Act 1987, provides

(1) It shall be the duty of any person who designs, manufactures, imports or supplies any article for use at work or any article of fairground equipment—

    (a) to ensure, so far as is reasonably practicable, that the article is so designed and constructed that it will be safe and without risks to health at all times when it is being set, used, cleaned or maintained by a person at work;

    (b) to carry out or arrange for the carrying out of such testing and examination as may be necessary for the performance of the duty imposed upon him by the preceding paragraph;

    (c) to take such steps as are necessary to secure that persons supplied by that person with the article are provided with adequate information about the use for which the article is designed or has been tested and about any conditions necessary to ensure that it will be safe and without risks to health at all such times as are mentioned in paragraph (a) above and when it is being dismantled and disposed of; and

(d)   to take such steps as are necessary to secure, so far as is reasonably practicable, that persons so supplied are provided with all such revisions of information provided to them by virtue of the preceding paragraph as are necessary by reason of its becoming known that anything gives rise to a serious risk to health or safety.

Section 6(1A) provides for similar duties in respect of the design etc. of fairground equipment.

Section 6(1) is far-reaching in that it applies to importers, manufacturers and anyone involved in the supply of the goods, supply in this context meaning the 'sale, lease, hire or hire-purchase, whether as principal or as agent for another'.

The essential weakness of s.6(1), however, is the level of the duty that it imposes. In this subsection (and indeed throughout other parts of the section) the phrase 'as far as is reasonably practicable' is used. This means that many of the offences created by the section are not absolute or even strict in nature but are similar to the civil law duties in negligence. Thus if a defendant can prove that further safety features were not practical, no offence will be committed. This duty is lower than that commonly found in consumer safety legislation which tends to impose strict liability offences subject to statutory defences.

Not all the duties imposed by s.6(1) carry this relatively light burden. Section 6(1)(b) provides an absolute duty to ensure that the appropriate testing has been carried out either by the person or another. Similarly, s.6(1)(c) contains an absolute duty to ensure that adequate information and warnings are provided to ensure that the article can be used safely and without risks to health both when it is being set, used, cleaned or maintained and when it is being disposed of or dismantled. Section 6(1)(d) emphasises that the defendant's responsibility for the product does not end when he supplies it. There is a continuing duty to provide further information about serious risks to health or safety, so far as is reasonably practicable, to people to whom goods have been supplied.

Section 6(2) places an absolute duty on the designers and manufacturers of articles for use at work, to ensure that all necessary research is done to eliminate or minimise, as far as is reasonably practical, any risk to health or safety posed by the article.

Section 6(3) turns to the installation or erection of articles for use at work by placing a duty on installers and erectors to ensure, as far as is reasonably practical, that nothing about the way an article is installed or erected will make it unsafe or a risk to health when it is being set, used, cleaned or maintained.

Thus far, the section has dealt with articles for use at work, but s.6(4) and (5) move on to place similar duties in respect of substances, defined as including 'any natural or artificial substance, whether in solid or liquid form or in the form of a gas or vapour'. This would include, for example, chemicals for use in school laboratories or substances used by local authority officers for the control of vermin. Section 6(4) provides that manufacturers, importers and suppliers must ensure, as far as is reasonably practical, that such substances are safe when being used, handled, processed, stored or transported. The remainder of the subsection echoes the s.6(1) duties of arranging for testing and the provision of information. Section 6(5) requires the carrying out of necessary research.

Defences

Section 6(6) to (8) provide some defences to persons to whom s.6 applies. First, s.6(6) makes clear that there is no need for a potential defendant to repeat any testing that has previously been carried out by someone else if it is reasonable for him to rely on such tests. Thus, for example, it would be reasonable for a defendant supplier to rely on the fact that an article carries the BSI Kitemark in respect of those factors to which the Kitemark applies. This is particularly pertinent to alleged offences against s.6(2) and (5).

Section 6(7) makes clear that the duty imposed by s.6 is restricted to a supplier who supplies 'in the course of a trade, business or other undertaking carried on by him (whether for profit or not) and to matters within his control'. However, the breadth of this phrase is far wider than under other Acts such as the Trade Descriptions Act 1968 where the course of a trade or business has been relevant. Here the duty extends beyond trade or business and into other undertakings under the defendant's control. Of particular note is the fact that the undertaking need not be profit making. It is difficult to envisage how someone supplying articles for use in work would be able to use this defence.

Finally, s.6(8) provides a defence if the designer, manufacturer, importer or supplier of an article (note substances are not included) has supplied the article to another person on the basis of a written undertaking that the other person will undertake the necessary steps to ensure that the article is safe. Note that it must be a written undertaking, an oral one will not suffice.

Enforcement

Enforcement of s.6 is undertaken primarily by inspectors from the Health and Safety Commission. Sections 20–26 of the Act stipulate the enforcement powers available to the inspectors. They include, as one would expect, powers of entry, examination and seizure. As under the Food Safety Act (see next chapter), enforcement officers can issue improvement notices requiring the remedy of contraventions of the Act and prohibition notices prohibiting the recipient from carrying on specified activities which breach the Act.

Civil liability

Section 47 of the Act makes clear that a breach of s.6 does not give a civil law right of action to anyone who has been injured as a result of the breach. In practice, however, it is likely that such an incident would give rise to action in negligence.

Recent regulations

Health and safety at work is being promoted further by the use of regulations which give force to EEC Directives. Six sets of such regulations came into force early in 1993 although there are delays in implementing them in existing workplaces for periods of up to four years in some instances. Some of the new regulations relate specifically to goods that will be used in the workplace, these being the Health and Safety (Display Screen Equipment) Regulations 1992 (S.I. 1992/2792), the Provision and Use of Work Equipment Regulations 1992 (S.I. 1992/2932), and the Personal Protective Equipment at Work (PPE) Regulations 1992 (S.I. 1992/2966). The remaining new regulations relate to the management of the work environment and are the Management of Health and Safety at Work Regulations 1992 (S.I. 1992/2051), the Workplace (Health Safety and Welfare) Regulations 1992 (S.I. 1992/3004) and the Manual Handling Operations Regulations (S.I. 1992/2793).

QUESTION

G Ltd is an importer of toys. He supplied Fred, a retailer, with some long haired dolls which had been manufactured outside the EEC. There was no recommended minimum age at which children should have access to one of these dolls. Mary bought one from Fred and gave it to her daughter, Jessica, aged two. A few hours later Mary discovered Jessica chewing a large piece of the doll's hair which had become detached from the doll's scalp. She reported the incident to Upshire Trading Standards Department.

Advise the Trading Standards Department about any possible offences contrary to Part II of the Consumer Protection Act 1987.

FURTHER READING

Goodman, M.J., *Health and Safety at Work : Law and Practice* 1988 (Sweet and Maxwell)

Harvey, B.W. and Parry, D.L., *The Law of Consumer Protection and Fair Trading* (4th ed) 1992 (Butterworth)

Janner, G., *Janner's Complete Product Liability* 1988 (Business Books Ltd)

Keenan, D. and Riches, S., *Business Law* (3rd ed) 1993 (Pitman)

Pitt, G. (ed), *Butterworth's Commercial Law Handbook* (Butterworth)

Royce-Lewis, C.A., *Product Liability and Consumer Safety* 1988 (ICSA)

Wright, C.J., *Product Liability – The Law and its Implication for Risk Management* 1989 (Blackstone Press)

CHAPTER 15

Food safety

INTRODUCTION

Food, like water, is in an unusual position in that it is both intended for internal consumption and is essential to the health and well-being of a normal healthy person. Given this status, the quality of food is an issue of particular importance.

Food quality has been subject to some measure of control since the passage of the Assize of Bread and Ale 1266. Modern food law dates from the mid-nineteenth century with the latest statute being the Food Safety Act 1990. This statute provides more extensive control than was the case previously and adopts a rationale of control 'from the plough to the plate'.

FOOD

Section 1 identifies food for the purposes of the Act as including:

(a) drink;
(b) articles and substances of no nutritional value which are used for human consumption;
(c) chewing gum and other products of a like nature and use; and
(d) articles and substances used as ingredients in the preparation of food or anything falling within this subsection.

It does not include live animals or birds, or live fish which are not used for human consumption while they are alive, animal, bird or fish fodder or feeding stuff, controlled drugs and medicinal products. These items are governed by other statutes including the Agriculture Act 1970 and the Medicines Act 1968.

The word 'substances' as used in s.1 is defined in s.53 to include 'any natural or artificial substance or other matter whether it is in solid or liquid form or in the form of a gas or vapour'. This acknowledges the trend in modern food production that a large percentage of foodstuffs supplied commercially will include an artificial substance of some sort be it colourant, preservative, anti-oxidant, emulsifier etc. Many of these have no real nutritional value but are used to make the food last longer, spread more easily or be more appealing to the eye or palate.

Section 3 contains a presumption that any food commonly used for human consumption shall, if sold or offered, exposed or kept for sale be intended to be sold for human consumption. This effectively reverses the burden of proof leaving it to the defendant to establish that the food was not so intended.

SALE AND COMMERCIAL OPERATIONS

The Act seeks to exert increased control both by the extension of the Act to persons not previously covered by food safety legislation and also by an extension to the meaning of the word 'sale' and thereby to the number and types of situations covered.

A 'business' is defined in s.1 to include 'the undertaking of a canteen, club, school, hospital or institution, whether carried on for profit or not, and any undertaking or activity carried out by a public or local authority'. Thus, for the first time, local authorities are subject to prosecution under food safety legislation, a significant burden given the volume and variety of food that may be purchased, stored and supplied by a local authority through its schools etc. Indeed, depending upon the contracting arrangements within any particular authority, individual schools may be classed as businesses and prosecuted for offences against the Act. Similarly, colleges and universities will be liable for the supply of food in their refectories and hospitals for the food they supply to their patients. A business becomes a 'food business' when commercial operations with respect to food or food sources (defined as growing crops, live animals, birds or fish from which food is to be derived by harvesting, slaughtering, milking, collecting eggs or otherwise) are carried out. At the moment all premises used for the purpose of a food business must be registered but this system seems likely to be withdrawn within the next year.

In considering the breadth of 'commercial operations' we must first address the definition of 'sale' which underlies both the meaning of commercial operations and the main offences under the Act. The meaning of 'sale' under the Food Safety Act 1990 is far wider than that considered previously under the Sale of Goods Act 1979. In addition to the accepted meaning of 'sale', it includes for the purpose of this Act

(a) the supply of food, otherwise than on sale, in the course of a business; and
(b) any other thing which is done with respect to food and is specified in an order by the Minister,

with references to purchasers and purchasing being construed accordingly. Further, the Act extends to any food offered as a prize or reward or given away in connection with entertainment (including social gatherings, amusement, exhibition, performance, game, sport or trial of skill), any food offered as a prize, reward or gift for the purposes of an advertisement or in furtherance of a trade or business and any food exposed or deposited in any premises for the purposes described above. Given the breadth of this definition, it seems likely that virtually any supply of food, other than in a purely private or domestic situation, is likely to fall within the definition of 'sale' and thus be subject to the provisions of the Act.

'Commercial operations' are defined as being any of the following, namely

(a) selling, possessing for sale and offering, exposing or advertising for sale;
(b) consigning, delivering or serving by way of sale;
(c) preparing for sale or presenting, labelling or wrapping for the purpose of sale;
(d) storing or transporting for the purpose of sale;
(e) importing and exporting.

Again, this is a very wide definition and would include virtually any activity in relation to food or contact materials carried out by a food business.

RENDERING FOOD INJURIOUS

The enforcement of food safety is promoted through two criminal offences and a selection of notices and orders that can be used to support and encourage food safety.

Section 7 of the Act makes it an offence to render any food injurious to health by any of the following means:

(a) adding any article or substance to the food;
(b) using any article or substance as an ingredient in the preparation of the food;
(c) abstracting any constituent from the food;
(d) subjecting the food to any other process or treatment with the intent that it shall be sold for human consumption.

In establishing whether food is injurious to health, regard must be given not only to the probable effect of the food on the person consuming it but also on the probable cumulative effect on the health of a person consuming it in ordinary quantities. Injury means any impairment whether temporary or permanent.

It seems unlikely that any food producer would wilfully render his food injurious because of the obvious resultant effects on publicity and future sales. However it is quite feasible that normal production processes may render the food injurious nonetheless. For example, a normal part of food production is the addition of additives. Suspicions have been raised about the long-term effect of some additives and the possibility that they may cause a variety of disorders such as hyperactivity in children or even cancer. Given the increasing sophistication of analytical techniques and advances in medical science it seems feasible that ultimately such a link will be established beyond doubt and that someone will be held criminally liable in respect of the addition of a normal additive. Note that it is a strict liability offence though subject to the statutory defences provided in the Act.

Of course, any food business, including local authorities, may be the victims of sabotage either by a disgruntled employee or by a blackmailer making criminal demands against the threat of introducing injurious articles into the food thereby affecting both production and sales. Clearly, such a person would be liable under s.7 although, in practice, they are likely to face far more serious criminal charges.

Food can only be rendered injurious to health by one of the methods specified in s.7. However, this does not include all the foreseeable methods. As Howells, Bradgate and Griffiths point out the section does not include rendering food injurious by failing to subject it to some process or treatment. Thus no liability under s.7 would arise in respect of such food.

THE FOOD SAFETY REQUIREMENT

Section 8 provides the more general offence of food not satisfying the food safety requirement. It reads:

> Any person who—
> (a) sells for human consumption, or offers, exposes or advertises for sale for such consumption, or has in his possession for the purpose of such sale or of preparation for such sale: or
> (b) deposits with, or consigns to, any other person for the purpose of such sale, any food which fails to comply with the food safety requirement shall be guilty of an offence.

Again, this is a wide reaching provision that is likely to cover all situations in which someone deals with food. There is no requirement that a sale has actually occurred for para. (a) extends to mere offers to sell or exposures for sale while para. (b) goes even further by including the mere deposit or consignment of food. Thus, the delivery of unsafe food to a school for preparation for supply would be an offence as would the storage of such food by a school. In practice, local authorities are likely to be the recipients rather than the creators of food that fails the safety requirement and, if in doubt about the quality of the food, should inform the duly authorised enforcement officers. If a school or other local authority institution were to continue to store unsafe food or serve it to diners, the authority would commit an offence itself.

Section 8, like s.7, creates a strict liability offence with no *mens rea* requirement. Thus, the knowledge and intentions of the defendant are irrelevant other than the intention to sell the food within the meaning of the Act.

Section 8 does not provide a general safety requirement in the way that s.10 of the Consumer Protection Act 1987 does. Instead it defines what constitutes unsafe food in this context. Section 8(2) stipulates the three ways in which food may be deemed to fail the food safety requirement, namely:

(a) it has been rendered injurious to health by one of the means mentioned in section 7(1);
(b) it is unfit for human consumption;
(c) it is so contaminated (whether by extraneous matter or otherwise) that it would not be reasonable to expect it to be used for human consumption in that state.

The first two appear clear cut while the third is worthy of comment. Food is likely to become contaminated by the growth of a mould or the development of an infestation such as, for example, maggots, or by the presence of a foreign object. With respect to the existence of a contaminant the section requires that the contamination means that it is not reasonable for the food to be used for human consumption. In respect of a mould growth this may be so even though the mould does not present a health risk to a human being (*David Greig Ltd* v *Goldfinch* (1961) 105 Sol Jo 307). With regard to an extraneous object, there is an implication that it must affect the food microbiologically such as to render it unfit for human consumption. An object such as, for example, a milk bottle top in a loaf of bread which would not have a microbiological effect on the food may not create an offence under this section. In practice, it would be prosecuted under s.14 as being food not of the nature or substance or quality demanded by the purchaser. Naturally, anyone storing food for sale must be careful to ensure that it does not become unfit through poor storage, a problem particularly pertinent to perishable food. Further, care must be taken to ensure that foodstuffs do not become contaminated by mould, infestation or through contact with extraneous objects.

As with s.7 matters, if purchasers (be it local authority or otherwise) are of the belief that food with which they have been supplied does not meet the food safety requirement, they should inform the duly authorised enforcement officers.

Enforcement of section 8

Enforcement of s.8 is carried out by authorised officers from the food authorities which include the district and county councils of the non-metropolitan counties, the London borough councils, the Common Council for the City of London and the appropriate Treasurer from the Inner and Middle Temple. In practice, therefore, the vast majority of enforcement work is undertaken by the Environmental Health Departments of district councils and the Trading Standards Departments of county councils. These arrangements will change, however, if the current proposals for local government reorganisation take effect.

Enforcement of food safety law emanates from two sources: regular routine inspection of both food and food premises by authorised officers and also as a result of complaints received from members of the public. Section 9 provides authorised officers with specific powers to enforce the s.8 food safety requirement (more general enforcement powers are available elsewhere in the Act). Officers have the power to inspect all food intended for human consumption at all reasonable hours. In practice, this probably means during normal business hours making allowance for the fact that business hours may vary between different businesses. The power is to inspect the food, not the premises, and thus would seem to extend to any location where the food is sold, stored etc.

Under s.9(2) there is also a right to act where the officer believes, otherwise than on inspection, that any foods are likely to cause food poisoning or any disease communicable to human beings.

In either of these situations the officer has the power to issue a notice to the person in charge of the food stipulating that the food is not to be used for human consumption and is either not to be moved or alternatively is to be moved to a place specified in the notice. In this case the officer has 21 days in which to decide whether the food does comply with the food safety requirement and either withdraw the notice or have it dealt with by a J.P. Alternatively, the officer may seize the food and seek an order from a J.P. for the food to be condemned and destroyed. In this instance, the owner of the food has a right to be heard in the hearing before the J.P.

If the notice is withdrawn or the J.P. refuses to condemn the food, the owner will be entitled to compensation.

NOTICES AND ORDERS

Time is often of the essence in the enforcement of food safety legislation. The preparation of criminal prosecutions takes time while more immediate action is necessary to control imminent health risks. Sections 10–13 of the Act provide for a range of notices and orders, some of which are exercisable by authorised officers and some of which need court involvement or Ministerial action. These provisions are given weight by the fact that a failure to comply with an improvement notice is a strict liability offence while knowingly failing to comply with an order is also an offence. Note that a degree of *mens rea* is needed in this case.

Improvement notice

Section 10 applies to any regulations which make provision

(a) for requiring, prohibiting or regulating the use of any process or treatment in the preparation of food; or
(b) for securing the observance of hygienic conditions and practices in connection with the carrying out of commercial operations with respect to food or food sources.

This would include regulations governing the cleanliness of kitchens and food preparation areas and the maintenance of machinery and utensils to be used in the preparation of food. Thus, the kitchens of restaurants, hospitals and school canteens are equally eligible for inspection and subject to improvement notices if found wanting. Where an authorised officer from an enforcement authority has reasonable grounds for believing that the proprietor of a food business is failing to comply with regulations he may serve a notice stating the grounds for his belief that there is a failure to comply, the matters that constitute the failure, the measures which in the officer's opinion must be taken to secure compliance and the period, being not less than 14 days, within which the measures (or their equivalent) must be undertaken. A failure to comply is an offence.

Prohibition orders

Section 11 deals with prohibition orders which potentially have a far greater impact than improvement notices. If the proprietor of a food business is convicted of breaching a regulation and the court is of the opinion that a health risk is posed by

(a) the use for the purposes of the business of any process or treatment;
(b) the construction of any premises used for the purposes of the business, or the use for those purposes of any equipment; and
(c) the state or condition of any premises used for the purposes of the business

the court may issue an order prohibiting the use of the process, treatment, premises or equipment as appropriate. Further, in similar circumstances, the court can prohibit the proprietor from participating in the management of any food business of a type specified.

When an order is made, the enforcement authority is under a duty to serve a copy of the order on the proprietor of the business and, where appropriate, affix a copy to the premises. An order relating to processes, treatments, premises or equipment continues in force until the enforcement authority certifies that it is satisfied that the risk no longer exists. An order relating to the proprietor of a business is terminated when the court gives a direction to that effect. After a period of six months, the proprietor may apply for such a direction although it is at the court's discretion whether to grant one.

Emergency prohibition notices and orders

Recent outbreaks of food poisoning including salmonella and listeria have proved the need for officers to be able to take immediate action to put an end to a health risk posed by food. Where an authorised officer is of the opinion that the health risk condition discussed above is fulfilled in respect of any food business, he can serve an emergency prohibition notice under s.12(1) on the proprietor of the food business. A magistrates' court if similarly satisfied can issue an emergency prohibition order under s.12(2). Before applying for an order, an officer must give one day's notice to the proprietor of the business. When a notice or an order has been made, a copy must be affixed to the premises and a copy of any order must be served on the proprietor of the business. A notice is effective for only three days unless an application for an emergency prohibition order has been made in which case it remains effective until the application for the order is decided. It is an offence to knowingly fail to comply with either a notice or an order.

Both emergency prohibition notices and orders cease to have effect when the enforcement authority issues a certificate confirming that they are satisfied that the health risk condition no longer exists. The certificate must be issued within three days of the authority being so satisfied. Alternatively, the proprietor of the business can apply for such a certificate, the authority then having fourteen days in which to make its decision and give its reasons for any refusal.

The proprietor of the business is entitled to compensation in respect of the service of the notice if either the enforcement authority fails to apply for an emergency prohibition order within three days or the court is not satisfied that a health risk condition existed at the time that the notice was issued.

Emergency control orders

It is in the nature of modern trading with widespread distribution of foodstuffs that a health risk may be posed across a wide geographic area, well beyond the jurisdiction of any individual enforcement authority. Section 13 provides a solution in the ability of the Minister to issue an emergency control order. Such an order is made when the Minister is satisfied that the carrying out of commercial operations with respect to food, food sources or contact materials involves or may involve imminent risk of injury to health. The Minister has the power to give such directions and do such other things as appear to him to be necessary or expedient to prevent any commercial operations involving food, food sources or contact materials which he reasonably believes are subject to the emergency control order. However, he also has the power to consent, either unconditionally or conditionally, to allow prohibited activities to be undertaken by particular individuals. Such a consent is a defence to any charge of knowingly contravening an emergency control order which normally is an offence.

CONSUMER PROTECTION

The two other major offences contained in the Act have as their rationale the protection of the purchaser rather than the general maintenance of food safety standards. There is a total of six offences created under this Part of the Act which seek to protect the purchaser in relation to quality, description, presentation etc. These provisions are of particular concern to anyone regularly involved in the purchasing of food as they deal with offences relating to specific purchases as opposed to general standards.

Food not of the nature or substance or quality demanded

Section 14 reproduces a provision that has appeared in food safety legislation since 1875 and thus is a well established part of food safety law in this country. Section 14(1) reads:

> Any person who sells to the purchaser's prejudice any food which is not of the nature or substance or quality demanded by the purchaser shall be guilty of an offence.

In this context 'a person' includes both individuals and bodies corporate and unincorporate. Thus any business, be it partnership or limited company, can commit this offence as can any individual. Employers will be liable for the acts of their employees as will principals for the acts of their agents.

The sale must be to the prejudice of the purchaser which will occur if the purchaser does not receive goods of the quality that he ordered and for which he has paid. Thus it follows that prejudice must be considered by reference to what the purchaser thought he was buying, i.e. the contract description. It effectively makes a criminal offence out of a breach of description. It is possible to prevent liability arising if the purchaser is aware of the deficiency in the goods. Thus in the Scottish case of *Brander* v *Kinnear* 1923 JC 42 it was held that a notice disclaiming the purity of the food will be effective if it is brought sufficiently to the attention of the purchaser and it makes clear the nature of the prejudice that he is being asked to accept.

Section 14(2) provides that it is no defence to argue that the purchaser was not prejudiced because he bought for analysis or examination. This is a very important provision given that much of the routine enforcement of s.14 involves the purchase of foodstuffs by enforcement staff for analysis by a public analyst. This is crucial to the enforcement of regulations relating to the constituent elements of products such as meat and spreadable fish products, milk and milk products and soft drinks all of which are subject to control as regards their percentage constituents but which can only be checked via analysis. Many of these regulations are being reviewed.

While s.14 ostensibly governs the sale of food, the decision of *Meah* v *Roberts* [1978] 1 All ER 97 makes clear that it covers anything that is sold as food. In that case liability existed when caustic soda instead of lemonade was supplied to a child.

The section creates three distinct offences as held in *Bastin* v *Davies* [1950] 1 All ER 1095. Thus the prosecution must decide which of the three, nature, substance or quality, it wishes to pursue. The terms do overlap to some extent and it is feasible for a prosecution to be brought equally successfully under more than one heading.

Food will not be of the nature demanded if it is different from that ordered even though the product supplied is pure. Thus, caustic soda is not lemonade, jam is not honey and milk is not cream.

It is not of the substance demanded if it fails to satisfy any regulations controlling its constituent elements as described above or if it fails to satisfy a generic description applicable to those goods. Thus in *Anderson* v *Britcher* (1913) 78 JP 65 there was no offence committed when sugar originating from Mauritius was described as 'Demerara sugar', it being held that 'demerara sugar' had become a generic term with which the sugar complied. Naturally, it would be an offence against s.1 of the Trade Descriptions Act 1968 to state that a foodstuff had been manufactured in a particular place if this was not true.

Milk is of the substance demanded even if the fat content is below that demanded by regulations as long as the milk is as it came from the cow. Such was held in *Few* v *Robinson* [1921] 3 KB 504.

Anness v *Grivell* [1915] 3 KB 685 held that 'quality' relates not merely to the description of the foodstuff but also to its commercial quality. Thus if the quality is inferior to that reasonably expected by the purchaser given the description, price etc., an offence would be committed.

Naturally, food will not be of the quality demanded if it is adulterated. Thus foodstuffs that contain extraneous objects such as string in a loaf of bread, glass in babyfood and a straw in a bottle of milk would all create offences under this section. There is some overlap with the food safety requirement in s.8 as discussed earlier.

Falsely describing or presenting food

Section 15 creates three offences relating to the false or misleading description, advertising or presentation of food. The offences are all linked to the nature or substance or quality of the food. Thus it is an offence to provide a label (whether or not attached to or printed on the wrapper or container) or to publish an advertisement which either falsely describes the goods or is likely to mislead as to the nature or substance or quality of the food. Further, s.15(3) creates a new offence of selling, offering or exposing food 'the presentation of which is likely to mislead as to the nature or substance or quality of the food'.

An offence relating to a label or advertisement can be committed even though the offending description contained an accurate statement of the composition of the food.

Section 15 is supplemented by the Food Labelling Regulations 1984 (S.I. 1984/1305)(as amended) which are probably the most important set of regulations relating to food. These require most foods to be marked with the name of the food, a list of ingredients in weight descending order excluding water, details of minimum durability, any special storage instructions and the name or address of the manufacturer, packer or seller.

The likely duration of foodstuffs in good condition is of importance particularly for perishable products. These must be marked with a 'use by' date, it being an offence to sell foodstuffs after the date specified. By contrast, 'best before' dates, found on a variety of foodstuffs, are merely to guide the purchaser as to the likely storage period of the goods, no offence being committed by selling goods after that date. 'Sell by' dates are no longer legal.

REGULATIONS

Regulations play a central part in the control of food safety. Section 16 of the Food Safety Act 1990 gives power to the Minister to make regulations governing every aspect of food production and sale including, *inter alia*, the composition of food, microbiological standards, processes and treatments, hygienic conditions, labelling, marking and securing compliance with the food safety requirement. Regulations enacted under previous statutes, e.g. the Food Labelling Regulations 1984 (as amended), have been adopted by the 1990 Act.

Sections 17–19 provide the Minister with other regulatory powers to regulate compliance with Community obligations, matters relating to novel foods and the registration and licensing of food premises.

DEFENCES

Section 21 provides for a 'due diligence' defence bringing defences for food safety legislation into line with those contained in other criminal regulatory legislation including the Trade Descriptions Act 1968 and the Weights and Measures Act 1985.

Section 21(1) creates a single strand defence requiring the defendant to show that he took all reasonable precautions and exercised all due diligence to avoid the commission of the offence either by himself or by someone under his control. However he is not required to establish the act or default of another, reliance on information, mistake etc. stipulated in the version of the defence found in the Trade Descriptions Act 1968 (see chapter 13). In practice, of course, it may be necessary to establish one of these as a means of demonstrating due diligence. A defendant cannot plead the act or default of another or reliance on information provided by another unless he has served a notice to that effect on the prosecutor at least seven days before the hearing and provided such information as he can to assist in identifying that other person. If the defendant has already appeared in court in connection with the offence, the notice must also be within one month of the first such appearance.

As under the Trade Descriptions Act 1968, reasonable precautions and due diligence would be established by showing that an effective quality control system had been set up and was functioning correctly. This would include an appropriate level of product sampling and testing by the defendant.

In addition to the general defence, s.21(2) provides a specific defence for persons charged with offences contrary to s.8 (food safety requirement), s.14 (selling food not of the nature or substance or quality demanded) and s.15 (falsely describing or presenting food). If such persons have neither prepared the offending food themselves nor imported it into Britain, they will be presumed to have satisfied the due diligence defence provided they can establish three things, namely

(a) that the commission of the offence was due to an act or default of another person who was not under his control, or to reliance on information supplied by such a person;
(b) that the sale or intended sale of which the alleged offence consisted was not a sale or intended sale under his mark; and
(c) that he did not know, and could not reasonably have been expected to know, at the time of the commission of the alleged offence that his act or omission would amount to an offence under the relevant provision.

Own-branders would not be able to satisfy para. (b) of this defence. However, a similar but stricter defence applies to them if in addition to (a) above an own-brander can also establish

(b) that he carried out all such checks of the food in question as were reasonable in all the circumstances, or that it was reasonable in all the circumstances for him to rely on checks carried out by the person who supplied the food to him; and
(c) that he did not know and had no reason to suspect at the time of the commission of the alleged offence that his act or omission would amount to an offence under the relevant provision.

As with Part I of the Consumer Protection Act 1987, own-branding exposes the trader to a more stringent legal liability and must be balanced against the potential marketing advantages that it offers.

Section 20 of the Act provides a by-pass procedure the same as that discussed previously in relation to s.23 of the Trade Descriptions Act 1968 (see chapter 13). It permits the prosecution to proceed directly against the person by whose act or default the offence was committed irrespective of whether proceedings are taken against the primary offender. As with the Trade Descriptions Act, the prosecution will need to establish the existence of a *prima facie* offence by the primary offender, it being irrelevant whether he would have a valid defence.

Finally, s.22 provides the standard defence for a person publishing misleading advertisements who can show that it is his business to publish or arrange for the publication of advertisements and also that he received the advertisement in the ordinary course of business and did not know and had no reason to suspect that its publication would constitute an offence.

ENFORCEMENT

As discussed earlier, enforcement of the Act is undertaken by the designated food authorities. In addition to the specific powers given by ss.9–12 to authorised officers from those authorities, more general enforcement powers are contained in Part III of the Act. These give an authorised officer the power to take samples, powers of entry, access to records and the right to seize and detain any records which he has reason to believe may be required as evidence of an offence against the Act or any regulations or orders made thereunder.

QUESTION

Jenny runs a catering business. She has a contract to supply the catering facilities in the factory canteen of H Ltd, a local manufacturer, and uses the factory kitchens to prepare hot snacks. One lunchtime, she served a hot sausage roll infested with maggots to Joe. The environmental health officer visiting the premises in response to a complaint from Joe, noticed that the 'use by' dates on some of the yoghurts on display had expired.

Discuss Jenny's criminal liabilities under the Food Safety Act 1990.

FURTHER READING

Harvey, B.W. and Parry, D.L., *The Law of Consumer Protection and Fair Trading* (4th ed) 1992 (Butterworth)

Howells, G., Bradgate, R. and Griffiths, M., *Blackstone's Guide to the Food Safety Act 1990* 1990 (Blackstone Press)

Stephenson, G., 'Due diligence and Food Safety' (1991) 155 JP 781

CHAPTER 16

Weights and measures

INTRODUCTION

Large purchases of goods are typically sold either by reference to a unit of length, area, volume, capacity, weight or, alternatively, by a specified number of pre-packs of goods each of a given amount. In either instance, purchasers will want to ensure that they have received the full quantity of goods for which they have paid under the terms of the contract of sale. The Weights and Measures Act 1985 is the statute which currently provides the framework for ensuring that purchasers do not receive short quantity when buying goods.

Goods bought by reference to a unit of size may be sold by length, area, volume, capacity, or weight, Parts I to V of Schedule 1 of the Act stipulating the units of measurement, both imperial and metric, that are legal for use for trade in the UK. The gradual metrication of our system of weights and measures means that both the imperial and the metric systems are currently in use although there is a move towards the total metrication of our system with all products being sold in metric quantities. At the moment some derogations exist whereby certain products may still be sold by imperial measure, e.g. draught beer until 1999.

OFFENCES OF SHORT WEIGHT OR MEASURE

The 1985 Act provides for various offences relating to the giving of short weight or measure when selling goods, although which Part of the Act applies depends on whether goods are sold by reference to quantity or whether they are sold in 'regulated packages', i.e. made up according to the average quantity principle. Where they are sold by weight, measurement or number Part IV of the Act will apply while Part V applies to goods sold in regulated packages. Hence Part IV offences relate to items such as bulk deliveries of coal and fuel oil, delivery of pre-packed goods in excess of the normal 10kg/10 litres upper limit for goods being controlled by the Part V average quantity requirements.

Goods sold by weight, measurement or number

Section 28(1) provides the general offence relating to short quantity goods and applies to the sale of goods sold by quantity. It reads

> Subject to sections 33 to 37 below (the statutory defences), any person who, in selling or purporting to sell any goods by weight or other measurement or by number, delivers or causes to be delivered to the buyer—
>
> (a) a lesser quantity than that purported to be sold; or
> (b) a lesser quantity than corresponds with the price charged,
>
> shall be guilty of an offence.

The section can apply both at wholesale and retail level but is restricted to incidents when the defendant is selling or purporting to sell the goods. In practice, local authorities are likely to be buying for use rather than resale and thus are unlikely to commit an offence under this section. By contrast, companies may be buying goods for the purposes of resale in which case an offence may be committed if short quantity were given at that time.

As the section states, it is an offence to provide a quantity less than that purported to be sold.

In *Frank H Mann (Torquay) Ltd* v *Womersley* (1972) (unreported, but quoted by O'Keefe) an offence was committed when a trader sold a box of apples accompanied by an invoice which stated '1 case of 30lbs of Bramleys' but which actually weighed 25lb 11 oz. The matter was complicated further by the fact that the purchaser, the Corporation of Torquay, had ordered 28lb of apples.

By the same token a deficiency in the amount of any of the following delivered pursuant to a contract would create an offence, e.g. heating oil by volume for use in schools, ballast sold by weight for use by a highways department, potatoes bought by weight for use in canteens or crayons sold by number for use in nursery schools.

If a purchaser believes that he has received short weight goods he can, of course, ask a duly authorised inspector of weights and measures to weigh the goods for him to establish the actual weight. Of course, the practical limitation to this power is that the goods delivered must be capable of identification and not have become mixed in any way with any other goods. Thus, for example, coal cannot be re-weighed if it has been deposited into a bunker in which some coal remains from a previous delivery. In addition, coal poses particular problems in that its weight will vary depending on how wet it is.

The purchaser has another line of action in very particular circumstances. Under s.41 where any road vehicle is loaded with goods for sale by weight to a single buyer, or for delivery to the buyer after they have been so sold, the buyer or seller of the goods can demand that the driver of the road vehicle gets the vehicle check-weighed to confirm the weight of the goods.

Thus, for example, if a lorryload of topsoil sold by weight is being delivered to a local authority leisure services department, the authority can demand that it be check-weighed. It is an offence to refuse to have a vehicle check-weighed if so requested by the seller or buyer of the goods.

An offence under s.28(1) is also committed if the goods supplied do not correspond to the price charged. Thus for example, if a contract was for '£30 worth of meat at £1-50p per lb' an offence would be committed if less than 20lb were delivered.

It must be remembered that the purpose of s.28 is to attach criminal liability for the delivery of a short quantity of goods. It does not provide the purchaser with compensation. The civil law remedies of the buyer are set out in s.30(1) of the Sale of Goods Act 1979 as discussed in chapter 9. It provides that where the seller of goods delivers a quantity less than that he contracted to sell, the buyer may reject the goods or alternatively may accept them and pay for them at the contract rate. Thus the contract price would be reduced to reflect accurately the quantity of goods actually delivered.

Sections 29–31 of the 1985 Act create other offences that are connected with the sale of short quantity. Section 29 makes it an offence in the sale or purchase of any goods or when offering goods for sale or purchase to make any representation, whether oral or otherwise, calculated to mislead anyone buying or selling the goods as to the quantity of the goods. In this context 'calculated to mislead' means 'likely to mislead' rather than 'intended to mislead'. Such a misdescription could also constitute an offence against s.1 of the Trade Descriptions Act 1968 and could give rise to civil liability under s.13 of the Sale of Goods Act 1979 and the laws governing misrepresentation.

Section 30(1) deals with statements made when goods covered by this Part of the Act are pre-packed in or on containers marked with a written statement as to the weight of the goods. An example would be where apples are pre-packed in a plastic sealed bag and labelled with the statement '5lb net'. If the goods weigh less than the declared weight, an offence will be committed by any person who has them in his possession for sale subject, naturally, to the statutory defences not being available. Further, if the deficiency cannot be accounted for by anything that has happened to the goods after they had been sold by retail sale to the buyer or his representative, an offence will have been committed by anyone who sold or agreed to sell the goods in their pre-packed state. Section 30(2) provides a similar offence for non-pre-packed goods.

Section 31(1) which provides the last offence in this group states that, in relation to goods which are required by Part IV of the Act to be accompanied by a document containing particular statements, it shall be an offence to make materially incorrect statements.

Defences

The two major defences in Part IV are to be found in ss.33 and 34 and relate to written warranties and due diligence.

Section 33 provides a written warranty defence similar to that provided previously under food safety legislation. The defendant can employ the defence if he bought the goods from some other person as being of the quantity represented and was provided with a written warranty that the quantity was correct. Further, the defendant must show that he believed that the statement in the warranty was accurate and had no reason to doubt its accuracy. If the warranty was provided by a person outside Great Britain, the defendant must also have taken reasonable steps to check its accuracy. If he wishes to rely on a warranty defence, the defendant must send a copy of the written warranty together with the name and address of the person who provided it to the prosecutor at least three days before the date of the hearing.

Section 34 contains the due diligence defence similar to that already discussed in relation to both the Trade Descriptions Act 1968 and the Food Safety Act 1990. In this Act it is a single strand defence requiring that the defendant took all reasonable precautions and exercised all due diligence to avoid the commission of the offence. The test promulgated by Fisher J in *Tesco Supermarkets Ltd* v *Nattrass* requiring the defendant to demonstrate that he had established an efficient quality control system and then ensured that it functioned correctly would be equally applicable here. This would include such factors as appropriate sampling of the product to ensure compliance as in *Garrett* v *Boots Cash Chemists Ltd* and *Sherratt* v *Gerald's The American Jewellers Ltd* discussed earlier. A case decided under the Weights and Measures Act 1979 is *Bibby-Cheshire* v *Golden Wonder Ltd* [1972] 3 All ER 738.

In the *Golden Wonder* decision, the defendant, a manufacturer of potato crisps, produced approximately 20 million packets per week. The case related to an individual packet which was weight marked 15 grams but only weighed 9 grams. The packets were filled by machine, it being shown that the defendant used the best machines available, that it was statistically impossible not to produce any underweight packets and that none of the machines in use consistently produced deficient packets. Further, an efficient system for the check-weighing of packets randomly was in use. It was held that the defendant had established the due diligence defence.

As with the Food Safety Act 1990 there is no need to demonstrate that the offence was due to the act or default of another or that the defendant had relied on information supplied by another. However if the defendant wishes to adduce such evidence as part of his defence, appropriate notice must be given to the prosecutor.

Sections 35 and 36 provide additional, more limited, defences. Section 35(2) provides for a defence to be available in respect of a deficiency in the quantity of goods as compared with a weight marking on a container or a statement in a document accompanying the goods. In either situation it is a defence to show that the deficiency arose after the marking of the container or statement in the document and further that it was attributable wholly to factors for which reasonable allowance was made when marking the container or making the statement. Section 35(3) provides a further defence if the deficiency is in non-pre-packed food if it can be shown that the deficiency arose through unavoidable evaporation or drainage.

Section 36 provides an unusual defence in that it covers the situation where the inaccuracy in the weight of goods provided is due to an excess of the goods. The defence exists when the defendant can demonstrate that the excess was attributable to the taking of reasonable measures to avoid a deficiency. The civil law position regarding an excess delivery is covered in s.30(2) of the Sale of Goods Act 1979 which provides that where the seller delivers a quantity of goods larger than the buyer had contracted to purchase, the buyer can (a) reject the whole consignment, (b) accept only the amount for which he contracted and reject the remainder or (c) accept the whole consignment and pay for it at the contract rate.

REGULATED PACKAGES

Part V of the Weights and Measures Act 1985 as supplemented by the Weights and Measures (Packaged Goods) Regulations 1986 gives effect to EEC Directives 75/106/EEC and 76/211/EEC which introduced the average quantity system into the UK in respect of certain pre-packed goods.

The introduction of this system constituted a marked shift in weights and measures law in Britain which had been based previously on the net weight concept under which the minimum weight of goods was that marked on the container/wrapper. Enforcement of the system by the weights and measures inspectorate took place largely at retail level.

The average quantity system considers the quantity of goods in a batch rather than individually and dictates that the average quantity of items in the batch as a whole will not be less than the quantity marked on the individual item. The system permits the quantity of some items in the batch to be greater than the nominal quantity while others are less than the nominal quantity. Provision is made for a 'tolerable negative error' (TNE) of approximately 2½% in individual items as long as the batch as a whole complies. While this ensures a consistent standard across a batch, there is no guarantee that any individual item will not be deficient. An individual item only becomes an 'inadequate' (a crucial concept in the system) when its deficiency exceeds twice the TNE (approximately 5%). The production of an inadequate is illegal. Goods that conform with the average quantity system will be 'e' marked.

Enforcement of the average quantity system by the weights and measures inspectorate occurs primarily at packer level where complete batches are available. A batch for this purpose consists of an identifiable collection of items produced by the same process from the same constituent parts. Alternatively, where goods are produced on a continuous production line, a batch can consist of one hour's production. It is impractical to undertake enforcement at retail or purchaser level unless the retailer/purchaser has taken delivery of an identifiable batch. This is unlikely though not unknown.

This Part of the Act places purchasers in both a weak and strong position. The weakness is that they have no comeback if they receive deficient pre-packed items covered by Part V unless they have purchased the whole identifiable batch and can arrange for it to be tested, an unlikely scenario, or if an item is inadequate. Thus, for example, if a local authority takes delivery of 1000 tins of baked beans some of which are deficient, nothing can be done unless some of the cans are inadequates. The strength of the purchaser's position is that as the strict controls in Part V of the Act are aimed at packers, it is unlikely that a purchaser would be guilty of an offence.

The offences in Part V are contained in s.50 and are aimed at the packer or importer of a product. However s.50(5) does provide one offence which could be committed by someone who has purchased with the intention of resale, though not by an ultimate purchaser. It reads

> If a person has in his possession for sale, agrees to sell or sells a regulated package which is inadequate and either—
> (a) he is the packer or importer of the package; or
> (b) he knows that the package is inadequate,
> he shall be guilty of an offence.

Note that there are three restrictions on liability, namely, that it is related to sale, that the item must be 'inadequate', i.e. deficient by more than twice the TNE, and that the defendant must know that it is inadequate. Given these strictures, the ultimate purchaser buying the goods for use cannot be guilty.

Packers and importers charged under s.50(5) can use the due diligence defence provided by s.51. The defence is not open to other defendants as the s.50(5) offence requires that the defendant knew that the item was inadequate, such knowledge being inconsistent with reasonable precautions and due diligence.

QUESTION

The Supplies Department of Westshire County Council ordered 2000 tins of sliced carrots from Vegetables Ltd. The carrots were for use in school canteens to which the County Council distributed them. Doris, a school cook, opened one of the tins in the presence of Lisa, one of her assistants. The tin was less than half full. There was a weight statement on the side of the tin which read 2kg e. Doris put the tin to one side to prevent it being disturbed and reported the matter to the Supplies Department. They, in turn, reported it to the Trading Standards Department.

Discuss whether any offences against the Weights and Measures Act 1985 have been committed.

FURTHER READING

Harvey, B.W. and Parry, D.L., *The Law of Consumer Protection and Fair Trading* (4th ed) 1992 (Butterworth)

Painter, A., (ed), *O'Keefe's Law of Weights and Measures* (Butterworth)

CHAPTER 17

Consumer credit

INTRODUCTION

The Consumer Credit Act 1974 was passed in response to the report of the Molony Committee. It regulates consumer credit as opposed to commercial credit although the term consumer has a far broader meaning in this context than that in the Unfair Contract Terms Act 1977 discussed earlier.

Section 8(1) of the Act defines a 'personal credit agreement' as being an agreement between an individual (the debtor) and another person (the creditor) by which the creditor provides the debtor with credit. An individual in this context includes a partnership or other unincorporated body of persons not consisting solely of bodies corporate. Thus any sole trader or partnership falls within the definition and attracts the protection of the Act even though their credit transactions may be solely for business purposes, there being no requirement that the credit transaction must be for private use. Limited companies and other corporate bodies fall outside the protection of the Act.

A 'consumer credit agreement' is a personal credit agreement under which credit not exceeding £15 000 is to be provided. Any such agreement will be 'regulated' unless exempt under s.16. Exempt agreements include mortgages secured on land provided by a variety of persons including, among others, local authorities, insurance companies, charities and building societies. Further, low cost credit agreements in which the interest rate does not exceed the greater of 13% or 1% above the base lending rate prevailing 28 days before the date of the agreement are exempt, as are agreements in which the total number of payments does not exceed four. This excludes both ordinary trade credit in which a trade customer is billed at the end of the accounting period for all goods supplied within that period, as it would charge card accounts such as American Express whereby payment must be made at the end of each charge period. Small agreements, i.e. those for less than £50 (£30 in some situations) are also excluded.

CATEGORIES OF CREDIT

Consumer credit and consumer hire agreements

Agreements under the Act will be either consumer credit agreements or consumer hire agreements. Credit includes cash loans and any other form of financial accommodation. Thus loans, hire-purchase, credit sale, conditional sale, credit cards, overdrafts, credit tokens etc. are all forms of credit. Any agreement for one of these falling within the relevant financial limits would attract protection. The common factor is that they are all means whereby the debtor acquires credit to finance the purchase of goods or services whereby title to any goods will pass ultimately to the debtor.

A consumer hire agreement is one whereby a person hires goods to an individual (the hirer) where the agreement is not a hire-purchase agreement, is capable of lasting for more than three months and does not require the hirer to make payments exceeding £15 000. Thus an agreement whereby a partnership hires a photocopying machine for a period of twelve months at a cost of £7500 would fall within the control of the Act. Under a consumer hire agreement there is no intention that the hirer will ever acquire the title to the goods.

The £15 000 limit applies to the amount of the credit received. Any deposit paid is ignored for this purpose as is the interest charged on the credit and any other administrative charges. Consider the following agreement:

Cash price	£25 000
Deposit	£10 000
Amount borrowed	£15 000
Total charge for credit	£ 3 500
Total price of the goods	£28 500

This is a regulated agreement, for despite the fact that the cash price of the goods was £25 000 and the total price including the total charge for credit (interest, administrative charges etc.) is £28 500, the amount actually borrowed is only £15 000 which falls within the range for a regulated agreement.

For running-account credit, e.g. credit cards and budget accounts, the relevant figure is the credit limit. If is does not exceed £15 000 the agreement will be regulated. Creditors cannot set the limit artificially high in order to avoid the controls in the Act for s.10(3) stipulates that an agreement will still be regulated if the debtor cannot draw more than £15 000 on any individual occasion, or must pay a higher rate of interest if he exceeds the £15 000 limit (or some other term favourable to the creditor takes effect) or that it is probable that, in all the circumstances, the debit balance will not exceed £15 000 at any time.

Fixed-sum and running-account credit

The Consumer Credit Act 1974 introduced new terminology into credit law including the distinction between fixed-sum credit and running-account credit. Fixed-sum credit occurs when the debtor receives a definite fixed amount of credit whether received in one payment or in instalments. Thus, a bank loan for £10 000 would be a fixed-sum agreement as would a hire-purchase agreement for £8000. In both situations, a definite sum is being borrowed.

Running-account credit occurs when the debtor is given a credit limit which he may not exceed but is permitted to use the credit facility repeatedly up to that limit which, allowing for regular payments made to the creditor, permits the debtor to receive continuous credit up to the limit. Examples include overdrafts and credit card agreements.

Debtor-creditor-supplier agreements

The 1974 Act further divides credit agreements into debtor-creditor-supplier (d-c-s) agreements and debtor-creditor (d-c) agreements.

D-c-s agreements involve credit for the purchase of goods under a pre-existing arrangement between the creditor and the supplier. Thus both hire-purchase and credit card sales fall into this category.

Under hire-purchase, the supplier of the goods introduces the debtor to the creditor as a potential source of credit. Thereafter, the supplier sells the goods to the creditor (typically a finance company) who as the new owner of the goods contracts with the debtor whereby the latter hires the goods for the duration of the agreement before ultimately exercising an option to purchase at the conclusion of the hire period. The title to the goods only passes to the hirer when the option is exercised.

Credit card sales are also d-c-s agreements whereby credit is provided by the credit card company under a pre-exisiting arrangement with the supplier. As part of the arrangement, the supplier is provided with the appropriate

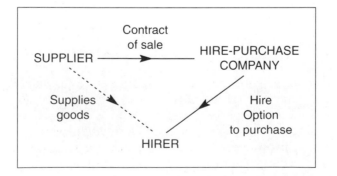

Figure 5   Hire-purchase agreement

machinery and credit forms paying a proportion of the purchase price of the goods to the credit card company by way of a fee. The provision of a credit card facility is seen as being an attraction to potential purchasers who may prefer to buy on credit rather than pay cash.

Debtor-creditor agreements

D-c agreements are those under which credit is provided by the creditor to the debtor without any pre-existing arrangement with any supplier of goods or services. This includes bank loans and overdrafts.

Restricted-use and unrestricted-use

Credit is further divided into restricted-use credit and unrestricted-use credit. The former occurs when the creditor has the ability to restrict the purposes for which the debtor uses the credit, while the latter allows the debtor total freedom to use the credit as he sees fit. A hire-purchase agreement under which a partnership purchases a particular car would be restricted-use while a bank loan under which the bank pays a cheque directly to the debtor would be unrestricted-use as the bank has lost the opportunity to control the use of the credit. By contrast, if a bank loan were to be used to buy a car with the bank drawing the cheque in favour of the car's supplier, the loan would be restricted-use. The distinction lies in control.

LICENSING

One of the major reforms introduced by the Act was the introduction of a licensing scheme covering anyone involved in the provision of regulated consumer credit agreements and/or regulated consumer hire agreements. In addition, a licence is required by anyone involved in ancillary credit activities. Local authorities do not need a licence.

A licence is required by anyone involved in the provision of regulated credit or other ancillary credit activity, however small a part of their business it may constitute. Thus, a retailer who offers a credit card facility which is used occasionally still requires a licence even though the vast majority of his business is for cash.

Ancillary credit activities include credit brokerage (introducing a debtor to a potential source of credit), debt counselling and debt adjusting, debt collecting and the operation of a credit reference agency. Debt counselling involves advising debtors about their credit situation while debt adjusting comprises active involvement in assisting the debtor to resolve his financial difficulties, e.g. helping him to arrange for a rescheduling of his payments. A credit reference agency is a business the purpose of which is to gather information about the creditworthiness of potential debtors which is then provided to the agency's members as and when they receive applications for credit.

The licensing system is organised by the Office of Fair Trading. The Director General is required by s.25(1) to grant a licence to any applicant if he satisfies the Director General that he is a fit person to engage in activities covered by the licence, and that the name or names under which he applies to be licensed is or are not misleading or in any other way undesirable. In deciding whether an applicant is a fit and proper person, the Director General takes account of whether the applicant has committed any offence involving fraud or dishonesty, contravened any regulation governing the provision of credit, practised discrimination on grounds of sex, colour, race or ethnic or national origins or been engaged in any deceitful, oppressive, unfair or improper business practices. If he is minded to refuse the application, he must inform the applicant who has a right of appeal. Once granted, the licence lasts for 15 years although the Director General has the power to vary or revoke the licence within that period. Again there is a right of appeal against such a decision.

Both criminal and civil sanctions exist in respect of a creditor trading either without a licence or outside of the terms of his licence. Section 39 makes it an offence to so trade but the more effective sanction is to be found in s.40. This provides that any regulated agreement made when the creditor or owner was unlicensed is unenforceable against the debtor unless the Director General makes an order rendering the agreement enforceable. In deciding whether to make such an order the Director General must consider whether and to what extent the debtor was prejudiced by the trader's actions, whether he would have granted a licence if an application had been received and the trader's degree of culpability for his failure to obtain a licence.

FORMS OF AGREEMENTS

Section 60 of the Act, as supplemented by the Consumer Credit (Agreements) Regulations 1983, stipulates the form and content of regulated consumer credit agreements. The regulations require that specified information must be contained in the agreement including a prominent heading that it is a credit agreement, the name and address of both creditor and debtor, details of any security, a signature box in the prescribed format, the cash price of the goods, any advance payment, the amount of the credit, the total charge for credit, the total price payable, the number and timing of repayments and the Annual Percentage Rate (APR). The APR is calculated according to a given formula and provides the means whereby prospective debtors can compare the costs of different credit facilities. It is permissible to include a variable interest rate clause whereby the interest rate payable under the agreement may rise or fall by the unilateral action of the creditor.

In *Lombard Tricity Finance Ltd* v *Paton* [1989] 1 All ER 918 the debtor, Paton, entered an agreement to buy a computer on credit terms from the plaintiff finance company. The agreement included a term that the interest rate was 'subject to variation by the creditor from time to time on notification as required by law' as may from time to time be notified'. The interest rate rose from 2.3% to 2.45% and, after the defendant fell into arrears, to 2.95%. The Court of Appeal held that the clause was valid and that there was no obligation on the plaintiff to specify in the agreement the situations in which the interest rate might be raised.

A regulated credit agreement which is not in the prescribed terms, or does not contain all the terms or is not legible when presented to the debtor or hirer for signature is not properly executed under s.61. An improperly executed agreement is not enforceable against the debtor without an order of the court. The agreement remains legal and is enforceable against the creditor by the debtor or hirer but not *vice versa*. Thus in an improperly executed hire-purchase agreement for goods, the hirer could enforce the agreement and sue the creditor if the goods were not merchantable but the creditor could not sue the hirer without an order from the court if the hirer were to default on payment.

Sections 62 and 63, the so-called 'copy provisions', stipulate the points in the contractual process at which the debtor or hirer is entitled to receive a copy of the agreement. If when the agreement is presented to or sent to the debtor or hirer for signature, the contract is not executed in that the creditor still needs to sign it, a copy of the agreement must be given to the debtor or hirer at the time of his signature. He is entitled to a second copy within seven days of the agreement being executed by the creditor signing it. However, if the agreement becomes executed when the debtor or hirer signs it, he is entitled to receive one copy only, that being at the time of his signature. If the copy provisions are not satisfied, the agreement is not properly executed and hence unenforceable without an order of the court as detailed above.

If the agreement is cancellable, a copy of the debtor's or hirer's cancellation rights must be included with every copy of the agreement or, again, it is improperly executed and unenforceable. Cancellable agreements deal primarily with the situation of unsolicited doorstep selling and thus fall outside the ambit of this text. However, briefly, an agreement will be cancellable if it was signed by the debtor or hirer away from trade premises as a result of antecedent negotiations in which oral representations were made in the presence of the debtor or hirer. The debtor or hirer may cancel the agreement within a period of five days commencing with the day on which he receives the second copy of the agreement.

As the rules regarding form and content only apply to regulated agreements, it follows that unregulated agreements are not so protected. Thus, for example, anyone signing a blank H.P. form for a non-regulated agreement will find it difficult to avoid the contract unless he can plead *non est factum* (see chapter 3).

Withdrawal and cancellation

A consumer credit agreement is subject to the normal rules of contract. The prospective debtor makes a contractual offer when approaching the creditor for credit terms which the company is at liberty to accept or reject. By normal contractual principles, the offeror (the prospective debtor) can validly withdraw the offer at any time prior to acceptance by the finance company. Section 57 of the Act provides that notice of withdrawal may be written or oral as long as it indicates clearly the intention to withdraw from the prospective agreement. The notice is effective if given to the creditor, any credit-broker or supplier who negotiated during the antecedent negotiations and anyone who, while in the course of a business, acted on behalf of the debtor or hirer in the antecedent negotiations.

The valid cancellation of a credit agreement applies only to cancellable agreements and occurs after the agreement has been concluded. Under s.69, a cancellation notice must be written, clearly indicating the intention to cancel and be given to either the creditor, anyone prescribed in the debtor's notification of cancellation rights, any credit-broker or supplier who negotiated in the antecedent negotiations and anyone who, while in the course of a business, acted on behalf of the debtor or hirer in the antecedent negotiations.

JOINT LIABILITY

There are two situations in which the creditor may be held liable for the actions of another person, typically a credit-broker or the supplier of goods under an agreement (these will often be the same person). The first relates to liability for antecedent negotiations, while the second involves liability for contractual actions that the debtor or hirer may have against the supplier of the goods.

Section 56 controls liability for statements made during antecedent negotiations, these being negotiations with the debtor or hirer conducted either by the creditor or owner or by a credit-broker in relation to goods that will be subject to a s.12(a) d-c-s agreement (e.g. hire-purchase) or by the supplier of goods subject to a s.12(b) or (c) agreement (typically, credit card purchases). The 'negotiator' means the person by whom the negotiations were conducted. Antecedent negotiations begin when the negotiator and the debtor or hirer first communicate (including by advertisement) and includes any representations made by the negotiator to the debtor or hirer and any other dealings between them.

Section 56(2) provides that where a credit-broker or supplier has negotiated as detailed above, they are deemed to have acted as an agent for the creditor as well as acting in their own behalf. By the normal rules of agency a principal is responsible for the acts of his agents and thus, in this context, the creditor would be liable if, for example, the negotiator misdescribed the goods. Similarly the creditor would be liable for any contractual terms agreed on his behalf by the negotiator. This clarifies the position that was unclear at common law where precedents differed over the relationship between the supplier of the goods and the creditor. Naturally, unregulated agreements are still subject to the normal rules of agency.

The liability of the creditor for antecedent negotiations is reinforced by s.56(3) which provides that an agreement is void to the extent that it seeks to provide that a person acting as or on behalf of a negotiator is to be treated as the agent of the debtor or seeks to exclude liability for the acts of a negotiator or anyone acting on his behalf.

Section 75 provides for joint liability between the creditor and the supplier of goods under a regulated d-c-s agreement falling under s.12(b) or (c). Thus it includes credit card transactions but would not include hire-purchase. The reason for this can be seen by analysing the contractual position in both hire-purchase and credit card transactions as in Fig. 6 and Fig. 7.

In hire-purchase the hirer has direct contractual rights against the creditor with the result that joint liability is not relevant. By contrast, in a credit card

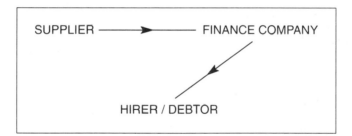

Figure 6   Hire-purchase transaction

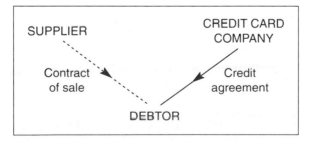

Figure 7   Credit card transaction

transaction the debtor has two separate contracts, one with the supplier and one with the creditor. Joint liability allows him to enforce rights acquired under the contract with the supplier against the creditor.

Section 75(1) stipulates that where the debtor would have a claim for misrepresentation or a breach of contract against the supplier he has a like claim against the creditor who is jointly and severally liable with the supplier. Thus, for example, if goods purchased by credit card are not of merchantable quality the debtor can sue either the supplier or the creditor. This is advantageous as it allows the debtor to choose which potential defendant is best able to meet his claim and also allows for an alternative defendant to be available if the supplier should go into liquidation.

Joint liability does not apply in non-commercial agreements (i.e. not made during the course of a business carried on by the creditor or owner) and is not applicable so far as the claim relates to any single item to which the supplier has attached a cash price of less than £100 or more than £30 000. Thus if a purchaser has bought a selection of four items on credit from the same supplier, the cash price of the individual items being £60, £75, £130 and £220, joint liability will only apply in respect of the last two. Claims in respect of the first two will be limited to those against the supplier. The fact that the debtor bought items with a total cash price of £485 is irrelevant for this purpose.

The section does not leave the creditor totally exposed, however, for he is entitled to be indemnified by the supplier of the goods for any loss that he (the creditor) has suffered under joint liability including costs reasonably incurred by him in defending proceedings instituted by the debtor.

Finally, as joint liability only applies in respect of regulated agreements, the debtor in any non-regulated agreement can only sue the supplier of the goods with whom he has contractual privity. Of course, in a hire-purchase agreement, the finance company will have been the legal supplier anyway.

IMPLIED CONDITIONS

The debtor or hirer acquiring goods on credit has a right to assume that the creditor has the right to sell the goods at the time that the property is to pass and that the goods will comply with the implied conditions of compliance with description, merchantable quality, fitness for purpose and compliance with sample. Which provisions apply will depend on the nature of the credit transaction. In a hire-purchase agreement, the implied conditions are to be found in ss.8–11 of the Supply of Goods (Implied Terms) Act 1973, these conditions being enforceable directly against the creditor as the owner and seller of the goods. In a credit card transaction, the implied conditions in ss.12–15 of the Sale of Goods Act 1979 are enforceable directly against the supplier of the goods and enforceable against the creditor by virtue of s.75 joint liability as described above.

The only implied condition worthy of particular note is that relating to the passage of title. Both s.8 of the Supply of Goods (Implied Terms) Act and s.12 of the Sale of Goods Act provide that the supplier/seller must have the right to sell at the time that the property is to pass. However, the timing of this will vary depending upon the nature of the agreement. In a credit card transaction or a credit sale agreement, property will pass immediately, while in an H.P. agreement it will not pass until the option to purchase has been exercised at the end of the hire period. Finally, under a conditional sale agreement property will pass when the agreement so stipulates, e.g. when two-thirds of the total price has been paid.

EXTORTIONATE CREDIT

The extortionate credit provisions of the Act are potentially far-reaching as they apply to all credit agreements between individuals and creditors and not simply regulated agreements. A credit bargain for this purpose means the credit agreement or where more than one transaction is to be taken into account when calculating the total charge for credit, all the transactions. A credit bargain is considered to be extortionate if it

(a) requires the debtor or a relative of his to make payments (whether unconditionally or on certain contingencies) which are grossly exhorbitant; or
(b) otherwise grossly contravenes ordinary principles of fair dealing.

Section 138 stipulates the factors to be taken into account when determining whether a bargain is extortionate. These include the interest rates prevailing at the time, the debtor's age, experience, business capacity and state of health, together with the nature of any financial pressure suffered by the debtor at the time of the agreement. Further the court must consider the degree of risk undertaken by the creditor in providing the credit, the creditor's relationship with the debtor and whether any colourable cash price was quoted for any goods or services included in the bargain. Where a credit bargain is held to be extortionate the court can, *inter alia*, rewrite the agreement inserting a lower rate of interest, require the creditor to return some or all of the monies paid under the agreement or direct the return of any security.

The provisions of the Act have proved to be of little value. In the nineteen years since the passage of the Act, only twenty four cases have reached the courts and only four agreements have been held to be extortionate. It is a reasonable assumption that no business, be it sole trader or partnership, would succeed in proving that any credit agreement that they entered was extortionate. Their 'business capacity' would count against them. The notable failure of these provisions has led to a proposal by the Director General of Fair Trading that the concept of the 'extortionate credit bargain' should be replaced by the 'unjust credit transaction'. A wider variety of factors could be used to determine whether an agreement was unjust, including whether payments were excessive and whether the creditor had exercised appropriate care and responsibility when making the loan. Further, the creditor's behaviour could be considered to determine if it was unfair, improper, deceitful or oppressive.

TERMINATION

The credit agreement may come to a premature end by:

(a) the debtor discharging his liability early and taking ownership of the goods, or
(b) the debtor exercising his right to terminate the contract, the ownership of the goods reverting to the previous owner, or
(c) the creditor bringing the agreement to an end because of the debtor's default.

Early settlement

Section 94 permits the debtor under a regulated agreement to discharge his indebtedness early by giving notice to the creditor and paying all amounts owing to the creditor under the agreement less any rebate to which the debtor is entitled. The Consumer Credit (Rebate on Early Settlement) Regulations 1983 stipulate a formula for calculating the rebate due to any debtor on early settlement of a debt. The rebate relates to the portion of interest under the agreement for which the debtor is no longer liable, the agreement having come to an end prematurely.

The decision of *Lombard North Central plc* v *Stobart* (1990) 9 Tr Law 105 confirmed that a creditor is estopped from denying the accuracy of an early settlement figure once the debtor has relied upon that representation. The defendant, Stobart, decided to settle his outstanding debt on a motor car. He was informed that the early settlement figure for the agreement was £1044, a figure subsequently confirmed by the creditor. Mr Stobart paid this sum in good faith. A week later the plaintiff credit company realised that the true figure should have been £5091. The Court of Appeal held that the original settlement figure must stand and that the plaintiff was estopped from enforcing the true sum.

Early settlement of the debt brings the agreement to an end and vests the ownership of the goods in the debtor.

Termination by the debtor

The debtor or hirer may wish to terminate a regulated hire-purchase agreement or regulated conditional sale agreement during its lifetime if, for example, the debtor no longer wants the goods or is unable to pay for them. Section 99 gives such a debtor the right to terminate the agreement at any time before the final payment by giving notice to any person who is entitled to receive payments under the agreement. However, the right does not extend to conditional sale agreements for land after the title to the land has passed to the debtor. Similarly, the right is lost in conditional sale agreements for goods where the title to the goods, having become vested in the debtor, has been transferred to a third party. Note the distinction between hire-purchase contracts and conditional sale contracts in that the title to the goods in a hire-purchase contract does not pass until the exercise of the option to purchase at the end of the agreement but the title passes under a conditional sale agreement at the time stipulated in the contract. Thus it may pass before the final payment is due. Where the title to goods has passed to the debtor under a conditional sale agreement but has not been transferred to a third party, the title reverts upon termination to the last previous owner.

Where the debtor terminates an agreement under s.99, he is liable to pay the creditor the difference between one-half of the total price and the amount he has already paid under the agreement, unless the agreement provides for a smaller sum to be paid or no payment at all (s.100). If installation charges were included in the agreement, the amount due is the sum of the installation charges plus one-half of the remainder due under the agreement less any monies already paid.

Despite the above provision, the court may substitute a lower figure if it feels that the lower sum reflects the actual loss suffered by the creditor consequent upon the termination. The sum may be increased to compensate the creditor for any loss suffered by the debtor's failure to comply with any obligation to take reasonable care of any goods or land subject to the agreement.

The creditor can terminate the agreement under s.98 by giving at least seven days' notice of the termination to the debtor and provided that there has not been any default by the debtor.

Regulated consumer hire agreements can be terminated under s.101 by the hirer after the expiration of eighteen months even if the agreement was for a longer period. Notice of termination can be given to any person entitled or authorised to receive payments under the agreement. The minimum period of notice is the shortest interval between the making of payments or three months, whichever is the shorter. However, the right to terminate under s.101 does not apply if

(a) payments under the agreement exceed £900 a year, or
(b) the goods were hired to the hirer for the purpose of his business and were acquired by the owner at the hirer's request for the purposes of the agreement from someone other than the owner's associate, or
(c) the hirer wanted, or purported to want, the goods for the purpose of hiring them out to other persons in the course of his business.

Default

A common cause for the termination of agreements, particularly in recessionary times, is default by the debtor. Default may bring about a variety of consequences depending on the terms of the agreement, including an accelerated payments clause whereby the whole of the outstanding debt becomes payable immediately, the enforcement of any security or even the creditor's right to repossess the goods. Which of the remedies is appropriate will depend to some extent upon the type of agreement. Thus in an agreement financed by a credit card in which the ownership of the goods has already passed to the debtor, default will be remedied by an action against the money rather than the goods. Ultimately, the creditor would sue for the outstanding amount. By contrast, in a hire-purchase agreement in which the title of the goods does not pass until the end of the hire period, the creditor may seek to repossess his goods.

For regulated agreements, the creditor's ability to enforce the contract terms on default are limited to some extent by the provisions of ss.87–91. Section 87 provides that the creditor or owner under a regulated agreement must serve a default notice on a debtor or hirer before he can do any of the following:

(a) terminate the agreement, or
(b) demand earlier payment of any sum, or
(c) recover possession of any goods or land, or
(d) treat any right conferred on the debtor or hirer by the agreement as terminated, restricted or deferred, or
(e) enforce any security.

These requirements do not prevent the creditor from restricting the debtor's right to further credit with immediate effect.

The default notice, which must be in prescribed form, must specify the nature of the alleged breach, what action must be taken to remedy the breach and the date by which it must be taken. Alternatively, if the breach is not capable of remedy, the notice must specify the sum (if any) that the debtor must pay by way of compensation and the date by which it must be paid. The creditor is prohibited from taking any further action until the specified period, which must be at least seven days, has elapsed.

If the debtor remedies the defect within the period specified in the notice, s.89 stipulates that the breach is to be treated as not having occurred. The agreement would then continue uninterrupted unless a further breach were to occur.

Sections 90 and 91 provide further protection to hirers who default on regulated hire-purchase agreements. Section 90 restricts the ability of the creditor of a regulated hire-purchase or regulated conditional sale agreement to repossess the goods in the event of the hirer's default. If the defaulting debtor has paid one-third or more of the total price of the goods (i.e. cash price plus all the interest, administrative charges etc.) and the property in the goods is still in the creditor, he cannot repossess the goods without a court order. If goods are recovered in contravention of these requirements, the regulated agreement will terminate and the debtor is entitled to recover all the monies already paid under the agreement. This may be a significant amount of money for the debtor may have nearly finished paying for the goods and yet be entitled to recover all the monies paid and effectively had free usage of the goods since he took possession of them. However these rights will be lost if the debtor voluntarily surrenders the goods to the creditor as long as the debtor had been made aware of the extent of his rights if he chose to refuse to surrender the goods. As Dobson points out, s.90 refers to seizing the goods 'from the debtor' and thus the creditor will not contravene s.90 if he seizes them either from a third party to whom the debtor had disposed of the goods or alternatively if the debtor has abandoned them.

The creditor also needs a court order if he wishes to enter premises for the purpose of recovering goods subject to a regulated hire-purchase or regulated conditional sale or regulated consumer hire agreement. Likewise, a court order is necessary for the recovery of land on default.

All of the above rights on default are limited to regulated agreements. Thus it follows that debtors in unregulated agreements, such as agreements where the amount borrowed exceeds £15 000 or agreements where the debtor is a limited company, do not attract the protection of the Act. Thus, for example, a partnership defaulting on a regulated hire-purchase agreement for a photostat machine having paid one-half of the total price would be entitled to receive a default notice with the resultant opportunity to remedy the default and would be protected against any attempt by the creditor to snatch back the goods. By contrast, a limited company defaulting in exactly the same way on a similar agreement would have none of these rights.

On receipt of a default notice, a debtor may apply to the court for a time order under s.129. A similar application can be made during a hearing in which the creditor is seeking to enforce a regulated agreement or any security, or recover possession of any goods or land to which a regulated agreement applies. It permits the court to reschedule payments under the agreement or any security having regard to the means of the debtor, hirer or surety. It also allows the court to grant the debtor or hirer an extended period in which to remedy any breach. The advantages of time orders are that they allow the debtor or hirer to fulfil his contractual obligations while taking cognisance of any difficulties he faces. Thus they are particularly useful for debtors who are suffering temporary cash flow problems but are basically sound, capable of ultimately fulfilling their contractual obligations and want the opportunity to do so. However, if the debtor has deeper financial problems a time order may only postpone the inevitable and ultimately be of no real benefit.

When considering whether to grant a time order, the court must also consider the interests of the creditor.

In *First National Bank plc* v *Syed* [1991] 2 All ER 250 the Court of Appeal refused to grant a time order to the defendant householder who had defaulted regularly on an agreement and who could only sustain a regular payment that would not even meet the accruing interest on the debt. Further, there was no prospect that the defendant's financial position would change such as to allow him to pay off any of the capital sum borrowed under the agreement. The time order was refused and the creditor was allowed to repossess the property constituting the security for the debt.

QUESTION

Mike, a sole trader, purchased a weighing scale from Weights Ltd for £560. The purchase was to be financed through an H.P. agreement with Easymoney Finance Ltd. Mike paid a deposit of £100, the remainder of the loan plus interest being repaid by twelve monthly instalments of £50. Having paid five instalments, Mike suffered from a cash flow problem and defaulted on the sixth and seventh instalments. Easymoney Finance Ltd have written to him saying that they want to repossess the goods.

Advise Mike.

FURTHER READING

Bradgate, R. and Savage, N., *Commercial Law* 1991 (Butterworth)

Dobson, A.P., *Sale of Goods and Consumer Credit* (4th ed) 1989 (Sweet and Maxwell)

Dobson, A.P. and Schmitthoff, C., *Charlesworth's Business Law* (15th ed) 1991 (Sweet and Maxwell)

Goode, R.M., *Consumer Credit Law* 1989 (Butterworth)

Harvey, B.W. and Parry, D.L., *The Law of Consumer Protection and Fair Trading* (4th ed) 1992 (Butterworth)

Pitt, G. (ed), *Butterworth's Commercial Law Handbook* (Butterworth)

Part V

Related legislation

CHAPTER 18

Competition law

INTRODUCTION

The rationale behind competition law is a determination to ensure fair competition among the providers of goods and services in any given sector and thereby protect users and consumers. This is achieved by controlling various aspects of the market to prevent practices designed to or likely to distort competition and which are held to be contrary to the public interest. Thus monopolies, mergers, restrictive trade practices, resale price maintenance and other anti-competitive practices are all subject to some degree of control.

MONOPOLIES

Monopolies are controlled in the United Kingdom by the joint efforts of the Director General of Fair Trading, who has powers under the Fair Trading Act 1973, and the Monopolies and Mergers Commission (MMC). The latter body, originally founded in 1948 as the Monopoly and Restrictive Practices Commission, comprises not fewer than ten or more than fifty members appointed by the Secretary of State.

A monopoly is defined in s.6 of the Fair Trading Act 1973 as occurring when

(a) at least one-quarter of all the goods of that description which are supplied in the United Kingdom are supplied by one and the same person, or are supplied to one and the same person, or

(b) at least one-quarter of the goods of that description which are supplied in the United Kingdom are supplied by members of one and the same group of interconnected bodies corporate, or are supplied to members of one and the same group of interconnected bodies corporate, or

(c) at least one-quarter of all the goods of that description which are supplied in the United Kingdom are supplied by members of one and the same group consisting of two or more persons as are mentioned in subsection (2) of this section, or are supplied to members of one and the same group consisting of two or more such persons, or

(d) one or more collective agreements are in operation, the result or collective result of which is that goods of that description are not supplied in the United Kingdom at all.

The first point to note is that the descriptions acknowledge that a monopoly may relate equally to the person supplying the goods or the person receiving them. A buyer may be in a monopoly situation and, as such, be able to dictate the price, quality etc. of the goods. Paragraphs (a) and (b) adopt a purely numerical approach to the existence of a monopoly relying on the premise that control of one-quarter of the market indicates a significantly powerful position. Paragraphs (c) and (d) take account of the behaviour of the person either in addition to or instead of his percentage control. A corresponding provision identifying a monopoly in the provision of services appears in s.7, while s.8 identifies monopoly situations as pertaining to exports. Finally, s.9 makes clear that a monopoly may be limited in effect to part of the United Kingdom and investigated as such.

It is not an offence to be a monopoly but the legislation recognises the ability of a monopoly to distort competition. Thus under s.2 of the 1973 Act the Director General of Fair Trading is required to collate evidence and information regarding commercial activities with a view to identifying monopoly situations. Having identified the possible existence of a monopoly the Director General can refer it to the MMC for investigation to determine whether the monopoly exists and, if so, whether it is operating contrary to the public interest. Again, there is no assumption that it will be.

When considering the 'public interest' element of the reference, the Commission must take into account all matters which appear to them to be relevant. Section 84(1) offers some guidance on this thorny issue by stipulating that the Commission should have regard to a variety of factors including the maintenance and promotion of effective competition, promoting the interests of consumers with regard to the prices charged for goods and the quality of them, the reduction of costs and development of new techniques and new products, maintaining and promoting a balanced distribution of industry and employment and the maintenance and promotion of competitive activity in markets outside the UK on the part of producers of goods, and of suppliers of goods and services in the UK. Further, under s.81 the Commission must take account of any representation made to it by persons appearing to have a substantial interest in the subject matter of the reference. The decisions of *R v Monopolies and Mergers Commission ex parte Elders IXL Ltd* [1987] 1 All ER 451 and *R v Monopolies and Mergers Commission ex parte Matthew Brown plc* [1987] 1 All ER 463 confirm that the MMC are under a duty to act fairly in the way that they conduct their investigations, though what constitutes fairness will depend to some extent on the circumstances of the individual cases.

On conclusion of their investigations, the Commission prepare a report of their findings to include their conclusions on the questions posed to them together with the reasons for those conclusions. Where the Commission find the existence of a monopoly which may be expected to operate against the public interest the report should specify the expected adverse results and, if the MMC think fit, recommendations of such action as should be taken to remedy the situation. Under s.56 an order may be made by the appropriate Minister to exercise any of the powers specified in Schedule 8 as a means of remedying the situation. These powers include outlawing the withholding of goods or services, the making of payments for services other than those received and charging prices different from those included in published lists. Further, the appropriate Minister may order the publication of price lists, regulate prices and prohibit the acquisition of another person's business.

The EEC approach to monopolies is found in Art.86 of the Treaty of Rome which seeks to prevent abuses of a 'dominant position' which may distort trade between Member States. Abuses include:

(a) directly or indirectly imposing unfair purchase or selling prices or other unfair trading conditions;
(b) limiting production, markets or technical development to the prejudice of consumers;
(c) applying dissimilar conditions to equivalent transactions with other trading parties, thereby placing them at a competitive disadvantage;
(d) making the conclusion of contracts subject to acceptance by the other parties of supplementary obligations which, by their nature or according to commercial usage, have no connection with the subject of such contracts.

These features would clearly have a serious impact upon competition but Art.86 will not apply unless an undertaking is shown to be in a dominant position. Unlike the UK, the EEC approach makes no reference to percentages of the market but rather considers the relative economic strength of the undertaking. If an undertaking can transact its business and act on its own decisions without the need to take account of its competitors' actions or the views of consumers, it will be in a dominant position. This will not necessarily equate with the same market share in all situations and hence this more flexible approach more accurately reflects the true situation.

The EEC Commission has wide powers to investigate suspected breaches of Art.86 and, if proved, has the authority to impose fines on the offending undertaking and to take such other actions as are necessary to prevent the continuation of the abuse.

MERGERS

Monopolies often result from mergers and thus the control of mergers itself militates against the creation of monopolies. A merger situation exists when two or more distinct enterprises unite thereby ceasing to be distinct entities. A merger will be subject to possible reference to the Monopolies and

Mergers Commission if the merged enterprise would have 25% or more of the market or where the value of the assets taken over exceeds £30m. As with monopolies, a merger may effect only part of the UK and yet be an appropriate merger for consideration. In *South Yorkshire Transport Ltd* v *Monopolies and Mergers Commission* [1993] 1 All ER 289 the House of Lords held that 'a substantial part of the UK' in this context should be decided by reference to whether the 'area was of such a size, character and importance as to make it worthy of consideration'. In the case, the merger of some bus companies to create a monopoly in an area that was 1.65% of the total UK and catering for 3.2% of the population was still substantial for this purpose.

There is no presumption that a merger is necessarily contrary to the public interest and no requirement that a reference takes place. Enterprises intending to merge can notify this fact to the Director General who then has a period of twenty days to decide whether to make a reference. This period may be extended by a total of twenty five days, during the last five of which the Secretary of State may institute a reference irrespective of the advice of the Director General. Once the period has expired no reference can be made provided that the merger takes place within six months of the expiration of the period.

As with monopoly references, the MMC have investigatory powers and must decide whether a qualifying merger exists and whether it is contrary to the public interest. The report of their findings must be presented within a specified period not exceeding six months. Where the merger is shown to be contrary to the public interest, the Secretary of State may use the same powers granted under Schedule 8 of the Fair Trading Act 1973 as are available to him in a monopoly situation to enable him to remedy the adverse effects of the merger.

As an alternative to a merger reference, the Director General may accept undertakings from the enterprises involved. These undertakings must address and remedy the potentially adverse effects which the proposed merger might have.

EEC control of mergers emanates from two sources, Art.86 of the Treaty of Rome and Commission Regulation 4064/89 (OJ 1989 L395/1) which came into effect in 1990. Article 86 is relevant in that a merger may create an enterprise that is in a dominant position that may lead to abuse. The more specific merger regulation applies to 'concentrations with a Community dimension'. This occurs where the world-wide turnover of all the enterprises involved in the merger exceeds ECU 5000m with the total Community-wide turnover of at least two of the enterprises exceeding ECU 250m unless each of the undertakings achieves more than two-thirds of that Community-wide turnover in the same Member State. In the latter instance, national legislation will apply.

Where EEC law applies the EEC Commission has the power to require any infringement to be remedied and to impose financial penalties. The remedy may involve separating the constituent enterprises of the merger.

RESTRICTIVE TRADE PRACTICES

The Restrictive Trade Practices Act 1976, as amended by the Restrictive Trade Practices Act 1977 and the Competition Act 1980, applies to agreements made between two or more persons carrying on business in the UK in the production or supply of goods or the supply of services and which contain restrictions accepted by two or more persons in respect of any of the following:

(a) the prices to be charged, quoted or paid for goods supplied, offered or acquired, or for the application of any process of manufacture to goods;

(b) the prices to be recommended or suggested as the prices to be charged or quoted in respect of the resale of goods supplied;

(c) the terms or conditions on or subject to which goods are to be supplied or acquired or any such process is to be applied to goods;

(d) the quantities or descriptions of goods to be produced, supplied or acquired;

(e) the processes of manufacture to be applied to any goods, or the quantities or descriptions of goods to which any such process is to be applied; or

(f) the persons or classes of persons to, for or from whom, or the areas or places in or from which, goods are to be supplied or acquired, or any such process applied.

An 'agreement' is defined as including 'any agreement or arrangement, whether or not it is or is intended to be enforceable (apart from any provision of this Act) by legal proceedings, and references in this Act to restrictions accepted or information provisions made under an agreement shall be construed accordingly'. Clearly, this is far broader than a legally binding contract and includes any agreement which dictates the way that the parties to it will be expected to act. A term in such an agreement is restrictive if it affects the ability of any party subject to it to freely make his own decisions regarding any of the specified matters The Act will apply where two or more persons are subject to the restriction or where a trade association recommends it (in which case all the members of the association are deemed to be subject to it individually).

Where an agreement falls within these definitions there is a duty under s.24 of the Restrictive Trade Practices Act to register it with the Office of Fair Trading. This involves registering all the documents that constitute the agreement. Registration must be effected within three months of the making of the agreement with the restrictions not taking effect in the interim. A failure to register means that the restrictions are void and unenforceable and that it is unlawful to attempt to enforce them. The Director General can seek a court order restraining the parties from enforcing the unregistered agreement or any other unregistered agreement.

Following registration, s.1 of the Act places a general duty on the Director General to refer such agreements to the Restrictive Practices Court unless the Secretary of State directs the Director General that the restrictions are not significant and do not merit reference or where the restrictions have already ceased to be effective. In the latter instance the Director General may still refer the agreement if he believes that the agreement may be revived or a similar one instituted.

The duty of the Court is to decide whether the restrictions are contrary to the public interest, the same yardstick as is used for monopolies and mergers. In this instance it is decided by reference to the eight 'gateways' set out in s.10 (goods) and s.19 (services) of the Act, of which the agreement must satisfy at least one if it is to be upheld and approved. The 'gateways' may be summarised thus:

(a) that the restrictions are reasonable given the character of the goods and the need to protect the public against injury from the consumption, installation or use of the goods;
(b) that the removal of the restrictions would deny the public as purchasers, consumers or users substantial benefits or advantages;
(c) that the restrictions are reasonable as a means of counteracting anti-competitive actions taken by a third party;
(d) that the restrictions are necessary to allow the parties to the agreement to negotiate fair terms for the supply of goods from a third party who controls a preponderant part of the business in those goods;
(e) that the removal of the restrictions would have a serious adverse effect on employment in areas where a substantial proportion of the business takes place;
(f) that the removal of the restrictions would cause a substantial reduction in the volume of or earnings from exports;
(g) that the restriction is reasonably required in order to maintain another agreement which the court has held is not contrary to the public interest;
(h) that the restriction does not directly or indirectly restrict or discourage competition to any material degree in any relevant trade or industry and is not likely to do so.

In addition the Court must be satisfied that the restriction is reasonable having regard to the balance between the gateways and any detriment likely to be suffered by the public or by any persons not parties to the agreement. If the agreement does not satisfy the gateways, the Court can order the parties not to enforce the offending agreement or any agreement of like effect.

The Restrictive Trade Practices Act 1976, while still good law at the time of writing, is due to be repealed. The replacement legislation which is currently being drafted will equate more closely to the approach adopted by Art.85 of the Treaty of Rome, the relevant EEC provision. As such, the new domestic legislation will contain a general prohibition against anti-competitive practices.

RESALE PRICE MAINTENANCE

Resale price maintenance involves manufacturers or suppliers of goods stipulating minimum prices at which goods can be resold at retail level. In the UK the Resale Prices Act 1976 provides a general prohibition against such practices.

Resale price maintenance can be either collective or individual. Collective resale price maintenance, which is outlawed by ss.1 and 2 of the 1976 Act, occurs when two or more suppliers of goods agree to withhold supplies of goods from a dealer who resells or has resold goods in breach of any condition as to the price at which those goods might be resold. It also occurs if suppliers agree to supply to dealers on terms less favourable than those offered to other dealers in the same business.

Individual resale price maintenance is governed by Part II of the Act. Section 9 renders void any term in an agreement by which the supplier of goods purports to establish a minimum price to be charged on the resale of goods. Further, s.11 makes it unlawful for a supplier to withhold goods from a dealer because the dealer has sold goods at a price below the resale price. However, one general defence is provided to offences against s.11, namely that the goods were withheld because the supplier has reasonable grounds to believe that the dealer had used the goods as a loss leader within the previous twelve months. A 'loss leader' is an item sold at a very low price to attract customers to the premises in the expectation that they will then buy other goods.

The Resale Prices Act 1976 will also be repealed in the foreseeable future as part of the new approach to restrictive trade practices. Agreements relating to the fixing of prices will be governed by the proposed new general prohibition on anti-competitive practices.

ARTICLE 85

Anti-competitive practices in the EEC are controlled under Art.85(1) of the Treaty of Rome which provides:

(1) The following shall be prohibited as incompatible with with the common market: all agreements between undertakings, decisions by associations of undertakings and concerted practices which may affect trade between Member States and which have as their object or effect the prevention, restriction or distortion of competition within the common market, and in particular those which:

   (a) directly or indirectly fix purchase or selling prices or any other trading conditions;
   (b) limit or control production, markets, technical development, or investment;
   (c) share markets or sources of supply;

(d) apply dissimilar conditions to equivalent transactions with other trading parties, thereby placing them at a competitive disadvantage;

(e) make the conclusion of contracts subject to acceptance by the other parties of supplementary obligations which, by their nature or according to to commercial usage, have no connection with the subject of such contracts.

Any agreement or decision which is contrary to this provision is prohibited and automatically void.

The scope of Art.85 is broad, covering all agreements between undertakings, decisions by associations of undertakings and concerted practices. There is no requirement that these undertakings are in competition with each other. Thus while Art.85 would clearly cover horizontal agreements (those between two or more competitors operating at the same level in the distributive process) it would also include vertical agreements (those between a supplier and a dealer).

Article 85 is concerned with the effect of the offending agreements. This highlights two aspects. First, the agreement must have as its object or effect the prevention, restriction or distortion of competition within the common market. This allows the EEC to be proactive in the enforcement of Art.85 by considering the likely effect of the agreement rather than waiting until the distortion occurs. The requirement is that competition is distorted, not that it is adversely affected. Thus it may be that competition is increased as a result of the agreement.

Second, the agreement must affect trade between Member States. Thus an agreement which only affects trade within one domestic market will not come within the ambit of Art.85. It is possible, of course, that what is ostensibly a domestic agreement may have an effect beyond the national boundaries as it may attract trade into the state or dissuade it depending on the circumstances.

While the breadth of Art.85 potentially encompasses virtually any agreement, it will only apply where the effect on competition is sufficiently serious. The EEC Notice on Agreements of Minor Importance provides that Art.85 will not apply if two criteria are satisfied:

(a) the products covered by the agreement do not constitute more than 5% of the products available in the area of the Common Market affected by the agreement; and
(b) the total annual turnover of the undertakings participating in the agreements does not exceed 200 million ECU.

In addition to providing exemptions for agreements that are not of sufficient significance, the EEC can also grant block exemptions by which exemptions covering categories of goods can be introduced thus negating the need for individual agreements to be cleared. Current block exemptions include patent licensing, maritime transport, motor vehicle distribution and exclusive distribution.

Unlike the requirements of the Restrictive Trade Practices Act 1976, there is no requirement to register agreements under Art.85. Nonetheless, firms may opt to submit their agreements to the EEC Commission for a ruling as to the legality of the agreement. This both establishes the legitimacy of the agreement and prevents liability arising for the period between the notification to the Commission and its ruling. Effectively, an undertaking may use a restrictive agreement without penalty for the period while the Commission considers its legality. If the agreement is rejected, the undertaking can cease using it immediately while having already obtained some benefit from it. This is of considerable benefit to undertakings given that the Commission can enforce financial penalties of up to 10% of the undertaking's annual turnover if the agreement is found to offend Art.85.

Limitations to the scope of Art.85(1) are to be found in Art.85(3). This provides that if an agreement can satisfy four criteria Art.85(1) will not apply. The criteria are that the restrictions contribute to improving the production or distribution of goods or to promoting technical or economic progress, that consumers receive a fair share of the resulting benefits, that the restrictions imposed are indispensable to achieving these objectives and that it does not afford undertakings the possibility of eliminating competition in respect of a substantial part of the products in question. The balance to be achieved is that the agreement must offer substantial benefits justifying overriding its anti-competitive tendencies.

Ultimately, if an agreement is found to offend Art.85, the Commission can impose financial penalties and require the undertakings to desist from enforcing the agreement which is void.

OTHER ANTI-COMPETITIVE PRACTICES

Other anti-competitive practices are governed by ss.2–10 of the Competition Act 1980.

Section 2(1) contains the basic prohibition against anti-competitive practices which occurs when a person in the course of a business pursues a course of conduct which, taken by itself or taken with the conduct of another person associated with him, is intended to, or is likely to or does have the effect of restricting, distorting or preventing competition in connection with the production, supply or acquisition of goods in the UK, or the supply or securing of services in the UK or any part of it. Agreements which would offend against the Restrictive Trade Practices Act 1976 are expressly excluded from the ambit of the Competition Act. Section 2(8) makes clear that local authorities are capable of committing anti-competitive practices and are subject to control.

If the Director General believes that a person is committing an anti-competitive practice, he can carry out an investigation under s.3(2) to establish whether this is so. Before commencing any such investigation, the

Director General is required to inform the Secretary of State and arrange for suitable publication of the investigation so as to bring it to the attention of persons affected by it or likely to have an interest in it. The Director General must publish a report as soon as practicable after the investigation is completed.

If the Director General concludes that the conduct complained of constitutes an anti-competitive practice, he can seek undertakings from the person concerned or alternatively refer the matter to the MMC. Any reference must occur between four and eight weeks after the publication of the Director General's report. The MMC must decide whether the person subject to the reference had engaged in any anti-competitive practice in the preceding twelve months and, if so, whether it was contrary to the public interest. If the MMC conclude that an anti-competitive practice contrary to the public interest occurred, the Director General may seek undertakings to control the anti-competitive behaviour or, alternatively, seek a court order to prohibit the continuance of the offending practice.

QUESTION

A Ltd, a coach company with 13% of the trade in South Wales, and B Ltd, another coach company with 14% of the trade in the same area, decide to unite so as to render their operations more efficient and potentially more profitable.

Discuss whether this decision is subject to review by the MMC and what actions the MMC may want to take.

FURTHER READING

Dobson, A.P. and Schmitthoff, C.M., *Charlesworth's Business Law* (15th ed) 1991 (Sweet and Maxwell)

Frazer, T., *Monopoly, Competition and the Law* (2nd ed) 1992 (Harvester Wheatsheaf)

Singleton, E.S., *Introduction to Competition Law* 1992 (Pitman)

Whish, R., *Competition Law* (2nd ed) 1989 (Butterworth)

Wilkinson, J., *Restraint of Trade* 1991 (Fourmat)

Office of Fair Trading, *Restrictive Trade Practices* 1990

CHAPTER 19

Intellectual property

INTRODUCTION

Information and designs can be as important, if not more important, to a business as the product it creates. A company has a vested interest in protecting the ideas, designs and processes that it creates and preventing exploitation of them by competitors. This concept does not sit easily with the controls on anti-competitive practices discussed in the previous chapter for the laws on intellectual property permit a company to create and protect a monopoly on ideas. The relevant controls relate to trade secrets, patents, copyrights, designs and trade marks.

TRADE SECRETS

Many employees gain access to confidential information at some point in their dealings with their employer. Similarly, independent contractors may acquire confidential information during the course of performing their contract for services. Such confidential information may relate to a variety of factors: designs, processes, corporate structures, marketing strategies etc., anything that a company might legitimately feel would be of benefit to a competitor. Such confidential information might reasonably be classed as trade secrets.

A company has a legitimate interest in seeking to protect such trade secrets from disclosure, deliberately or inadvertently, by employees who have knowledge of them. This may be achieved expressly through the use of a restraint-of-trade clause in the recipient's contract of employment. Such clauses are, of course, void at common law (see chapter 3) unless they are reasonable as regards the geographic area covered, the scope of the restriction and its duration. The protection of trade secrets by this method would be reasonable for the period for which it is reasonable to expect the information to remain secret. Thus, for example, in respect of a manufacturing process the information would be protected until the point where it would be reasonable to assume that any competitor would have developed the process independently.

Irrespective of any contractual term protecting trade secrets, a common law duty of confidentiality exists, the breach of which would give rise to an action for breach of confidence, in which a claim for an injunction to prevent further disclosure, damages etc. could be pursued. A successful breach of confidence action requires the plaintiff to show that the information is confidential, was given to the defendant in a situation suggesting confidentiality and that there has been either an actual disclosure of it or a threatened disclosure.

Central to the enforcement of this concept is the meaning of confidential and where the dividing line must be drawn between confidential information deserving protection and non-confidential general knowledge and skills that the recipient is entitled to use freely both during and after his employment with the owner of the information. The test for assessing confidentiality was considered in *Thomas Marshall (Exports) Ltd* v *Guinle* [1978] 3 All ER 193 in which it was held that the owner of the information must reasonably believe that the information is not public knowledge and that its release would be harmful to him or advantageous to his competitors. Finally, the information must be judged by the standards and practices appropriate within the relevant industry.

This distinction between confidential and non-confidential information and the duties that arise from it was discussed further in *Faccenda Chicken* v *Fowler* [1986] 1 All ER 617 in which the following factors were considered relevant:

(a)   the nature of the employment, i.e. whether the defendant regularly had access to confidential information such as to mean that he should have been aware of its confidential nature

(b)   the nature of the information, i.e. was it sufficiently confidential to justify being treated as a trade secret

(c)   whether the confidential nature of the information was brought sufficiently to the attention of the employee.

PATENTS

The granting of patents is subject to the Patents Act 1977, as amended by the Copyright, Designs and Patents Act 1988. A patent is granted on application to the inventor of a new or novel invention enabling him to control the usage of his invention for a period of twenty years from the date of the application. Effectively, it allows him a twenty-year monopoly in which to recoup his development costs and make a profit from his invention before it enters the public domain in which anyone can use it freely.

To attract a patent, the inventor or someone acting on his behalf must demonstrate that the invention, be it a product, component or process etc., for which the patent is sought represents a new addition to the previous state of the art and further that it is not something that would be obvious to a large number of people. The decision as to whether it is novel is decided by searches and examinations undertaken by the Patent Office. If it is held to be novel, a patent will be granted, while if it is not, the application will be refused. Whether the invention would be obvious to a lot of other people is more difficult to decide and is ultimately a matter for the court to decide taking into account the prevailing state of the art as applied by a person skilled in the art. This approach has attracted some criticism and is different from that adopted in the EEC. Finally, the invention must be capable of being made or used in industry. If granted, the patent lasts for a period of twenty years from the date of the application subject to the payment of an annual fee. In the event of two similar applications being made, priority is given in date order of the application dates. Thus the first application lodged will be granted the patent assuming that it satisfies the criteria while any later applications will be refused.

The granting of the patent does not guarantee that the inventor will be able to produce or profit from the invention. It may be that in practice it is not viable to produce the item at a competitive price, or there may be legislation in force at the time the patent is granted or introduced subsequently that renders illegal its manufacture, sale or usage. The only thing that a patent guarantees to the inventor is that he will have control over who, if anyone, is to be allowed to use or produce the invention during the twenty-year period. Thus, in a business context, its real value lies in the inventor's ability to prevent competitors using the invention. In practice, of course, competitors will invent alternative systems or products, although clearly this will involve the expenditure of both time and money.

Three issues are of interest to businesses in the usage of patents: their enforcement, the position regarding employee inventions and the protection of patents overseas, particularly in the EEC given the increased movement of goods and the removal of trade barriers.

Enforcement of a patent to prevent its abuse is by civil action with the owner of the patent seeking an injunction to prevent further abuse, an account for profits and damages. An actionable infringement arises under s.60 of the Patent Act 1977 if a person does any of the following without the consent of the patent owner at a time when the patent is still in force:

(a) where the invention is a product, he makes, disposes of, uses or imports the product or keeps it for disposal or otherwise;
(b) where the invention is a process, he uses the process or he offers it for use when he knows, or it is obvious to a reasonable person in the circumstances, that its use would be an infringement;
(c) he disposes of, offers to dispose of, uses or imports any product obtained directly by means of that process or keeps any such product whether for disposal or otherwise.

In addition to these primary offences, it is also an offence for a person to provide another person with the means to work a patent when the first person knows, or it would be obvious to a reasonable person, that the item can be used to put the invention into use in the UK.

Many inventions are made by employees during the course of their employment. The obvious issue is whether the patent belongs to the employee or to his employer. Section 39 of the Patents Act 1977 provides that where an employee makes an invention in the course of his employment or while he is undertaking duties specifically allocated to him although not in his normal course of employment, any resultant invention is the property of the employer. The invention will only belong to the employee if he developed it in his own time. However, the Act seeks to be equitable between the legal rights of the employer and the reasonable expectations of the employee inventor. Section 40 of the Patents Act provides that where an employer gains outstanding benefits from patenting an employee invention, the employee is entitled to receive fair compensation. The difficulty, of course, is in establishing what constitutes an outstanding benefit. Any attempt to use the employee's contract of employment to limit his rights under s.40 is unenforceable.

Finally, the issue arises of protecting patents in other jurisdictions, particularly in the EEC. Application for a patent can be made under the European Patent Convention and lodged at the European Patent Office. A successful application has the effect of granting enforceable patents in every member country listed in the application. This can include all the members of the EEC.

COPYRIGHT

Original literary, dramatic, musical or artistic works etc. invest automatic copyright in the creator without the need to register the item or take any other positive actions. Computer software is treated in exactly the same way and thus a business creating original documents or designs on software will automatically acquire the copyright in them. Copyright law is currently governed by the Copyright, Designs and Patents Act 1988 with the copyright lasting for the author's life and fifty years from the end of the calendar year in which he died.

Protection spreads further than might first appear, for literary work is defined in s.3(1) to include any work, other than a dramatic or musical work, which is written, spoken or sung, and accordingly includes a table or compilation and a computer program and preparatory design material for a computer program. By s.4(1) artistic work includes graphic work, photographs, sculpture or collage, irrespective of its artistic quality, with graphic work including painting, drawings, maps, charts or plans.

Thus, in a normal business using everyday business techniques and mediums, office manuals, product catalogues, advertising literature, computer programs etc. would all attract copyright protection. If the company produces any promotional videos they too would attract copyright.

Copyright is vested in the owner who is the person who created the work though, where the article is computer generated, the author is the person who made the arrangements necessary for its creation. Where a literary, dramatic, musical or artistic work is made by an employee in the course of his employment, his employer is the first owner of the copyright subject to any agreement to the contrary. To acquire copyright the author must be from the UK or be a body corporate registered in the UK or another appropriate country. Alternatively, the work must have been first published in the UK.

Section 16 of the Act stipulates the rights of the copyright owner as being to have the exclusive right to do the following in the UK:

(a) to copy the work;
(b) to issue copies of the work to the public;
(c) to perform, show or play the work in public;
(d) to broadcast the work or include it in a cable programme service;
(e) to make an adaption of the work or do any of the above in relation to an adaption.

These rights are infringed by anyone doing or authorising another to do any of the above restricted acts, directly or indirectly, in relation to the whole work or a substantial part of it without the licence of the copyright owner. However, the Copyright (Computer Programs) Regulations 1992 (S.I. 1992/3233) state that it is not a breach of copyright for a lawful user of a computer program to make back-up copies or to adapt the program for his lawful use. Similarly, it is acceptable for such a person to copy a program while in the process of converting it from low level language to high level language provided that certain criteria are met.

Further, secondary infringements occur when a person without the consent of the copyright owner imports an infringing copy into the UK otherwise than for his private or domestic use. Of equal concern to a business is the s.24 offence of facilitating a breach of copyright by a third party. This occurs where a person makes or imports into the UK or possesses in the course of a business, or sells or lets for hire, or offers or exposes for sale or hire an article specifically designed or adapted for making copies of the work, knowing or having reason to believe that it is to be used to make infringing copies.

In *CBS Songs Ltd* v *Amstrad Consumer Electronics Ltd* [1988] 2 All ER 484 the House of Lords found Amstrad not liable under s.21 of the Copyright Act 1956 (a provision having similar effect to s.24 of the 1988 Act). The case related to a tape-to-tape facility on twin deck tape recorders which were advertised in a way likely to encourage home taping of copyright material although Amstrad did warn that copyright permission might be needed that they were not authorised to give. The court held that Amstrad had warned customers of the copyright permission requirement and that they were helpless to control that use of the machines after sale.

Infringement of copyright is enforced by actions for an injunction to prevent further abuse and a claim for damages or an account of the profits made through the breach.

In addition to the exclusive use of the material, the owner of a copyright acquires three moral rights in relation to his work. These are the right of paternity, the right to object to derogatory treatment of the work and the right to protection from false attribution. The right of paternity, given under s.77, gives the author the right to be identified whenever the work is published commercially, performed in public, broadcast or included in a cable programme service, or where the copies of a film or sound recording including the work are issued to the public. This right does not extend to computer programs, the design of typeface or any computer generated work. The right not to have the work treated in a derogatory manner prevents the distortion or mutilation of the work or its treatment in any other way prejudicial to the honour or reputation of the author or director. The final right is not to have literary, dramatic, musical or artistic work falsely attributed to him as author. This is a matter of protecting reputation. While the other moral rights last for fifty years after the death of the author, a claim for false attribution must be made within twenty years.

In addition to civil liability, criminal offences also arise from a breach of copyright. Under s.107 an offence is committed by any person who, without the licence of the copyright owner,

(a) makes for sale or hire, or
(b) imports into the United Kingdom otherwise than for his private or domestic use, or
(c) possesses in the course of a business with a view to committing any act infringing the copyright, or
(d) in the course of a business:
    (i) sells or lets for hire, or
    (ii) offers or exposes for sale or hire, or
    (iii) exhibits in public, or
    (iv) distributes, or
(e) distributes otherwise than in the course of a business to such an extent as to be prejudicial to the owner of the copyright,

an article which is, and which he knows or has reason to believe is, an infringing copy of a copyright work.

Such offences are liable on summary conviction to imprisonment not exceeding six months or a fine not exceeding level 5 on the standard scale. Where the offence is committed by a body corporate, directors, managers, company secretaries or other similar officers are liable as well.

DESIGNS

Protection for designs exists by two methods, the unregistered design rights introduced by ss. 213–235 of the 1988 Act and the system for registered designs under the Registered Designs Act 1949, as amended by ss. 265–273 and Schedule 4 of the 1988 Act.

Unregistered designs

'Design' is defined for these purposes as being the design of any aspect of the shape or configuration (whether interior or exterior) of the whole or part of an article. Unlike registered designs, there is no requirement that an unregistered design appeals to the eye and thus it may be purely functional. Notably design does not extend to a method or principle of construction, or to a surface design or to any other features of shape or configuration which:

(i) enable the article to be connected to, or placed in, around or against, another article so that either article may perform its function, or

(ii) are dependent upon the appearance of another article of which the article is intended by the designer to form an integral part.

These are the so-called 'must fit' and 'must match' exceptions whereby no infringement occurs if an item is designed deliberately to fit or match with an existing product. This is of most concern in industries producing spare parts for machinery, cars etc. where the design of the spare part is predetermined by the product onto or into which it must fit.

A design is not original for these purposes if it is commonplace in the design field in question at the time of its creation.

To create an unregistered design right, the design must either have been recorded in a design document or an article must have been made conforming to the design. An unregistered design creates an automatic right of ownership in the same way as a copyright and subsists for a period of fifteen years from the end of the calendar year in which it was designed or ten years from the end of the calendar year in which articles made to the design were first available on sale or hire anywhere in the world by or with the licence of the owner. However, under s.237 any person has a right to a licence during the last five years permitting them to do anything that would otherwise be an infringement.

As with copyright, the rights are vested in the designer, i.e. the person who created it or, in the case of a computer generated design, the person who undertook the arrangements for the creation of the design. A design created in the course of employment belongs to the employer. To attract protection the designer must be a person, body corporate or other body having a legal personality resident in the UK or formed under the laws of or having substantial business in the UK, EEC or other approved country. Alternatively, rights may be claimed by the first person exclusively authorised to put the product onto the market.

The designer has the exclusive right to reproduce the design for commercial purposes either by making articles to the design or by making a design document. An infringement occurs if anyone breaches these rights without the licence of the designer. A secondary infringement occurs under s.227 where a person without licence imports into the UK for commercial purposes, or has in his possession for commercial purposes or sells, lets for hire, or offers or exposes for sale or hire, in the course of a business, any article which is, and which he knows or has reason to believe is, an infringing copy.

The breach of an unregistered design right gives the designer the right to sue for an injunction and damages or an account for profits. Further, the designer can ask the court for an order instructing the offender to deliver up any infringing articles.

Registered designs

Registered designs are covered by the Registered Designs Act 1949 as amended. 'Design' means features of shape, configuration, pattern or ornament applied to an article by an industrial process, being features which in the finished article appeal to and are judged by the eye. For this purpose an industrially produced pattern means one that is applied to fifty items not constituting a single set. Design does not extend to features of shape or configuration dictated by function or by the appearance of another article.

The registered proprietor of the design is its author or the person who commissioned it, or an employer if the design was created in the course of employment. Computer generated designs where there is no human designer belong to the person by whom the arrangements for the design were made. The proprietor acquires rights similar to the designer of an unregistered design, namely the exclusive right to make or import for sale or hire or expose for sale or hire any article conforming to the registered design or any design not substantially different. This prevents a person making minimal alterations to the design in an attempt to circumvent the proprietor's rights. The prohibition also extends to kits which if assembled would infringe the registered design. The rights last initially for five years which can be extended under s.8(2) in five-year periods up to a total of twenty five years. The normal remedies of an injunction and damages or an account for profit follow an infringement unless the defendant can show that he did not know of the registration.

TRADE MARKS

Words and symbols associated with the particular producers or suppliers are protected against abuse both by the Trade Marks Acts and by the tort of passing off.

Trade marks

At the time of writing trade marks are subject to the Trade Marks Act 1938 and the Trade Marks (Amendment) Act 1984. However, reform is imminent with a Trade Marks Bill currently before parliament, the purpose of which is to give effect to First Council Directive No 89/104 of 21 December 1988 to approximate the laws of the Member States relating to trade marks. It seems likely that it will be passed in the foreseeable future.

Currently, trade marks may be registered under either Part A or Part B of the register. Part A is more prescriptive but also offers the greater protection to the owner of the trade mark. This division will be abolished if the new Act takes effect. To register under Part A the applicant must demonstrate that the mark contains one of the following:

(a) the name of a company, individual or firm, represented in a special or particular manner;
(b) the signature of the applicant for registration or some predecessor of his in business;
(c) an invented word or words;
(d) a word or words having no direct reference to the character or quality of the goods, and not being according to its ordinary meaning, a geographical name or surname;
(e) any other distinctive mark, but a name, signature or word, other than those covered by (a) to (d) above, is not registrable except on evidence of distinctiveness.

This list achieves the balance between allowing registration of words or symbols that are inextricably identified with the one person's products while not preventing other persons from using other words or marks appropriate to their own products, e.g. the word 'Cornish' as applied in John's Cornish Cream would not be registered such as to prevent anyone else describing their goods as Cornish cream, Cornish fudge etc. Similarly, any person is entitled to use his own name or that of his place of business or any *bona fide* description of the quality or character of his goods.

Naturally, an application for a trade mark will be refused if it would be likely to be confused with an existing registered trade mark. However, despite the refusal, users of the mark will have a defence to an allegation of breach of trade mark if they can demonstrate that they had used the mark before its first use by the proprietors of the registered mark or prior to its registration.

A trade mark gives the proprietor the exclusive right to use the mark and thereby distinguish his goods from those of another person. An infringement occurs if someone else uses his mark or one that is so similar that it is likely to cause confusion. The usual remedies of an injunction to prevent further abuse and damages or an account for profits can be claimed.

The Council Directive stipulates that a trade mark consists of any sign capable of being represented graphically, particularly words, including personal names, designs, letters, numerals, the shape of goods or their packaging provided that they are capable of distinguishing the goods or services from those of another person. Under Arts. 3–4 registration of a trade mark will be refused for a variety of reasons including that it might deceive the public, it is contrary to public policy, it is identical to an earlier trade mark (be it a Member State or a Community trade mark) or is so similar that it could cause confusion.

Registration of the mark gives the proprietor exclusive rights to the mark allowing him to prohibit third parties from using it without his consent including affixing the sign to goods or packaging, displaying the goods near a sign, importing or exporting goods under the sign and using it on business papers and advertising.

A trade mark can be revoked if it is not put to genuine use for a period of five years or if, due to the acts or inactivity of the proprietor, it has become the commonly used name in the trade for a product or service in respect of which it is registered.

Passing off

Passing off is the tort by which a producer or supplier can protect the goodwill attached to his business. The action is not to protect the symbol etc. under dispute but rather to protect the goodwill attached to it, the object being to prevent a person from misleading the public by passing off his goods as those of another person.

The protection extends to names, words, symbols and even the get-up of a product, anything that is sufficiently distinctive to identify the goods as being of one person's manufacture. The offending mark etc. does not need to be identical to the complainant's but must be sufficiently similar to cause confusion in the mind of a prospective purchaser.

In *White Hudson & Co Ltd* v *Asian Organisation Ltd* [1964] 1 WLR 1466 the plaintiff, a producer of medicated cough sweets wrapped in red cellophane wrappers, obtained an injunction to prevent the defendant using a similar wrapper that would confuse purchasers. Although the defendant put a different name on the wrapper, it was shown that purchasers relied on the get-up of the product and not the name.

Generic words can also be controlled, e.g. the use of the word 'champagne'.

In the Court of Appeal decision of *Taittinger* v *Allbev (1993) The Times,* 28 June 1993 the Court dealt with the use of the phrase 'Elderflower champagne'. The Court held that the term 'champagne' is not a generic term that can be applied to any sparkling wine but is restricted to wines coming from the Champagne region of France. The defendant was liable for passing off and was restrained by injunction from using the term again. This decision reinforced the 1960 decision of *Bollinger* v *Costa Brave Wine Co* [1960] Ch 262 which had held the same view regarding the use of the word 'champagne'.

Some names can cause difficulties because a manufacturer's name has fallen into common usage as a generic name for a particular type of product. Examples might be 'Yale' locks or 'Hoovers'. Arguably, in the public mind, the former now relates to a type of lock rather than the products of a particular manufacturer, while the latter is used in common parlance to mean any vacuum cleaner. Naturally, the onus is on the defendant to show that a situation exists such as to justify his use of the name.

To establish liability the words, mark etc. must have been used in the course of a business, been likely to mislead a prospective purchaser and caused actual damage to the plaintiff. If successful the plaintiff can seek damages, an injunction to prevent further abuse and an order for the obliteration of the offending mark or get-up.

QUESTION

Joe was the Managing Director of X Ltd, a small manufacturer. Joe's contract included a restraint-of-trade clause in which he agreed not to set up a competing business within five miles of X Ltd's premises for a period of two years. X Ltd was taken over by Y Ltd who immediately sacked Joe. Joe started a new firm four miles away from X Ltd's premises and started to manufacture an item that he had designed while working for X Ltd and which X Ltd had patented.

Advise Joe about his legal position.

FURTHER READING

Cornish, W.R., *Intellectual Property : Patents, Copyrights, Trade Marks and Allied Rights* (2nd ed) 1989 (Sweet and Maxwell)

Dobson, A.P. and Schmitthoff, C.M., *Charlesworth's Business Law* (15th ed) 1991 (Sweet and Maxwell)

Dworkin, G. and Taylor, R.D., *Blackstone's Guide to the Copyright, Designs and Patents Act 1988* 1989 (Blackstone Press)

Keenan, D. and Riches, S., *Business Law* (3rd ed) 1993 (Pitman)

Wilkinson, J., *Restraint of Trade* 1991 (Fourmat)

CHAPTER 20

International trade

INTRODUCTION

International trade in which goods cross national boundaries forms an important part of the trading network of many companies, this being particularly true in 1990s with the establishment of the single market in the EEC. Further, government policy exhorts producers to develop overseas markets as a means of earning foreign currency. But international trade is not without its problems. Typically, the seller resides in one nation state while the buyer is based in another. This breeds difficulties as regards the transfer of title, the opportunity to inspect goods and, most importantly from the seller's perspective, the guarantee of payment. International trade law has responded by developing a range of contracts and payment methods specifically designed to deal with these problems.

BILLS OF LADING

In an international contractual sale in which seller and buyer are unlikely to ever meet, documentary evidence of sale achieves an importance not found in domestic sales. Indeed the international sales of goods has been referred to as more of a sale of documents relating to goods. There are three common forms of documentation: bills of lading, sea waybills and a ship's delivery order, although the bill of lading is the one used most commonly.

A bill of lading serves three purposes: it is a document of title, evidence of a contract of carriage and a receipt. As a document of title its significance lies in the fact that it can be used to buy and sell the goods covered by it while they are in transit. Whether the bill of lading actually constitutes a document of title depends upon the wording of the individual bill. At the very least, however, it gives rights of constructive possession to the person who acquires it lawfully with that person having the right to expect the carrier to deliver the goods up to him upon presentation of the bill.

The contractual impact of a bill of lading arises from the inclusion within it of the details of the contract of carriage under which the goods are being transported. Typically, this will comprise the standard terms of carriage subject to any acceptable variations agreed by the shipper (usually the seller of the goods) and the carrier. At present, the relevant rules in the UK are the so-called Hague Visby Rules adopted by the Carriage of Goods at Sea Act 1971 which apply to every contract of carriage for goods leaving a UK port irrespective of their destination. These Rules will also apply to any other contract of carriage if the parties so agree. This will include every contract which is stated to be subject to English law.

The Hague Visby Rules lay down the basic requirements made of both shipper and carrier. The shipper must agree to pay the freight costs (i.e. the costs of carriage) plus the General Accident Contributions (GAC). The GAC is a form of indemnity whereby all the shippers with goods on any particular ship share the cost of any loss pro rata if the goods lost were discarded to protect the remainder. GAC can usually be recovered via marine insurance. The remaining duties on the shipper are to inform the carrier if any dangerous goods are being loaded and to arrange for the collection of all goods at their port of destination. Where the seller is transporting to an overseas buyer, this latter responsibility would be satisfied by ensuring that the buyer knows where and when to collect the goods. In an f.o.b. contract (see later) in which the buyer arranged the carriage he would already be aware of these details.

The carrier for his part is obliged to provide a seaworthy vessel which is equipped to receive and stow the goods and thereafter put to sea. Once at sea, the carrier is under an obligation to proceed without delay to the port of destination and not to deviate from the prescribed or agreed route except in an attempt to save life or property or where the deviation is reasonable.

The role of the bill of lading as a receipt is crucial to the contract of carriage for it is good evidence as to the identity, quantity and condition of the goods loaded under it. The bill, if governed by the Hague Visby Rules must provide details of:

(a) the leading marks on the goods. These are the identification marks which allow the goods to be identified as those to which the bill relates. This identifies them as the ones to be surrendered by the carrier to the holder of the bill of lading at the port of destination. The marks must be sufficiently permanent to prevent their obliteration during the voyage.

(b) the quantity of goods loaded. The ship's master is under an obligation to account for the full quantity of goods to the buyer at the port of destination. Thus, his signed statement in the bill is important as it stipulates the amount for which the carrier accepts responsibility. If a lesser amount is delivered, the carrier is liable. Section 4 of the Carriage of Goods at Sea Act 1992 provides that a bill of lading signed by the ship's master or any other duly authorised person is conclusive evidence against the carrier of the shipment of the goods.

(c) the condition of the goods when loaded. In an action by the buyer for the goods being damaged or not of merchantable quality, the bill is proof of their condition at the time of loading. If the goods are in a good condition, the carrier will sign the bill to that effect, the bill being said to be 'clean'. However, if the goods or packaging are damaged at the time of loading, the carrier must detail those defects on the bill of lading which is then described as 'claused'. This aspect of the bill is crucially important for it can be used as a means of allocating liability for goods delivered damaged at the port of destination. If the bill is clean, the carrier will be liable for the damage which must, *prima facie*, have occurred during the voyage. He will not be liable though for any damage detailed in a claused bill for which the buyer would need to seek redress from the seller. Whether the bill is clean or claused will also be vital to the ability of the holder of the bill to resell the goods during transit as a claused bill will militate against resale.

Claims against the carrier

The major conceptual difficulty with bills of lading has been their enforcement by the buyer. The bill of lading evidences a contract of carriage between the shipper (the seller) and the carrier to which the buyer is not a party. Normal rules of contractual privity clearly prevent the buyer suing to enforce this contract. This may be crucial if, as is usual, the risk in the goods passes to the buyer when the goods cross the ship's rail at the port of loading. Thus, while the contract exists between the seller and the carrier, it is the buyer who is affected by the performance of the contract.

Section 1 of the Bills of Lading Act 1855 was passed expressly to address this problem by providing that if certain criteria are satisfied the buyer should be able to enforce the contract of carriage as if he were a party to it. However, the wording of the section is seriously flawed as it appears to limit its impact to those situations where the transfer or endorsement of the bill causes the property in the goods to pass simultaneously. There are potentially many situations in which this will not occur and where therefore the Act would not apply. Bradgate and Savage have identified eight example situations, the three most significant of which are arguably:

(a) where the bill has been endorsed such as to facilitate delivery of the goods but where the passage of property is subject to a retention of title clause. Remember that where the contract is subject to English law, ss.16–19 of the Sale of Goods Act 1979 apply.

(b) where the goods are being transported in bulk. Here they will be unascertained goods in which the property cannot pass by virtue of s.16 of the Sale of Goods Act 1979 until such time as they are ascertained.

(c) where the property in the goods has passed under the contract before the goods are shipped.

Section 1 of the Bills of Lading Act 1855 was supplemented by the court's ability to construe an implied contract between the carrier and the buyer. This approach developed out of the leading case of *Brandt* v *Liverpool, Brazil and River Plate Steam Navigation Co Ltd* [1924] 1 KB 575 which relies on the premise that the buyer will pay the carrier any outstanding freight charges at the time of presenting the bill of lading and collecting the goods. Such a payment would evidence a contract based on the bill of lading. However, it is clear from the Court of Appeal in *The Aramis* [1989] 1 Lloyd's Rep 213 that this approach cannot be extended unduly. In that case, in which there were no outstanding debts for the buyer to settle, no implied contract arose. Given this decision, allied to the fact that most freight contracts are prepaid, it means that the potential use of *Brandt* contracts is severely limited.

These identified weaknesses have been addressed by s.2 of the Carriage of Goods at Sea Act 1992 which applies to all bills of lading, sea waybills and ship's delivery orders issued on or after 16 September 1992. In this context, s.1(2) of the Act states that a bill of lading does not include a document which is incapable of transfer either by endorsement or, as a bearer bill, by delivery without endorsement but, subject to that, includes 'received for shipment' bills of lading.

Section 1(3) defines a 'sea waybill' as a document which is not a bill of lading but which is a receipt which contains or evidences a contract for the carriage of goods by sea and identifies the person to whom delivery of the goods is to be made in accordance with that contract.

Section 1(4) defines a 'ship's delivery order' as a document which is neither a bill of lading nor a sea waybill but which contains an undertaking given for the purposes of a carriage of goods by sea and is given by the carrier to a person identified in the document and promises to deliver the goods to that person.

Section 2 which encompasses the main provision of the Act provides that the lawful holder of a bill of lading, the person entitled to delivery under a sea waybill or the person entitled to delivery under a ship's delivery order will be vested with all the rights to enforce the contract of carriage as if he had been a party to it. The advantage of s.2 over the Bills of Lading Act 1855 is that the new enforcement rights are not linked to the transfer of property (though they can be linked to possession) but arise merely by virtue of being the lawful holder of the appropriate documents, irrespective of the capacity in which they are held. This circumvents the difficulties posed by the Bills of Lading Act 1855 and the uncertainties of implied contracts under *Brandt*. However, a demand for delivery under the documents or the exercise of the contractual rights makes the plaintiff liable on the contract as if he had been a party to it. He gains not merely the benefits but also the burdens.

Where a third party with an interest or right in the goods subject to a bill of lading, sea waybill or ship's delivery order suffers loss as a result of a breach of the contract of carriage, the person vested with contractual rights under s.2(1) of the Act may sue on their behalf.

There is a limitation however on the person's ability to claim contractual enforcement rights under s.2(1). If the bill of lading does not give the lawful holder the right to possession of the goods as against the carrier, the holder will not acquire the right to sue on the contract of carriage unless he became the holder of the bill either as a result of a contract made before the bill lost its possession rights or as a result of the rejection of goods or documents delivered by him to another person under any contractual or other arrangements.

In addition to contractual rights, the holder of a bill may also have rights in tort – in conversion and possibly negligence. Conversion arises if the carrier delivers the goods to the wrong person at the port of destination. The difficulty arises if the goods arrive at the port of destination before the bill of lading. This is likely to happen if documentary credits are being used as the method of payment (see later) with the need for one and probably two banks to examine and approve the documentation. Any delay in the documentation can leave the buyer seeking delivery of the goods from the carrier at the point of destination but without the supporting documentation. Naturally, the carrier, wary of laying himself open to a claim for conversion, will be reluctant to surrender the goods. In practice, this is resolved by the buyer providing the carrier with an indemnity against any possible legal action.

The other potential source of tortious liability lies in negligence if the goods have been lost or damaged in transit. However, the scope of this tort appears to be very limited in this context with the decision of *The Aliakmon* [1986] 2 All ER 145 confirming the traditional view that a negligence action can only be brought if the buyer has the property in the goods or, at the very least, an immediate right to possession.

Multi-modal transport

Transport has changed significantly in recent years with the advent of containerised transport. From the seller's point of view, containerisation has much to offer: a secure easy-to-load method in which his goods are well protected from weather and theft throughout the whole of the journey from his premises to those of the buyer. However, the contracts of carriage for such containers do pose some difficulties. If the sea voyage is subject to a bill of lading, it is impossible for the carrier to confirm the quantity or condition of goods in a sealed container at the time of loading. Thus, if the goods delivered to the buyer are damaged, it is virtually impossible to specify when the damage occurred. Such problems have given rise to a new style of multi-modal transport contract which governs all aspects of the transportation from the seller's premises to the buyer's premises and thus includes the road/rail transport to the port of departure and, if relevant, the road/rail transport from the port of destination to the buyer's premises. It would also cover the loading and unloading of the container from the ship. The need for such multi-modal contracts is recognised, the voyage part of which may be subject to some form of bill of lading, but as yet no standard form of contract is in force.

C.I.F. AND F.O.B. CONTRACTS

As international contracts necessarily involve transporting the goods across at least one national boundary, it follows that seller and buyer must agree where the responsibility lies for making the arrangements and financing the carriage. A mere contract of sale of the type used for domestic sales is totally inadequate. The two most common forms of international contract are c.i.f. contracts and f.o.b. contracts.

C.i.f. contracts

A c.i.f. (carriage, insurance and freight) contract is the most common type and places the responsibility on the seller to arrange for the shipment of the goods and to insure them against loss or damage during the voyage. Thus the price charged to the buyer is inclusive of these services. In a fluctuating market it is in the buyer's interests to agree to a c.i.f. contract where the seller bears the risk of any increase in transport or insurance costs.

A c.i.f. contract places duties on both the seller and buyer. Naturally, if the contract is governed by English law this will include statutory duties arising from compliance with the Sale of Goods Act 1979. The duties placed on the seller may be summarised thus:

(a) the duty to provide goods that conform with the contract both as regards description and quantity and are of a merchantable quality and fit for their intended purpose. A breach of any of these requirements would constitute a breach of condition justifying repudiation of the goods and termination of the contract.

(b) the duty to deliver the goods to the correct port of loading during the contractually specified period. Time is of the essence in this situation as it is a contractually agreed term and thus to deliver the goods too early or too late will justify a termination of the contract.

(c) the duty to arrange for the necessary shipping to deliver the goods to the correct port of destination and to ensure that the vessel used can offer any special facilities needed, i.e. a refrigerated hold for the transport of some foodstuffs.

(d) to insure the goods against loss or damage during the voyage.

(e) to accept liability for the payment of the freight charges and the insurance charges.

(f)   to ensure that the appropriate documentation is available and forwarded to the buyer, or if relevant, the bank, to enable the buyer to take delivery at the port of destination.

(g)   to arrange for any other necessary documentation such as export licences.

The duties placed on the buyer again include some terms that are derived from his obligations under the Sale of Goods Act 1979 and some that are peculiar to international contracts:

(a)   the duty to take delivery of the goods when they arrive at the port of destination, assuming that they comply with the contract description and with the statutory implied terms.

(b)   the duty to accept the bill of lading if it is in proper form and pay for the goods delivered under it.

(c)   to pay for any additional freight or demurrage (costs incurred through a delay in loading at the port of departure) if the contract so specifies.

(d)   to arrange for the transportation of the goods after their arrival at the port of destination if the contract so provides.

(e)   to inform the seller of the date and place of destination of the goods if the contract so requires in sufficient time to allow the seller to make the necessary shipment arrangements.

(f)   to arrange and pay for any necessary import licences/customs duties etc.

F.o.b. contracts

The alternative form of contract is an f.o.b. (free on board) contract which places the responsibility on the buyer to arrange for the shipment of the goods and their insurance cover for the voyage. Thus the responsibilities of the seller cease when the goods have been loaded. In some ways the duties placed on the seller and buyer by an f.o.b. contract are the same as under a c.i.f. contract. Thus the seller is under an obligation to deliver goods complying with the contract and with the statutory implied terms, while the buyer is under a duty to take delivery of the goods and the documents of carriage and pay for the goods. The duties placed on the seller and buyer relating to the transport of the goods differs however from those under a c.i.f. contract.

The duties placed on the seller are:

(a)   to arrange for the transportation of the goods to the port of departure.

(b)   to deliver them to the appropriate vessel during the contractually agreed period for loading.

(c)   to obtain a mate's receipt when the goods are loaded and hand it to a forwarding agent for transmission to the buyer.

The duties placed on the buyer are:

(a) to book appropriate shipping space on a suitable vessel.
(b) to inform the seller of the port and date of departure and the name of the vessel in sufficient time to allow the seller to make the transport arrangements necessary to ensure that the goods are loaded on time. A failure to do this will allow the seller to terminate the contract, see *Bunge* v *Tradax* [1975] 2 Lloyd's Rep 235.
(c) to insure the cargo against loss or damage during the voyage.
(d) to pay the freight charges.

The potential advantage to a buyer in contracting on f.o.b. terms is that it allows him the choice of vessel. If the buyer regularly imports goods he may have a block insurance policy or have his own shipping contacts who can provide cheaper shipping. From a governmental point of view, f.o.b. contracts offer the opportunity to use domestic ships, both encouraging the shipping industry and saving foreign currency.

The passage of risk

As discussed in chapter 10, the risk in goods under s.20 of the Sale of Goods Act 1979 usually passes with the passage of the property in the goods. However, s.20 provides that this presumption does not hold true if there is an agreement to the contrary. In contracts for international trade it is usual to provide that the risk in the goods passes to the buyer at the time that the goods cross the ship's rail during loading irrespective of when the property in the goods passes. Therefore, if the goods are damaged during loading but before they cross the rail the seller must bear the risk. Equally, if there is a valid retention of title clause in the contract or if the goods have not been ascertained, the risk in the goods will pass to the buyer while the goods are still owned by the seller.

DOCUMENTARY CREDITS

The financing of international sale contracts poses particular problems. The seller will be reluctant to part with the goods until he is guaranteed payment of the purchase price for, should the buyer fail to pay, the seller would be faced with the difficulty of suing to enforce the debt in a foreign jurisdiction. While the position is not as onerous if the buyer is based in another EEC Member State, because the provisions of the Civil Jurisdiction and Judgments Act 1982 permit judgments to be enforced throughout the EEC, it is still a situation which a seller would rather avoid. The buyer for his part will not prepared to part with the money for the goods until he has received them and had the opportunity to inspect them. Both parties are bound to be wary of dealing with a contracting party with whom they may not have dealt in the past and who is beyond the jurisdiction of the courts.

This potential breakdown has been addressed by the development of the irrevocable Banker's Documentary Credit which permits the sale to be completed while minimising the risk faced by both parties.

Typically, the arrangement of an irrevocable Banker's Documentary Credit will involve the use of two banks, one in the buyer's country and one in the seller's country.

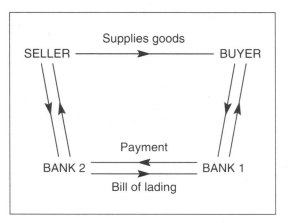

Figure 8   An irrevocable banker's documentary credit arrangement

As can be seen from Fig. 8, while the goods are sent directly from the seller to the buyer, the bill of lading or other shipping documents and the payment for the contract both pass through the hands of both banks. The arrangement works thus. Having agreed the terms of the contract of sale, the buyer instructs the bank in his country, Bank 1, to issue a documentary credit in favour of the seller. Once Bank 1 has confirmed to the seller that this has been done, the seller can safely ship the goods, certain that he will be paid. Bank 1 then instructs Bank 2 which is based in the seller's country about the credit. Bank 2 will confirm the arrangement. The seller having shipped the goods will be in possession of the bill of lading. He presents the bill of lading to Bank 2 who after checking and accepting the documents will pay the seller. Bank 2 will, in turn, present the documents to Bank 1 and receive payment, Bank 1 forwarding them to the buyer for payment.

The system clearly has advantages for both seller and buyer. The seller is assured of payment as the documentary credit is irrevocable, but should any difficulties arise the seller has an identifiable defendant (Bank 2) based in his own jurisdiction. The buyer for his part acquires the bill of lading as soon as Bank 1 has paid the debt to Bank 2, thus allowing the buyer to claim delivery of the goods at the port of destination or even sell the goods while they are still in transit. This latter facility is important for the buyer may need to sell the goods via the bill of lading in order to settle his indebtedness to Bank 1.

Because of the number of people involved in a documentary credit transaction, it is not uncommon for the goods to arrive at the port of destination before the buyer receives the bill of lading from Bank 1. This places the buyer in an invidious position. Naturally he will want to take possession of the goods as soon as possible to allow him to use them or arrange for their resale if that is his intention. However, in the absence of a bill of lading, the carrier may be reluctant to release the goods in case he is subsequently sued in conversion by anyone who has an immediate right to possession. The difficulty is resolved typically by the buyer providing the carrier with an indemnity against any claim in conversion that may be lodged against him.

QUESTION

Virgo Ltd, a manufacturer of goods in England, agreed to sell them to Cancer, a company in France. The contract was a c.i.f. contract with the goods being transported by sea from Southampton to Le Havre. It was agreed that payment would be by documentary credit through Bank A in France and Bank B in England. Virgo Ltd arranged for the loading of the goods and gave a clean bill of lading to Bank B. The goods were damaged in a heavy storm during the crossing. The goods arrived at Le Havre before the bill of lading.

Advise Cancer about obtaining possession of the goods and claiming for the damage caused to them.

FURTHER READING

Bradgate, R., and Savage, N., *Commercial Law* 1991 (Butterworth)
Schmitthoff, C.M., *Schmitthoff's Export Trade* (9th ed) 1990 (Stevens)

CHAPTER 21

Insurance

INTRODUCTION

Throughout this text this author has referred to situations in which the supplier/manufacturer of goods or services would have civil law liability in circumstances in which it would be possible to protect himself from the full rigours of liability by the use of insurance. Thus, for example, this would include liability for damage caused by goods proving unmerchantable or not fit for their purpose, injuries sustained from defective goods with consequent product liability, negligence, a failure to provide title to goods, accidental damage to goods and the loss of or damage to goods during transit by sea. It is noticeable that all the liabilities mentioned here refer to civil law liability. It would, of course, be contrary to public policy to allow the defendant in a criminal case to protect himself against the effects of such liability by the use of insurance.

Insurance has much to offer from the insured's perspective. It protects him from full liability for his actions by allowing him to contract with an insurance company for them to run the risk on his behalf. Further, the insured can spread the responsibility among his customers by treating the insurance premium, the cost of the contract, as another cost of production. This can be recouped from his customers through a marginal increase in the product price. Ultimately, therefore, insurance provides the insured trader with a means to avoid the financial implications of civil liability at minimal cost or inconvenience to himself.

TYPES OF INSURANCE

Insurance risks fall into two categories, indemnity insurance and contingency insurance. The former, indemnity insurance, provides indemnity, i.e. full financial cover, if a particular situation arises. Thus, for example, fire insurance is an indemnity insurance which will pay for the full cost of fire damage, assuming that the property was fully insured. By comparison, contingency insurance occurs when the insurer promises to pay an agreed sum upon the happening of the contingent event. The most common form of contingency insurance is life insurance under which the insurer agrees to pay a fixed sum upon the death of the person whose life was insured (not necessarily the policy holder). Life insurance is beyond the remit of this text and will not be considered in detail. The common feature to both indemnity insurance and contingency insurance is that there is a degree of uncertainty. With indemnity insurance the uncertainty is whether the event will ever happen. A company may have fire insurance on its factory and offices for twenty years and never have a fire. Similarly, it may have accident insurance on a company car and never have it involved in an accident. With life insurance, the uncertainty is of a different nature. The contingent event, death, is bound to happen, the uncertainty is when it will happen.

Insurance can also be divided into first party insurance and third party insurance. First party insurance protects the insured from the damage that he will suffer if the event occurs. Fire insurance is a good example where the insured person protects his own property against the risk of fire in order to receive indemnity against his own loss. Third party insurance provides compensation to third parties affected by the insured's actions. Thus, product liability insurance taken out by a producer to cover claims made by persons injured by defective products is third party insurance. It is possible to mix the two in one policy as, for example, where a company (or anyone else) insures a car 'fully comprehensive'. Such insurance protects the insured against the first party risks of damage to or loss of the vehicle itself through accident, theft etc. and protects it against third party liability owed to anyone injured by the car in an accident.

INSURABLE INTEREST

In order to effect valid insurance the insured person must have an 'insurable interest' in the subject matter of the policy. The lack of any insurable interest will render the contract void under the Gaming Act 1845.

An insurable interest was defined in the landmark decision of *Lucena* v *Craufurd* (1806) 2 B & PNR 269 as being 'a right in the property, or a right derivable out of some contract about the property, which in either case may be lost upon some contingency affecting the possession or enjoyment of the party'. The most obvious insurable interest is ownership of the goods or property insured but any legal interest in the subject matter will suffice. Thus, in a contract of sale involving a retention of title clause the seller retains an insurable interest in the goods until the property in them passes although he may already have parted with the possession of the goods. The buyer in that situation who has possession but not property has an insurable interest as a person who has bought or agreed to buy the goods and who has a potential liability to the owner should the goods be damaged while they are in his possession. Similarly, both creditor and hirer in a hire-purchase agreement would have insurable interests. A lien over goods will suffice to create an insurable interest such that the unpaid seller of goods will have such an interest. A person has an insurable interest in marine insurance if he will benefit from the safe arrival of the vessel and its cargo and suffer loss by its failure to arrive safely. These examples all relate to first party liability but the same would hold true of third party liability. Hence the seller or manufacturer of goods would have sufficient insurable interest to cover liability to third persons should the goods prove to be faulty.

The insurable interest must exist at the time of the loss, an expired interest or one yet to mature being insufficient.

In *Macaura* v *Northern Assurance Co Ltd* [1925] AC 619, Macaura was the owner of timber on his estate in County Tyrone. He sold the timber to a company in return for 42 000 fully paid shares in the company, which made him the principal shareholder, all other shares being held by his nominees. He was also an unsecured creditor of the company in the sum of £19 000. He continued to insure the timber in his own name rather than in the company's name. Two weeks after the sale the timber was destroyed in a fire. The House of Lords held that although Macaura was the principal shareholder and creditor of the company and as such had a genuine interest in the well being of the company, the timber was owned by the company and not by him in any capacity. As he had no legal interest in the property, he had no insurable interest and the insurance company were correct in refusing to pay upon his claim.

Macaura is also good authority for the proposition that mere possession of the goods does not amount to an insurable interest. A legal interest of some sort is necessary.

Lucena v *Craufurd* is evidence that a legal interest which has not yet matured does not constitute an insurable interest and will defeat an insurance claim.

In *Lucena* v *Craufurd* some enemy ships were captured on the high seas by some British ships. The Crown Commissioners were authorised to take control of such ships when they reached a British port. Meanwhile, the Commissioners sought to insure the ships, some of which were lost at sea before reaching port. The House of Lords held that at the time of loss the Crown Commissioners did not have an insurable interest in the vessels and thus could not claim on the insurance policy.

The insured's ability to recover is limited to the extent of his own interest. However, in some situations, it may be possible for the insured to claim the full value of the lost or damaged goods and hold the balance on trust for the owner of the remaining insurable interest. This is particularly so if the third party is named in the policy.

In *Hepburn* v *A. Tomlinson (Hauliers) Ltd* [1966] AC 451 a carrier of goods insured them for the duration of carriage naming the owner of the goods as a party to the insurance and including some first party cover. The court held that the owner of the goods was entitled to recover when the goods were stolen from the carrier with the latter being in no way responsible for the theft.

THE CONTRACT

A contract of insurance is at root a contract subject to the same rules as any other contract. Thus, there is a requirement for offer, acceptance, consideration etc. In insurance, the contractual offer is made by the insured person presenting details of the insurance required to the insurance company. This is commonly done by the completion of a standard proposal form which will include details of the party to be insured, the nature of the risk, the duration of the insurance and any special factors which are to be brought to the attention of the insurance company. As stated, this is done typically in a proposal form but there is no obligation to this effect. An offer made orally as, for example, where a motorist arranges for the insurance of a different car over the phone, is both legal and binding if accepted. If the proposal is the contractual offer, it follows that the insurance company is at liberty to accept or reject the offer, the contract becoming effective if the company accepts the offer. The consideration for the contract is the insurance premium.

An insurance contract is a contract *uberrimae fidei* and thus the parties are under an obligation to inform each other of all matters relevant to the insurance contract. This duty of disclosure is particularly pertinent to the provision of information by the insured person when proposing the contract. The insurance company obviously need all the relevant information to enable it to decide whether to accept the insurance proposal and provide the insurance cover required. In practice, the crucial information will be almost exclusively in the hands of the person seeking the insurance cover who is subject to an obligation to provide it to the insurance company. A failure to disclose all the material information will render the contract voidable at the behest of the insurer in the same way that any contractual misrepresentation affects the resultant contract. However, the Association of British Insurers and Lloyd's have indicated that they will not avoid non-commercial insurance contracts as a result of an innocent misrepresentation or non-disclosure in a proposal.

This duty of disclosure begs the obvious question as to what information must be disclosed. Clearly, any question on the proposal form must be fully and truthfully answered but the duty of disclosure goes beyond this. The insured is under a duty to disclose all material facts, which are considered to be any facts that a prudent insurer would take into consideration when deciding whether to insure the risk. Cases suggest, for example, that a previous conviction of the insured is a material fact even if the conviction is in no way related to the risk for which insurance cover is being sought.

In *Woolcott* v *Sun Alliance & London Alliance Ltd* [1978] 1 All ER 1253 the insured arranged for insurance for his house. He failed to disclose that he had previous convictions for robbery but stated that, if asked, he would have disclosed details of the convictions. The house was subsequently destroyed by fire. The court held that the insurance was entitled to avoid the insurance because of the insured's failure to disclose a material fact.

The decisions of *Regina Fur Co Ltd* v *Bossom* [1957] 2 Lloyd's Rep 466 and *Roselodge Ltd* v *Castle* [1966] 2 Lloyd's Rep 113 would both support this proposition.

A refusal by another company to provide insurance for the insured is also a relevant material fact as can be seen in the decision of *Glicksman* v *Lancashire & General Insurance* Co [1927] AC 139.

In the *Glicksman* decision a firm of which Glicksman was a partner applied for some burglary insurance. The firm had never been refused insurance cover although Glicksman personally had been. It was held that the insurer was entitled to avoid the policy for non-disclosure of a material fact.

The duty of good faith and disclosure in insurance is a mutual duty and thus is also owed by the insurer to the insured. The House of Lords decision of *Banque Financière de la Cité SA* v *Westgate Insurance Co Ltd* [1990] 2 All ER 947 confirmed this point although holding that the insured has no right to damages in this situation, his remedy being recission of the contract.

An insurance contract can be assigned in the same way as any other contract. With insurance contracts however there must be compliance with certain criteria. As explained earlier only a person with an insurable interest can insure goods. It follows therefore that if that person ceases to have an insurable interest the insurance policy will cease. The disposal of the goods, for example by sale, would defeat the insurance policy unless it is assigned to the buyer of the goods simultaneously with the passage of property in the goods. Further, as an insurance contract is a contract *uberrimae fidei* any assignment must be agreed by the insurance company. The insured person cannot simply foist a new contractual party on the insurance company without its consent.

Contracts of marine insurance are assignable by indorsement. This flexibility is essential to the smooth running of international trade contracts particularly c.i.f. contracts.

TERMS OF CONTRACT

The terms of an insurance contract fall into three headings: warranties, conditions and terms descriptive of the risk. Rather confusingly, the use of terminology in insurance contracts is in direct opposition to its use in other contracts. Thus in the insurance context, warranties are the most important and significant terms, the breach of which gives the insurer the option of rescinding the contract. Conditions are the lesser terms the breach of which gives rise to an action for damages or perhaps the right to avoid liability for one particular claim. Terms descriptive of the risk are as the name suggests terms which add to the understanding of the risk insured but which do not give rise to any remedy if breached.

Warranties are often derived from the information contained in a proposal form with the form typically including a statement that such information will form the basis of the contract. It follows that if the information on the proposal is incorrect the insurer can terminate the policy.

In *Dawsons Ltd* v *Bonnin* [1922] 2 AC 413 the proposal form for vehicle insurance on a lorry asked for the address at which the lorry would be garaged. The insured inadvertently gave an incorrect address. Although this mistake had no effect on the risk being insured the court nonetheless held that the insurers could avoid the contract for a breach of warranty as the proposal form clearly stated that the answers would form the basis of the contract.

This provision is of most importance in respect of commercial insurance, for the Association of British Insurers and Lloyd's agreed in 1986 that in non-commercial insurance they would not convert statements in proposal forms into warranties of either past or present fact.

Breaches of condition in this context refer to relatively minor breaches and may allow the insured to evade liability for one incident. A prime example would be the condition typically included in insurance policies which requires that the insured must inform the insurer of a likely claim within a specified period after the occurrence of the event. A failure to comply with such a term allows the insurer to avoid liability for that event while not interrupting the continuation of the insurance policy.

Terms descriptive of the risk are by way of being explanatory rather than enforceable which may go some way towards mitigating the effect of a breach of warranty.

In *C.T.N. Cash & Carry Ltd* v *General Accident Fire & Life Assurance Corporation plc* [1989] 1 Lloyd's Rep 259 the policy on the insured's premises stated that the cash kiosk would be attended and locked during business hours. The court held that this term was descriptive of the risk and that the insurer could repudiate a claim arising at a time when this term was not being complied with without repudiating the whole insurance contract.

THE ROLE OF AGENTS

A significant proportion of insurance business is conducted through independent agents or brokers registered under the Insurance Brokers (Registration) Act 1977. Much of the relationship is subject to the normal rules of agency but the key question in the insurance context is on whose behalf the agent is working. Is he the agent of the insurer to sell insurance policies or the agent of the insured looking for insurance cover? This is particularly important with regard to the insured's duty of disclosure for if the agent is acting for the insurer disclosure to him will satisfy the duty. If however the agent is acting for the insured, disclosure to him will be of no effect. As a general rule of thumb, agents canvassing business on behalf of an insurer will be presumed to be acting for that insurer. Equally an independent insurance broker providing advice about possible alternative sources of insurance to the insured will be presumed to be acting as his agent. Both however would seem to act as the agent of the insurer for the purpose of issuing cover notes. Further, the decision of *Newsholme Bros* v *Road Transport and General Insurance Co* [1929] 2 KB 356 specified that if the agent of the insurer for the sake of convenience fills in the proposal form for the insured this does not make him the agent of the insured particularly if the insured signs the proposal form after it has been completed.

CLAIMS

The insured party is entitled to make a claim under a policy when and if the event insured against occurs and causes damage or loss to the insured. Thus payment is due on a fire policy if the property insured is damaged by fire. Similarly a life insurance policy is payable upon the death of the person who was the subject of the policy.

The policy typically provides that monetary compensation will be paid upon the occurrence of the event but there is no legal requirement to this effect. Hence it would be perfectly legal to stipulate that the insurer is responsible for replacing a lost item or rebuilding a damaged property. The latter would be of particular value in the current economic climate where the market value of property (which is the sum that the insured would be likely to receive upon destruction of the property) would not cover the cost of rebuilding it.

For indemnity insurance the insured will receive the market value of the property at the time of its destruction, this being so both for real property and goods. Thus second-hand goods will only attract their current value and not the cost of a new replacement. It is possible to obtain new-for-old policies whereby for an additional premium the insured will receive the cost of new goods rather than the market value of the old ones. Where the goods have not been destroyed merely damaged the insurer will receive the cost of repairing them. It should be noted that total loss justifying payment under a marine insurance policy includes 'constructive total loss' in which the goods or vessel have been abandoned in a situation where actual total loss was inevitable.

These statements about payment have been made on the basis that the property is fully insured, i.e. that its full market value was insured. However, in practice property is often underinsured, either inadvertently because property values have risen without the insured making appropriate alterations to the insurance cover or deliberately as a means of reducing the cost of insurance premiums. It would be inequitable to allow an insured person who is underinsured to recover the full cost of any damage that he suffers. It is normal practice for insurance contracts to contain an average clause which provides that where the property subject to the policy is undervalued the insured person will only receive the equivalent percentage of compensation. Thus, for example, if property worth £10 000 is insured for £6000 the insured will only receive £6000 if the property is totally destroyed as a result of an insured event. If the same property were to suffer damage valued at £5000 (50% of its market value) the insured would only receive £3000 in compensation (50% of its insured value).

With liability insurance, the insured person is entitled to receive the full amount to cover his liability to third parties injured by the insured item. Thus, for example, in product liability insurance the producer will receive the full amount of his civil liability to the injured user of a defective product. This payment will be subject only to any maximum cover stipulated in the contract.

The right to full payment may be mitigated by the existence of an excess on the policy. Such a provision, very common in motor insurance, requires the insured person to accept liability for some of the damage, perhaps, for example, the first £100. If damage of less than the excess is occasioned the insured person is liable for all of it. If the damage exceeds the excess, the insured pays the excess with the insurer paying the remainder.

A basic tenet of insurance as stipulated in *Castellain* v *Preston* (1883) 11 QBD 380 is that the insured will receive full indemnity but not receive more than the value of his loss. It may be, however, that the property or goods are covered by more than one insurance policy with the net result that if all the relevant policies paid out fully, the insured would be overcompensated. In a purchasing and supply situation this could happen, for example, if the owner and the carrier of goods both insured the goods for the duration of the contract of carriage. If the goods should be lost or stolen during the carriage, payments could be claimed under both insurance policies. The same situation would occur with goods in storage if both the owner and the warehouseman insured them. When one of the insurers pays out the full claim in this situation, he is entitled to seek a contribution from any other insurer covering the same risk. This is so even if, as happened in *Legal and General Assurance Society Ltd* v *Drake Insurance Co Ltd* [1992] 1 All ER 283, one of the insurers would have been able to avoid liability on the claim because the insured had not complied with the condition about the giving of notice of a claim.

SUBROGATION

Subrogation deals with the rights of the insurer to recover money from the insured if he has been overcompensated and to enforce the rights of the insured against any third party responsible for the loss.

The first part of subrogation, that relating to the opportunity for the insurer to reclaim some money from the insured, arises if the insured has been overcompensated. As explained earlier the insured has a right to receive full indemnity for his losses assuming that he was fully insured but does not have a right to be overcompensated. This situation might arise if, for example, the damaged goods had been insured by two insurance companies both of whom, unaware of the existence of the other, had paid out full indemnity. The insured would then have received double indemnity. Similarly, it might arise if the insured receives full indemnity from his insurance company and then receives compensation from any third party responsible for the event, e.g. a negligent driver under motor insurance. In any situation in which the insured has been overcompensated the insurer is entitled to recover the excess payment from the insured. However the insurer may not recover more than the amount for which he was responsible under the policy. Any further excess is a windfall for the insured.

The second aspect of subrogation relates to the right of the insurer to adopt any legal action to recover compensation that would have been open to the insured. Thus, for example, if the owner of goods has received indemnity from his insurance company for their loss, the insurer could then sue anyone whose negligence caused the loss. This right of subrogation effectively means that the insurer steps into the shoes of the insured as regards legal claims. Therefore, the insurer is bound by any restrictions that would have applied to the insured. Hence, if any legal defence could have been raised against the insured, it can be raised against the insurer. Similarly, the insurer will be subject to any counterclaim of contributory negligence. Finally, the insurer cannot sue any other party to the insurance policy as that would involve the insured effectively suing himself.

QUESTION

Z Ltd want to insure their factory against the risk of fire damage. Consider each of the three issues raised:

(a) do they have an insurable interest?

(b) must they tell the insurer that they were refused burglary insurance for the factory?

(c) Z Ltd, being short of capital, can only afford to insure the factory for 80% of its value. What is the inherent risk of this strategy?

FURTHER READING

Birds, J., *Modern Insurance Law* 1982 (Sweet and Maxwell)

Dobson, A.P. and Schmitthoff, C.M., *Charlesworth's Business Law* (15th ed) 1991 (Sweet and Maxwell)

Bradgate, R. and Savage, N., *Commercial Law* 1991 (Butterworth)

PART VI

Employment law

CHAPTER 22

Employment law

INTRODUCTION

Employment law is an enormous subject with many different facets. A comprehensive examination of the subject is well beyond the remit of a text of this nature. Hence, this chapter will concentrate on the contract of employment, being the feature of employment law that is of most direct relevance to individual employees.

TERMS OF THE CONTRACT

A contract of employment is at root a contract subject to the normal requirements of offer, acceptance, consideration and an intention to be legally bound. In essence, the agreement is that the employee will attend for work during the requisite hours and undertake the work lawfully required of him by his employer in exchange for his weekly wage or monthly salary. However, that description paints an extremely simplistic view of the true position for numerous statutes have made significant inroads into the contractual relationship.

The Employment Protection (Consolidation) Act 1978 as amended (most recently by the Trade Union Reform and Employment Rights Act 1993) requires that written particulars of the terms of the contract must be given to an employee no later than two months after he commenced employment. This provision applies to all employees who work at least eight hours a week and who have worked for at least one month. If the employer fails to provide the particulars or provides some that the employee believes to be inaccurate, either party can refer the matter to an industrial tribunal. The tribunal can order that the particulars be given and stipulate the content of the particulars based on the evidence from employer and employee about their agreement.

The written particulars must contain the following information:

(a) the names of the employer and employee,
(b) the date when the employment commenced. This is significant for determining periods of notice, rights to redundancy payments,

entitlement to maternity pay/leave etc. when the total length of employment is crucial.

(c) the job description. Again this may be important if questions of redundancy arise.

(d) the normal working hours,

(e) the scale, method and timing of payment,

(f) entitlement to paid holidays, both the annual amount of leave that may be taken and any restrictions on the periods during which such entitlement may be used,

(g) periods of notice to terminate. There are statutory minimum periods of notice that must be given but the contracting parties can agree to longer periods.

(h) whether there is a pension scheme,

(i) sickness entitlement,

(j) whether the employment is to be added to a previous contract of employment and be treated as one period of continuous employment. This again is important for matters such as redundancy payments, maternity rights, pension rights etc. Schedule 13 of the Employment Protection (Consolidation) Act 1978 provides that the following will be treated as periods of continuous employment: continuous employment with a partnership where the partners have changed, continuous employment by two or more associated employers, e.g. companies within the same group, successive contracts with the same employer, and contracts where the employer has changed but the change is subject to the Transfer of Undertakings (Protection of Employment) Regulations 1981. These regulations state that where an employee is employed by an undertaking immediately before its transfer to a new owner, the period of employment is deemed to be continuous and the new employer takes over the employment protection responsibilities of the old employer. There were attempts to avoid this provision by sacking all the employees of the old employer before the undertaking was transferred permitting the new employer to re-employ such of the employees as he wanted. However the House of Lords in *Litster* v *Forth Dry Dock and Engineering Co Ltd* [1989] 1 All ER 1134 held that where an employee is sacked before the transfer of an undertaking for a reason connected with the transfer his contract will be transferred and his period of employment be continuous. This does not prevent an employer dismissing an employee at that time for genuine organisational or technical reasons that necessitate a change in the workforce. Unfortunately, the position does not appear to be so clear cut with regard to the employees of public authorities.

(k) where the work is not permanent, the period during which the employment is expected to continue and the date when it is due to end,

(l) details of relevant collective agreements.

If the employment will involve a period overseas exceeding one month the employee must also be told the period of that employment, the currency in which he will be paid during that period, additional pay or benefits offered and the terms of employment that will apply upon the employee's return to the UK.

THE DUTIES OF EMPLOYER AND EMPLOYEE

Not all the terms of an employment contract will be express and the law does impose some implied duties on both the employer and the employee.

Duties of the employer

(a) **To provide work.** Surprisingly, there is no general duty on the employer to provide work for his employees. If an employer is prepared to pay his employees to do nothing, they have no cause for complaint. The one exception to this is that employees possessing a particular skill, the maintenance of which needs regular practice, must be given the opportunity to maintain their skills.

(b) **To pay the employee.** The employee has a right to receive payment for his labours. In practice, an express agreement about payment is one of the basic terms of any employment contract, be it written or oral. However, in the unlikely event of no agreement existing, an employee is entitled to receive reasonable payment for his work. Employers must provide employees with an itemised payslip showing any deductions made from the wages although this right does not extend to employees working less than eight hours a week. Section 27 of the 1993 Act provides that employees working between eight and sixteen hours a week have the same right as those working longer hours unless they are employed in a company with fewer than twenty employees in which case the right does not exist until the employee has completed five years' continuous service.

(c) **To allow the employee certain paid absences from work.** Employees may be absent from work for a variety of reasons including sickness, holidays, ante-natal care, attending to trade union matters and looking for a new job if facing redundancy. The employer is statutorily required to provide time off and payment for ante-natal care, for redundant employees looking for new work and for trade union officials attending to union matters. Similarly, employees are entitled to receive statutory sickness pay for the first 28 weeks of sickness in a three-month period via their employer although there is no obligation on the employer to provide contractual sick pay. By contrast, there is no statutory right to paid holidays, any such provision being governed by the terms of the contract. If it does allow for such paid leave, the employee has a right to receive it and on leaving the employment may be entitled to receive payment in lieu of any leave entitlement not used.

(d) To provide a safe system of working. This duty was recognised by common law but has been reinforced by the provisions of the Employer's Liability (Defective Equipment) Act 1969 and the Health and Safety at Work Act 1974. The 1969 Act makes the employer strictly liable for the equipment that he provides for his employees and for any injuries that they may suffer through the equipment proving to be defective. The employer has a right to sue the manufacturer of such defective equipment to recover any damages that he has had to pay to an injured employee.

The Health and Safety at Work Act 1974 stipulates the basic requirements concerning safety in the workplace and places responsibilities upon both employer and employee. Employers with five or more employees are required to decide a policy regarding health and safety in the workplace, update it as necessary and inform employees. Health and safety has recently been reinforced by the coming into force on 1 January 1993 of six sets of regulations promulgated to adopt EEC Directives as discussed in chapter 14.

(e) To indemnify the employee against any expenses or other costs incurred during the course of his employment.

(f) Not to discriminate against the employee. Discrimination is likely to be either sexual or racial and can occur at the time of appointment, during the course of employment or at termination. This topic will be considered more fully later in the chapter.

Duties of the employee

The contract of employment depends upon the personal performance of the employee, a fact reflected in the duties placed upon him.

(a) To perform the contract himself. An employee is appointed because of the particular skills that he can bring to the employer's business. Hence the employer can reasonably expect that the employee will undertake the tasks himself and not send a substitute. Naturally, when performing his functions the employee is under a duty to use his skills carefully and correctly as the employer will be vicariously liable for any damage caused by the employee acting in the course of his employment.

(b) To obey his instructions. An employer has the right to stipulate the work that the employee is to undertake and, in some situations, the manner in which it is to be done. The latter will not be possible if the employee is a highly skilled professional person who must be allowed to use his own judgement about the best way to perform his functions. It was this difficulty that led to the demise of the 'control' test as a means of deciding whether a person was an employee or an independent contractor (see chapter 11). The employer has a right to place restrictions on the way that the work is to be carried out, a not unreasonable right given that the employer will be vicariously liable for any damage caused by his employee performing his job in a forbidden manner as occurred in *Limpus* v *London General Omnibus* (1862) 1 H & C 526.

In *Limpus* the defendant bus company had instructed its drivers that they were not to race or obstruct buses belonging to rival companies. In contravention of this instruction, the defendant's driver obstructed the plaintiff's bus and caused it to overturn. The defendant was held vicariously liable for the actions of its driver who was acting in the course of his employment even though he was undertaking his work in a manner that the employer had expressly forbidden.

The failure by an employee to obey lawful and reasonable orders gives the employer the right to dismiss him.

Of course, the employee is entitled to refuse to obey an instruction that is unlawful because, for example, it would involve a criminal act or an order that is unreasonable.

(c) A duty of good faith. An employee may during the course of his employment gain knowledge about his employer's business including the way that it is organised, details of customers and details of products and processes. The employee must not abuse this knowledge and owes a duty of good faith to his employer in respect of such information. Thus, an employee should not allow himself to become involved in a conflict of interests whereby his own interests conflict with those of his employer. This duty exists both during his employment and after it. In practice, if an employee is likely to come into contact with sensitive or confidential information, the employer will insist on a restraint of trade clause in the employment contract specifically restricting the employee's ability to use such information. As discussed in chapters 3 and 18, such clauses are construed restrictively by the courts but are legal and enforceable, if reasonable, having regard to the breadth of the restriction, the size of the geographic area included and the duration of the restriction.

This duty will also extend to the duty to account to his employer for all monies received by the employee on behalf of the employer during the course of his employment along the lines discussed in chapter 6 on the law of agency. The duty to account extends to property that the employee uses during his employment, so that on termination of the employment the employee is required to return any of the employer's goods in his possession. Theft of the employer's goods by the employee would justify immediate dismissal.

DISCRIMINATION

Discrimination is likely to be either sexual or racial in origin and is governed by the provisions of the Sex Discrimination Acts 1975 and 1986, the Race Relations Act 1976, the Employment Act 1989 and the Trade Union Reform and Employment Rights Act 1993.

Sex discrimination

Sex discrimination may occur at the time of appointment by actively discriminating against potential employees of one particular sex. The most obvious discrimination at this stage would be against women of childbearing age because of the risk that a female employee may seek maternity leave (and possibly pay) at some point in the future with consequent disturbance to the employer's business. Concern by employers may be acute given that to dismiss an employee for reasons related to pregnancy is potentially unfair and may give the employee a right to claim damages for unfair dismissal. Under the Trade Union Reform and Employment Rights Act 1993 this is so irrespective of the length of service or the number of hours worked per week.

Section 6 of the Sex Discrimination Act 1975 makes it unlawful to discriminate against a woman in an employment context. Thus, for example, if a woman employee is subjected to different working hours, pay scales, promotion or training opportunities or access to company facilities because of her sex an actionable discrimination will have occurred.

Certain sexual discrimination is permitted however by s.7 of the Act which provides that in specified situations being a man may be a Genuine Occupational Qualification (GOQ). The examples quoted in that Act include jobs that require men for physiological reasons (excluding physical strength or stamina), dramatic performances or entertainment for purposes of authenticity, jobs that need to be done by a man for reasons of decency or privacy, jobs involving a man living in a private home where objection might reasonably be taken to allowing a woman such proximity, jobs in hospitals, prisons or other establishments catering for men, jobs providing personal services in education or welfare that can most effectively be provided by a man, jobs overseas in countries where the duties could not be done effectively by a woman, and where the job is one of two to be held by a married couple.

Further protection against sex discrimination is to be found in the Equal Pay Act 1970 as amended, s.1 of which implies an equality clause into any contract of employment that does not contain one either expressly or as a result of a collective agreement. Section 2 provides that the clause applies in three situations, namely, where a woman is employed on like work with a man in the same employment, where the woman is employed on work rated as equivalent with a man in the same employment and where a woman is employed on work not otherwise covered where the demands made of her are of equal value to those required of a man. In each situation if a clause in the woman's contract is less favourable than a similar clause in the man's contract, the woman's contract will be modified so that it ceases to be less favourable. Similarly, if a woman's contract does not contain a term similar to one in a man's contract which bestows a benefit on him, the woman's contract will be treated as including such a term. Naturally, there has been some case law on the meaning of phrases such as like work and demands of equal value although those terms are defined in s.1(4) and s.1(5). Essentially, like work involves work of a broadly similar nature where the differences between the woman's job and the man's job are not of any practical importance. Work is to be regarded as being equivalent if the demands made of the woman under headings such as effort, skill or decision are of an equal value. All of these measures apply equally to protect men.

Maternity rights

Maternity rights is an area where the employee's rights are naturally directly related to their sex. As explained above, a woman has a right not be discriminated against at the time of appointment because of the possibility that she might want maternity leave in the future. If in employment, a woman has statutory rights relating to maternity leave and pay should she need them, as well as rights protecting her from redundancy or dismissal on the grounds of pregnancy.

Section 27 of the Trade Union Reform and Employment Rights Act 1993 gives all pregnant employees regardless of their length of service or hours of work the right to 14 weeks' statutory maternity leave during which all their non-wage contractual rights must be maintained. This section is due to come into force in October 1994 along with proposed changes to maternity payment rights. At present there is no such right.

Of more significance to the pregnant employee is her right to return to work. At present an employee who at the qualifying date has worked for her employer for sixteen hours a week for a period of at least two years, or has worked between eight and sixteen hours a week continuously for five years has a right to forty weeks' maternity leave returning to work twenty nine weeks after the birth of the child. The qualifying date for assessing this entitlement is the beginning of the eleventh week before the expected date of confinement. To take advantage of this protection, the employee must give written notice to her employer at least twenty one days before the maternity leave is due to begin confirming the reason for her forthcoming absence and her intention to return. Despite giving such notification, there is no obligation on the employee to return at the end of the period. If she wishes to do so however she merely gives written notice to her employer at least three weeks before the date on which she is intending to return. Thereafter she can only delay her return if taking certified sick leave. The employer for his part can delay her return for up to four weeks for reasons such as industrial action provided that he informs her of this.

A refusal by the employer to allow the woman to exercise her right of return is unfair dismissal actionable through the industrial tribunal. A specific exception to this exists in relation to small firms, i.e. those with five or fewer employees, if it is not practical for the woman to have her previous job back. Further, if for reasons other than redundancy, e.g. reorganisation, it is not possible for the woman to undertake her previous job then the employer must offer her suitable alternative employment. If he does and the employee refuses to accept it the dismissal will not be unfair. Allied to this is the possibility that the woman will have been made redundant during her absence. In that situation, if there is no suitable alternative work to offer the woman she can claim redundancy rights.

Sections 24 and 25 of the 1993 Act give new rights to women against being dismissed or selected for dismissal on maternity related grounds and to be offered suitable alternative employment if they have to be suspended from work for health and safety related reasons because they are pregnant, have recently given birth or are breastfeeding. This would include, for example, women whose normal occupation involves them dealing with X-ray machinery. When these provisions take effect, the dismissal of a woman for pregnancy related reasons will be automatically unfair irrespective of her length of service or the number of hours she works. The rights relating to suspension for pregnancy related reasons only apply to women who have worked for at least one month. The right to receive full pay during such suspension lasts for twenty six weeks except for any period during which the employee was offered suitable alternative work and refused it.

Racial discrimination

Controls against racial discrimination are contained in the Race Relations Act 1976, s.4 of which makes it unlawful to discriminate in relation to employment in Great Britain. Discrimination by an employer is evidenced in the arrangements he makes for determining who should be offered employment, the terms on which the employment is offered, by the employer refusing or deliberately omitting to offer employment or by the way the employer offers or refuses to offer access for promotion, transfer, training, or other benefits, facilities or services.

As with sexual discrimination, there are certain situations when racial discrimination is acceptable if the racial group of the employee is a Genuine Occupational Qualification. While the range of exceptions is not as extensive as in sex discrimination, there are marked similarities in the exceptions. Section 5 provides that racial grouping will be a GOQ for a dramatic or other entertainment where racial grouping is required for authenticity, or where the employee is working as an artist's or photographic model and authenticity is needed. Further, a racial grouping requirement is acceptable for jobs involving work in a place where food or drink is provided, whether or not for payment, and consumed by members of the public or a section of the public in a setting in which persons of that racial group are needed for authenticity. Thus, to use the oft-quoted example, it would not be discriminatory to require applicants of Chinese origin for work in a Chinese restaurant.

TRADE UNION RIGHTS

Rights relating to trade union membership are to be found in the Trade Union and Labour Relations (Consolidation) Act 1992 as amended. Section 37(1) makes it unlawful to refuse a person employment either

    (a) because he is, or is not, a member of a trade union, or
    (b) because he is unwilling to accept a requirement—
        (i) to take steps to become or cease to be, or to remain or not to become, a member of a trade union, or
        (ii) to make payments or suffer deductions in the event of his not being a member of a trade union.

Further, under s.37(3) if any job advertisement indicates or might reasonably be taken to indicate that a restriction of the type mentioned above would apply, any person who does not satisfy the condition or is unwilling to comply with it and is refused employment shall be presumed conclusively to have been refused employment for that reason. Any person so refused under s.37(1) or (3) can make a claim for compensation via the industrial tribunal. Any such claim must be made within three months of the date on which the complaint arose although the tribunal does have the discretion to extend this period in some situations.

Similar restrictions are placed upon a refusal by an employment agency to offer their services to a person or to decline a person responding to an offending advertisement.

As explained earlier, trade union officials have a right to paid time off work in which to perform their trade union functions. Further, s.146(1) of the 1992 Act provides all employees with protection against action short of dismissal taken by the employer for reasons relating to trade union membership or activities. Specifically the protection covers three situations:

    (a) preventing or deterring the employee from being or seeking to become a member of an independent trade union, or penalising him for doing so,
    (b) preventing or deterring the employee from taking part in the activities of an independent trade union at an appropriate time, or penalising him for doing so, or
    (c) compelling the employee to be or become a member of any trade union or of a particular trade union or of one of a number of particular trade unions.

For the purposes of (b) above, 'appropriate time' means a time outside the employee's working time or a time within his working hours when, in accordance with arrangements agreed with or consent given by his employer, it is permissible for him to take part in the activities of a trade union. A breach of any of the above provisions gives the employee the right to seek compensation through an industrial tribunal. If during a claim under s.146 the employer or complainant alleges that the employer so acted because of pressure put on him by a trade union or other person, the complainant or employer can seek to have that third party added to the proceedings. If the case is proven and the tribunal considers the third party to be responsible, damages can be awarded against them.

Dismissal from employment because of trade union membership will give rise to a claim for unfair dismissal as discussed below.

TERMINATION OF THE CONTRACT

Agreement

Termination of an employment contract can arise in the normal contractual manner. Thus it may be terminated by the parties agreeing to do so. The common means by which such agreement may be reached is through a contractual term stipulating the periods of notice that can be given by either party so as to bring the contract to a lawful end. Minimum periods are imposed by the Employment Protection (Consolidation) Act 1978 which stipulates that a period of one week's notice must be given to an employee who has been employed for four weeks. Thereafter a minimum of one additional week's notice must be given for every year of employment up to a maximum of twelve weeks. Note that these are minimum periods and that the parties are free to contract for longer periods of notice to be given. A failure by an employer to abide by such periods of notice would give rise to a claim for wrongful dismissal to be heard in the High Court (although in the future they may be heard in an industrial tribunal if an order is made under s.38 of the Trade Union Reform and Employment Rights Act 1993). The damages to be awarded will be the wages or salary due for the outstanding portion of the contractual notice period. In practice, an employer wishing to dispense with the contractual period is likely to pay the employee the relevant sum as 'pay in lieu of notice'.

Periods of notice and payment for breach will not be relevant if the employer summarily dismisses the employee for misconduct such as theft of the employer's property.

Frustration

An employment contract may be frustrated by the employee's inability to attend for work for reasons other than certified sickness. Further contractual frustration will occur on the death of either party to the contract, where an employing company goes into liquidation or otherwise ceases trading, or where a partnership is dissolved.

Fixed-term contracts

A contract may be for a fixed term such as two years. The expiration of the period will bring the contract to an end automatically. The fixed term is the maximum intended duration of the contract but not necessarily the minimum for the contract may include a term relating to periods of notice that can be given in the interim.

DISMISSAL

Most people would recognise dismissal as occurring when the employer informs the employee that he is no longer needed for work. This may arise through the employee being made redundant, in which case there is no suggestion of improper behaviour by employer or employee and the latter will be entitled to any redundancy pay for which he is eligible. Redundancy is considered later. Alternatively the employee may have been wrongfully or unfairly dismissed. Wrongful dismissal occurs when the contractually agreed mechanism for termination, e.g. periods of notice, have not been complied with. Thus, wrongful dismissal gives rise to an action for contractual breach. By contract, unfair dismissal exists when there is no legitimate reason for the dismissal and gives rise to an action in the industrial tribunal.

Dismissal may also occur constructively where the behaviour of the employer is such as to justify the employee treating the conduct as being indicative of a rejection of the employment contract by the employer. The employee can accept the termination and seek damages.

Unfair dismissal

Some dismissals will automatically be deemed unfair. Thus dismissal for a reason relating to pregnancy, or for joining or refusing to join a trade union or when transferring an undertaking is unfair, as is making an employee redundant in contravention of an agreed procedure. Dismissing an employee for taking strike action is not necessarily unfair as the employee is in breach of his contract of employment and, as such, the employer is within his rights to dismiss him. However, dismissals in a strike situation become unfair if only some of the striking employees are dismissed as this demonstrates an attempt to use the strike as a cover for dismissing selected employees without appropriate compensation. Similarly, if all the striking employees are sacked and only some of them are re-engaged at the cessation of the industrial action, those not re-engaged are unfairly dismissed.

The right to complain to an industrial tribunal about dismissal has been extended by the Trade Union Reform and Employment Rights Act 1993. Section 28 gives all employees, irrespective of their length of service, hours of work or age, the right to complain to an industrial tribunal if they are dismissed, selected for redundancy or suffer some other detriment because of some action they have taken in respect of health and safety at work. Such dismissals will be automatically unfair. Scenarios covered by the provision include carrying out designated health and safety duties, bringing to the employer's attention circumstances at work that pose a health and safety risk and leaving the premises and/or making appropriate arrangements for the safety of himself and others in the event of a danger that he reasonably believes to be serious and imminent. Section 29 provides a more general right of complaint to an industrial tribunal by an employee irrespective of the length of service, hours worked or age if the employee has been dismissed or selected for redundancy for asserting his statutory rights by either taking proceedings against the employer or alleging that the employer had infringed his rights.

Not all non-contractual reasons for dismissal will be unfair. Thus a person will be fairly dismissed if he is incompetent or has lied about his qualifications. Similarly, some serious misconduct such as theft of his employer's property would justify summary dismissal without compensation.

A claim for unfair dismissal must be lodged with the tribunal within three months of the dismissal (six months if it has arisen from a strike). The remedies for unfair dismissal are monetary compensation and a claim for reinstatement or re-engagement. Reinstatement involves the employee being returned to his previous work on the same conditions while re-engagement is an appointment on different terms. In practice, many employees would not wish to return to a post from which they have been unfairly dismissed working for the employer who dismissed them. Hence, such claims are relatively few.

Generally, the employee's claim will be for monetary compensation. The award may be in two parts, the basic award which is calculated in the same way as redundancy pay, although age is not relevant, and an additional award where the employer fails to comply with an order for reinstatement or re-engagement. Under s.30 of the 1993 Act this may equal the arrears of pay due and any other benefits even though this may exceed the normal level of awards. Further, a special award may be made where the dismissal was automatically unfair and the employee sought reinstatement or re-engagement. This special award will be increased if the employer was ordered to reinstate or re-engage the employee and unreasonably refused to do so. The contributory negligence of the employee will be taken into account and may result in a reduction in the award.

Redundancy

Where an employer ceases trading or restructures or reorganises the business with the effect that some jobs are abolished, the employees are said to be redundant. Under the Employment Protection (Consolidation) Act 1978 redundant employees are entitled to compensation provided that they have completed two years' continuous service with the employer since attaining the age of eighteen.

Certain employees are not eligible for redundancy payments, for example, employees who have reach the retirement age cannot claim. Part-time workers working fewer than sixteen hours a week are not eligible, although this figure drops to eight hours after five years' continuous service. Further, employees who work outside Great Britain cannot claim, neither can employees under fixed-term contract of two or more years' duration who have agreed to forego redundancy rights.

A redundant employee will lose his right to redundancy pay if he has been offered suitable alternative work by his employer and has refused it, or alternatively, has accepted an alternative job.

Any agreed formula for selecting employees must be followed, e.g. last-in first-out. If the procedure is not followed, those employees who have been wrongly selected for redundancy can sue for unfair dismissal. Under s.34 of the 1993 Act employers are required to consult with appropriate recognised trade unions about proposed redundancies at the earliest opportunity. This must be a minimum of at least 30 days before the first redundancy if the proposal is to dismiss 10–99 employees from one establishment within 30 days, and at least 90 days if the proposal is to dismiss 100 or more employees within 90 days.

Redundancy pay is calculated by reference to the age of the claimant and the period of continuous service. Those aged 18–21 receive half a week's pay for every year of service, those aged 22–40 receive one week's pay for every year and those aged 41–65 receive one and a half week's pay for every year of service. The claimant receives a maximum of twenty years at a weekly rate not exceeding £205.

QUESTION

Advise G Ltd, who have approached you about the following three employment related issues:

(a) Mary who is a full-time employee has been working for six weeks. She has complained that she has not received any written details of her terms of employment.

(b) Jenny who has been working for the company for three years has complained that she is not receiving the same training as her male colleagues.

(c) During a recent strike, G Ltd sacked 15 employees out of a workforce of 62. The sacked employees are threatening to make a claim for unfair dismissal.

FURTHER READING

Department of Employment, *The Trade Union Reform and Employment Rights Act 1993*

Keenan, D. and Riches, S. *Business Law* (3rd ed) 1993 (Pitman)

Savage, N. and Bradgate *Busines Law* (2nd ed) 1993 (Butterworth)

Selwyn, N.M., *Selwyn's Law of Employment* (8th ed) 1993 (Butterworth)

Suggested solutions to questions

Chapter 1

This question raises two issues: first, the question of competitive tendering and any obligation on the person seeking the tender to accept one of the tenders, and, second, the battle of the forms.

(a) Congo Computers Ltd feel that they should have been awarded the contract as their referential bid was lower than the tender of £360 000 made by Niger Computers Ltd. Certainly, Ace Ltd had committed themselves to accepting the lowest offer and thus would be bound to do so in accordance with the decision in *Harvela Investments Ltd* v *Royal Trust Co of Canada Ltd*. However, the *Harvela* case also held that a referential bid is not legitimate in that situation. Therefore, Ace Ltd were right to award the contract to Niger Computers Ltd and Congo Computers Ltd have no grounds for complaint.

(b) Niger Computers Ltd want to raise the contract price from £360 000 to £370 000. Whether they can do this will depend on whose standard terms were adopted as the contract. It is a battle of the forms situation in which both Ace Ltd and Niger Computers Ltd have each attempted to contract on their own standard terms. Applying *Butler Machine Tool Co* v *Ex-Cell-O Corpn*, Niger Computers will win as their terms were the last ones proposed and were accepted by Ace Ltd when their employee signed and returned the tear-off slip. Therefore, the price variation clause is enforceable and Niger Computers Ltd can raise the price.

Chapter 2

The question relates to the use of two types of express clauses in contracts: *force majeure* clauses and liquidated damages clauses. A *force majeure* clause stipulates what will happen if certain contingent events occur, while a liquidated damages clause seeks to agree a genuine enforceable pre-estimate of contractual loss in the event of a breach. In the question, the *force majeure* clause has included industrial action and thus covers the situation in hand. Hence the supplier Red-Telephones Ltd will not be liable for the delay in completion of the contract. However, if he had been, the validity of the liquidated damages would have become an issue and whether 1% of the contract price for each week's delay was a genuine pre-estimate of loss or a penalty. Only the former is enforceable.

Chapter 3

The two parts of this question deal with two different situations in which the consent to the contract has not been genuine.

(a) Part (a) deals with a situation in which the buyer of goods has misrepresented his identity so that the seller is not aware of the true identity of the purchaser. The solution depends on whether the identity of the buyer was essential to the formation of the contract. There is a presumption that the seller intended to deal with the person with whom he actually dealt and that the identity of the buyer did not matter. Where this is so, the contract will only be voidable. Where the identity was crucial the contract will be held void for mistake. In this question, applying *Kings Norton Metal Co Ltd* v *Edridge, Merrett & Co Ltd*, it will be held that Hippo Ltd intended to deal with Jeremy. As such the contract is only voidable and if Hippo Ltd are to regain the coats they must avoid the contract before Jeremy sells the coats to an innocent third party.

(b) On the facts, Hippo Ltd have had no alternative but to complete the contract with Worm Silks Ltd despite the price being raised by £800 otherwise they will be in breach of their retail contracts. However the decision to continue the contract with Worm Silks has resulted from duress and Hippo Ltd would be entitled to claim for a return of the £800.

Chapter 4

The exclusion clause in this contract must be examined from two perspectives: first, the type of damage that it seeks to exclude and, second, the nature of the injured person.

Emily wants to claim for the injury caused to her back by the fall. We are told that the chair broke because of negligent workmanship by an employee of Tiger Office Furniture Ltd. This is crucial for s.2(1) of the Unfair Contract Terms Act 1977 forbids any exclusion which attempts to restrict liability for physical injury caused by negligence. Hence, the clause is invalid as regards Emily's claim and she can claim compensation.

Leopard Ltd's claim is for property damage. They have two potential causes of action. They can make a claim in negligence or, alternatively, they can claim for a breach of the implied condition of merchantable quality in s.14(2) of the Sale of Goods Act 1979. Where there are two potential actions, one contractual and the other tortious, the exclusion clause will apply only to the contract action and not to the tort action unless the clause specifically says so. Applying *White* v *John Warwick Ltd* the clause can be pleaded for the claim under the Sale of Goods Act but will have to satisfy the test of reasonableness as required by s.6(3) of the Unfair Contract Terms Act 1977 as Leopard Ltd are not 'dealing as a consumer'. (If they were 'dealing as a consumer' the clause would be void under s.6(2) of UCTA.) The clause cannot affect the negligence action.

Chapter 5

(a) Danny's contract with Eric Ltd for the purchase of the window frames is probably a divisible contract. While this issue is never clear cut, the fact that each instalment carries with it a right to payment suggests that it is divisible. Despite their failure to complete the contract, therefore, Eric Ltd will be entitled to be paid for the four instalments that they have delivered. Danny should be advised to pay for them. However, he may be able to claim some compensation for the fact that Eric Ltd are not intending to complete the contract. Their statement means that there is an anticipatory breach and Danny can sue for damages immediately without waiting for the completion date of the contract.

(b) Plumbers Ltd have completed the contract by performance. However, the fact that Danny had to employ another plumber to do some necessary remedial work means that the performance was substantial rather than complete. As such, Danny is entitled to deduct the cost of the remedial work from the contract price but he is liable to pay the remainder. Applying *Hoenig* v *Isaacs*, Danny must pay Plumbers Ltd the outstanding £1000 less the £350 for the remedial work.

(c) The contract with Flooring Ltd contained a liquidated damages clause effective if the floor tiles were late being delivered. The issue is whether the clause is a genuine pre-estimate of the loss or a penalty. If it is a genuine pre-estimate, Danny will entitled to claim £300 from Flooring Ltd for the three-day delay, irrespective of whether his actual loss was more or less than £300.

Chapter 6

This question addresses the rights and obligations of both principal and agent in the agency set-up. The major point from the question is that the agreement is for two years from 1 January and thus will be affected by the passage of the Commercial Agents (Directive) Regulations 1993 which are due to come into effect on 1 January 1994. Therefore, the first year of this agreement will be governed by the normal common law position but will be amended automatically on 1 January 1994 to take account of the new regulations. Thus, thereafter, C Ltd will be entitled to receive their remuneration on the due dates, receive statements about the amount of commission to which they are entitled etc. Further, if after 1 June 1995 they continue to act as B Ltd's agent, the contract will automatically change under reg.14 into an indefinite contract carrying with it a right to remuneration and to appropriate periods of notice.

Chapter 7

This question involves the application of ss.13, 14(2), 14(3) and 15 of the Sale of Goods Act 1979. Jeremy is a sales representative for Carpets Ltd which means that the sale is happening 'in the course of a business'. While this does not matter for ss.13 and 15, it is vital for ss.14(2) and 14(3) which only apply to business sales.

The carpet was described as 'heavy industrial quality'. This does make definite statements about the quality of the goods and its likely durability. If the carpet is not 'heavy industrial quality' as Andrew suspects, there will have been a breach of s.13 entitling X Ltd to terminate the contract.

There has also been a *prima facie* breach of section 15, sale by sample. The section states that the bulk will correspond with the sample, that the buyer will have the reasonable opportunity of comparing the bulk with the sample and that the goods will be free from any defect rendering them unmerchantable which would not be apparent on reasonable examination. Here there is clear suggestion that the bulk does not correspond with the sample and that Andrew has had no opportunity to compare the carpet with the sample.

The merchantability issue appears in both s.14(2) and s.15. We are told that tufts are coming out of the carpet and that faded patches are appearing. Applying the s.14(6) definition it may be that the faded patches will not have any effect as they do not affect the usability of the carpet. However, if Andrew can persuade the court to apply the *Rogers* v *Parish* decision etc., it may be that the goods will be unmerchantable because they are unacceptable. However, in the circumstances this is a relatively weak argument. The fact that tufts are coming out of the carpet is probably a stronger case and may show both that the carpet is unmerchantable and that it is not fit for its intended purpose.

Irrespective of what the court decides on s.14, Andrew's real problem lies in the fact that he may be deemed to have accepted the carpet under the authority of the *Bernstein* decision. If this is so, X Ltd will have lost the right to terminate the contract and will only be able to sue for damages. As Andrew's suspicions were raised when the carpet was delivered, he should have queried it then before allowing the carpet to be laid. The laying of the carpet could be seen as an act of acceptance.

Chapter 8

This problem involves the supply of goods and services and raises three points: the length of time taken to do the job, the price charged and the subsequent fault with the system.

The length of time will depend to some extent on whether the fact that Brian said the job would take two days means that time has become of the essence in this contract. If it has, the failure to complete on time would be a contractual breach giving rise to damages. If it has not, there is the possibility that s.14 of the Supply of Goods and Services Act 1982 would apply, which states that the work must be completed within a reasonable time. It is suggested that a reasonable time here would be two days and that A Ltd could claim for compensation after this. On the facts, the former of the two seems most likely.

Brian has not quoted a price, merely that it will be more than £50. Therefore, A Ltd can look to s.15 of the 1982 Act for relief, which states that where no agreement has been made about price a reasonable charge must be paid. Reasonable in this context would be £250. However, as A Ltd have already paid the £400 Brian requested it is now too late to complain. The act of paying will be seen as contractual acceptance which will not be overturned unless A Ltd can show that they paid under duress. Alternatively, the court might hold that the statement about the price depending on any new parts etc. is a mechanism for deciding the price under the terms of the contract. If this is so, s.15 will not apply anyway and A Ltd will be bound by the contract price. Any complaint about the price should have been settled before payment was made.

The system failed after three weeks. This might be due to a lack of skill and care on Brian's part when doing the job in which case there is a breach of s.13 of the 1982 and A Ltd will be entitled to a remedy. Remember that ss.13–15 of the 1982 are implied terms not implied conditions and thus there is no automatic right to terminate. Alternatively, it may be that one of the replacement parts was either not of merchantable quality or not fit for the purpose, in which case there has been a breach of the implied conditions in s.4 of the 1982 Act.

Chapter 9

(a) The first contract involves a delivery of the wrong amount. C Ltd ordered 20 tons of sand and has received 20 tons and 18 cwt. There are three options open to C Ltd all of which are to be found in s.30 of the Sale of Goods Act 1979. Under s.30(2) C Ltd can either reject the consignment as a whole or can accept the contract amount of 20 tons and reject the excess. Alternatively, under s.30(3) C Ltd can accept the whole of the delivery but is then under an obligation to pay for all the goods delivered at the contract rate.

(b) C Ltd want to reject the wood delivered in the third instalment. As each instalment carries with it a right to payment, it will probably be classed as a divisible contract. As such, if one instalment is faulty C Ltd would be able to reject the one consignment without it interfering with the continuance of the contract.

Chapter 10

These three contracts with Angus concern the passage of title and therefore the passage of risk, because under s.20 of the Sale of Goods Act 1979 risk passes with property unless there is an agreement to the contrary. Along with risk will go the decision as to whether to cover the risk with insurance.

(a) These are unascertained goods as the contract is to supply 30 bags of fertilizer out of a stock of 90 bags. The issue therefore is whether unconditional appropriation has taken place such as to permit title to pass to Angus under s.18, Rule 5. We know that the bags have been put to one side, labelled and a delivery note sent to Angus. Although there are conflicting authorities, this is probably enough to constitute unconditional appropriation, particularly if the delivery note makes reference to specific bags. If this is so, the risk is with Angus who must bear the loss.

(b) The rotovator was sold subject to a retention of title clause which is valid under s.19 of the Sale of Goods Act 1979. Therefore, *prima facie*, the risk is with F Ltd, the seller. However, there are two further possibilities. One is that the contract of sale included a term agreeing that the risk would pass to Angus along with possession of the goods. If this is so Angus will have to bear the loss. The other possibility is that the contract included a term requiring Angus to insure the goods while they were in his possession. If this is so, a claim can be made against the insurance company irrespective of who owned the goods at the time. Both F Ltd and Angus would have sufficient insurable interest to permit them to insure the goods.

Chapter 11

This question involves the vicarious liability of Y Ltd for the actions of their employee, Bill, and the type of person who can make a claim in a work based accident.

Employers are vicariously liable for the actions of their employees while those employees are acting in the course of their employment. This is so even if the employee is doing his appointed task in a manner specifically forbidden by the employer as in *Limpus* v *London General Omnibus*. The employer only ceases to be liable if the employee is on a frolic of his own, i.e. doing something other than his appointed job.

Bill is employed to drive a fork lift truck and was doing so when the accident occurred. Therefore, Y Ltd are vicariously liable for his actions despite their instructions and despite providing him with appropriate training. Naturally, Bill is also liable for his actions.

Clearly, there is a duty of care owed to other people on the premises as it is foreseeable that such people could be hurt if Bill performed his job negligently. This duty has been breached with the result that Fred and David have been hurt. Both of them are entitled to claim for their injuries. Under common law there was no duty owed to fellow employees with the result that Fred would have been unable to claim. However, this position no longer exists and a duty of care is owed to fellow employees. Fred has a valid claim.

Therefore, both Y Ltd and Bill will be liable in negligence.

Chapter 12

Elsie is interested in what claim, if any, she has under Part I of the 1987 Act for the injuries and damage she has suffered as a result of the faulty television.

Product liability under Part I of the 1987 Act is strict and hence Elsie will only need to demonstrate that the set was faulty and that she suffered loss as a result. Given the facts it should not be difficult to prove this. She can sue either Screen Ltd, the producer of the item, or Components Unlimited because it was their defective item that caused the problem. She has suffered personal injury and property damage. The claim for personal injury is straightforward. However the claim for property damage is slightly more complicated. Under s.5 of the Act the property must be of a type ordinarily intended for private use or consumption and so intended by the actual user. Again, Elsie should have no difficulty with this. The issue is over the value of the damaged property. Section 5(4) states that you cannot claim unless the value of property exceeds £275. Applying this, the cost of the video (£300) can be claimed but the curtains (£175) fall below this threshold. However, the section seems to allow for the total property damage to be added together in which case Elsie's loss is £475 and can be claimed.

Finally, she cannot claim the cost of the defective item under the 1987 Act. The original purchaser of the item will have to make a claim against the seller under s.14 of the Sale of Goods Act 1979.

Chapter 13

The jackets ordered by Downshire County County have been ordered by reference to a description. The description 'waterproof' has been applied to them and Clothes Ltd have sold them as complying with that description. In fact, the jackets are only showerproof and therefore the description is false. The first issue is whether the description is false to a material degree as required by s.3 of the Trade Descriptions Act 1968 and whether the description is of a type controlled by the Act. It is a controlled description for it would fall within the category of 'fitness for purpose' specified in s.2. It also appears to be false to a material degree for its falsity affects the suitability of the item.

There are two potential defendants, the manufacturer who applied the original description and has committed an offence against s.1(1)(a) of the Act and Clothes Ltd who may have committed offences of offering to supply and supplying under s.1(1)(b). Clothes Ltd may be able to claim a defence under s.24 in that they relied on information supplied to them by the manufacturer. However, they will still need to prove reasonable precautions and due diligence, which is more difficult after the decisions of *Garrett* and *Sherratt* as the court may hold that a simple test would have proved the falsity of the statement.

Downshire County Council might receive compensation under s.35 of the Powers of Criminal Courts Act if Clothes Ltd are convicted. Alternatively, the County Council could sue for compensation under s.13 of the Sale of Goods Act 1979.

Chapter 14

Upshire Trading Standards Department will be considering possible criminal offences against G Ltd, the importer of the dangerous toy, and Fred, the retailer who sold it. There is a potential for offences against the general safety requirement contained in s.10 of the Consumer Protection Act 1987 and/or under the Toys (Safety) Regulations 1989 made under s.11 of the Act. In fact, there is no offence against the Toy (Safety) Regulations in respect of the choking hazard posed by the doll as this hazard is not included in the regulations. Despite this both importer and retailer have committed offences against the general safety requirement and can be convicted under s.10 of the Act as the goods are consumer goods which are not reasonably safe. The position might have been different if the goods had included a warning stipulating a lower age for the safe use of the product.

Chapter 15

Jenny is a food business for the purposes of the Food Safety Act 1990 and therefore is subject to the controls contained both in the Act and in any regulations made under the Act or adopted by it.

She has sold a sausage roll infested with maggots. This will constitute an offence against the food safety requirement contained in s.8 of the Act. This section makes it an offence to sell for human consumption any food which is so contaminated (whether by extraneous matter or otherwise) that it would not be reasonable to expect it to be used for human consumption in that state. Jenny may be able to claim a due diligence defence if she can show that she took all reasonable precautions and exercised all due diligence to avoid the commission of the offence. Whether she did will depend on all the facts of the case.

She has also committed an offence by offering to sell yoghurts on which the 'use by' date has expired. This may have arisen because of poor stock rotation on her behalf or because of an oversight. Either way she will find it very difficult to establish any defence.

Chapter 16

Section 50(5) of the 1985 Act makes it an offence to have in possession for sale, to agree to sell or sell a regulated package that is inadequate if the defendant is either the packer or importer of the package or, alternatively, knows that the package is inadequate. An inadequate package is one that is deficient by over 2TNE (approx 10% deficiency).

The tin of carrots is a regulated package subject to the average quantity system as it is 'e' marked. As it was less than half full, it is a reasonable assumption that it is an inadequate and therefore illegal.

The school will not have committed an offence as they have not sold it and did not know that it was inadequate. The same is true of the Supplies Department of the County Council. The first possible offence may have been committed by the wholesaler who sold it to the County Council, although they will only be liable if they knew that the tin was inadequate. As it is a sealed product, this is highly unlikely. The primary offence will have been committed by the packer or importer at the place that the product was first sold. It will be the responsibility of the Trading Standards Department in that area to decide whether to prosecute.

Chapter 17

Mike is an individual for the purposes of the Consumer Credit Act 1974 as he is not a body corporate. Therefore, he can claim the protection offered by the Act in respect of any regulated agreements. The agreement in hand is an H.P. agreement for £460 (the amount actually borrowed) and therefore is regulated.

The question concerns Mike's rights when he is in default. The total price of the goods is £700 of which he had paid £350 when he went into default. Under ss.87–88 of the Consumer Credit Act 1974, Easymoney Finance Ltd must serve a default notice on Mike before they can take any action against him including recovering the goods. The notice must stipulate the default and what must be done to remedy it. If Mike complies with the requirements of the notice, the default will be expunged.

If Easymoney Finance Ltd want to recover the goods, they must get a court order for the weighing scale is an item of 'protected goods' within s.90 of the Act as Mike has paid one-third of the total price. Hence the goods cannot be recovered without either his agreement or a court order. If Easymoney recover the goods in contravention of this requirement, Mike will be entitled to a total refund of all the monies paid under the agreement. If he wants to keep the weighing scale, he can apply to the court for a time order under s.129 of the Act giving him extra time to meet his commitments under the agreement. If his cashflow problem is temporary, this may be the perfect solution.

Chapter 18

The uniting of A Ltd and B Ltd will result in a new company which will have 27% of the coach trade in the South Wales area. Because of the percentage of the trade under their control, this merger is subject to review by the Monopolies and Mergers Commission to consider whether it is contrary to the public interest. There is no presumption that it is.

Although the merger only effects one area in the UK rather than the whole country this is sufficient to justify a reference to the MMC if it will create a monopoly in the area. This was held in the decision of *South Yorkshire Transport Ltd v Monopolies and Mergers Commission.*

Instead of referring the matter to the MMC the Director General of Fair Trading can accept undertakings from A Ltd and B Ltd that they will address any presumed risks posed by the merger. However, if the merger is referred to the MMC, it can require a variety of possible solutions as listed in Schedule 8 of the Fair Trading Act 1973.

Chapter 19

Joe wants to be able to use an item that he designed in order to set up a new company. The question raises a few issues: the existence of a restraint-of-trade clause, whether it is enforceable by Joe's new employer and his use of a patented item.

As discussed in previous chapters, restraint-of-trade clauses are enforceable if they are protecting some legitimate interest and are reasonable as regards both their duration and their geographic impact. This restraint-of-trade clause is *prima facie* valid.

The clause was between X Ltd and Joe. However, Y Ltd who took over X Ltd and then sacked Joe are seeking to enforce it. The decision of *Morris Angel & Son Ltd v Hollande* confirms that they can do this. Y Ltd have acquired all the contractual rights of X Ltd including the right to enforce the restraint-of-trade clause.

Joe is producing an item that he created while working for X Ltd. As an employee invention the product belongs to X Ltd under s.39 of the Patents Act 1977, as is evidenced by the fact that they patented it. However, Joe would have been entitled to some compensation under s.40 of the Patents Act. He cannot make the item without the patent holder's agreement as this would be contrary to s.60 of the Patents Act. The company have a right to seek an injunction to prevent further abuse of the patent as long as the patent is still in force.

Chapter 20

The goods are being transported c.i.f. Thus the obligation was on Virgo Ltd to arrange for the freight and insurance of the goods. They were duly despatched in good condition as evidenced by the clean bill of lading. The risk in the goods will have passed to Cancer when the goods crossed the rail of the ship on loading in London. Therefore, when the goods arrive damaged the responsibility is on Cancer to arrange for a remedy.

The goods arrived before the bill of lading which will have to pass through the hands of Bank B and Bank A before reaching Cancer. Cancer can actually obtain possession of the goods from the carrier by providing the carrier with an indemnity against any claims in conversion. Thereafter Cancer can make a claim against the insurer under the policy of marine insurance arranged by Virgo Ltd but which will have been transferred by endorsement to Cancer as part of the transfer of the bill of lading. They remain liable to pay the contract price for the goods to Virgo Ltd via Bank A and Bank B as the goods were in good condition when shipped.

Chapter 21

Z Ltd have raised three issues regarding the insurance of their factory:

(a) An insured person must have an insurable interest in the subject matter of the insurance. Where insurance of property is concerned this is most obvious if the insured owns the property. The facts given here mean that Z Ltd will have an insurable interest either as the owner or the tenant of the property.

(b) An insured person is under an obligation to tell the insurer of any material facts that may affect the insurer's preparedness to accept the policy. The fact that Z Ltd have been refused burglary insurance is clearly a material fact for it suggests that the property is at risk from burglary and therefore perhaps from arson. If Z Ltd do not tell their insurer of this fact, the insurer can avoid the policy.

(c) Insurance policies typically contain an average clause. Thus in the event of a claim the insured only receives the full value of the claim if the property was fully insured. If it was underinsured the claim will be reduced by a corresponding percentage. Thus if Z Ltd only insure the property for 80% of its value they will only receive 80% of any claim whether the property is destroyed or merely damaged.

Chapter 22

G Ltd have three employment issues to resolve:

(a) Mary has complained about not receiving her written particulars of employment. As yet, G Ltd have not done anything wrong. Under the Trade Union Reform and Employment Rights Act 1993, G Ltd have eight weeks in which to give Mary her written particulars.

(b) If Jenny's complaint is true, G Ltd have committed an offence against s.6 of the Sex Discrimination Act 1975 which makes it unlawful to discriminate against a woman in the employment context. This would include not permitting a woman the same training opportunities as a male colleague doing the same job.

(c) The sacked workers have a claim for unfair dismissal. While striking is technically a breach of contract giving the employer a right to dismiss the striking workers, a strike cannot be used as a means of dismissing selected workers. Thus these dismissals are *prima facie* unfair and the workers can claim compensation through the industrial tribunal.

INDEX

Also available from Pitman Publishing and published in association with the Chartered Institute of Purchasing and Supply (CIPS)

PURCHASING PRINCIPLES AND MANAGEMENT

7th edition

Peter Baily, David Farmer, David Jessop and David Jones

"The authors are to be congratulated that their book has been the premier text upon purchasing for more than a decade." *Business Educational Journal*

The seventh edition of this core text continues to develop and reinforce the conception of purchasing as a dynamic and managerial process and includes new material which reflects the now more general view of purchasing as a strategic function.

The book provides a pro-active managerial view of the purchasing function and is written in a clear and practical style.

Purchasing Principles and Management:

- gives increased consideration to strategic issues, purchasing evolution, purchasing education and green issues
- contains an additional section on purchasing policy
- includes new chapters on buying for manufacturing and services.

It is aimed at undergraduates on purchasing or management courses and on masters programmes, as well as those taking the professional examinations of the Chartered Institute of Purchasing and Supply (CIPS).

Peter Baily lectured at the former Polytechnic of Wales and has served as a chief examiner for the CIPS.

David Farmer is Emeritus Professor and former Deputy Principal at Henley Management College.

David Jessop is Professor of Purchasing and Supply at the University of Glamorgan.

David Jones is Head of the Management Division, Blackburn College.

0 273 60319 1   352pp

STORAGE AND SUPPLY OF MATERIALS

6th edition

David Jessop and Alex Morrison

"... there is no doubt that this is a most useful book for the beginner and expert alike. Its scope is monumental and few are the areas which escape its attention ... there is probably no better introduction to the logistics process available today." *Logistics Today*

This well established text provides an authoritative and comprehensive overview of the storage and supply of materials, from elementary principles and simplest methods, to the most sophisticated automated operations.

The sixth edition deals with the provision of materials for all kinds of organisations including the service sector. It contains sections on the relevant procedures, as well as covering the physical processes of storage, handling and movement of materials.

Storage and Supply of Materials:

- covers the new European directives on handling
- gives a greater emphasis on strategic issues
- contains additional coverage of logistics
- pays increased attention to computer techniques such as EPOS
- contains a broader treatment of materials, referring not only to stocked items but also to the direct supply of materials
- includes a new chapter on health and safety.

The text is aimed at CIPS supervisory and professional students as well as degree students of business finance taking materials management and purchasing courses.

David Jessop is Professor of Purchasing and Supply at the University of Glamorgan.

Alex Morrison has held a number of distinguished posts in the field of stock control, including that of stores controller with the National Coal Board.

0 273 60323 X   352pp

STRATEGIC PURCHASING AND SUPPLY CHAIN MANAGEMENT

Malcolm Saunders

This exciting new text provides students wlth an understanding of the scope and potential of purchasing strategy in a variety of international organisations. It examines the changes taking place in the business world and looks at their implications for purchasing and supply management.

The text takes an integrated approach to the strategic management of the supply chain and sees this as a central component of the management function. It attempts to link developments in the field of purchasing to changes that have been taking place in both corporate and business strategy generally and in other functional areas such as marketing strategy and manufacturing strategy.

Strategic Purchasing and Supply Chain Management:

- links ideas to action, theory to practice
- draws upon a wide range of sources, both business and academic
- includes objectives in each chapter and case studies at the end of the book
- contains notes and references for further reading.

The book is ideal for Chartered Institute of Purchasing and Supply (CIPS) Professional Diploma students taking the unit in 'purchasing and supply management: planning, policy and organisation'. It is also suitable for undergraduate and masters students of purchasing and supply.

Malcolm Saunders is Principal Lecturer in Materials Management, Coventry Business School, Coventry University.

0 273 60326 4   320pp